THE GLOSSARY OF
ACCESSIBILITY DESIGN

Compiled & Edited By:
Vimal Gupta
Manasi Pathak

Rhythm

Independent
Publication

THE GLOSSARY OF ACCESSIBILITY DESIGN

Compiled & Edited By:
Vimal Gupta
Manasi Pathak

ISBN:9798862336405

9798862336405

Published by:

Rhythm Independent Publication,

Jinkethimmanahalli, Varanasi, Bengaluru, Karnataka, India - 560036

For all types of correspondence, send your mails to the provided address above.

The information presented herein has been collated from a diverse range of sources, comprehensive perspective on the subject matter.

ADA Accessibility Guidelines

ADA Accessibility Guidelines are a set of standards and guidelines established by the United States Access Board to ensure that digital content and physical spaces are accessible to individuals with disabilities. These guidelines outline specific requirements that must be met to provide equal access and usability for everyone, regardless of their abilities. In terms of accessibility design, the ADA Accessibility Guidelines focus on providing clear and concise instructions for developers and designers to follow when creating digital content or physical spaces. These guidelines cover a wide range of areas, including websites, software applications, mobile devices, and physical elements such as ramps and elevators. The ADA Accessibility Guidelines provide instructions on various aspects of accessibility design, such as the use of alternative text for images to ensure that individuals who are blind or have low vision can understand the content. They also specify requirements for captions and transcripts to make audio and video content accessible to individuals who are deaf or hard of hearing. Additionally, the guidelines address issues like color contrast to ensure that individuals with visual impairments can perceive the content correctly. They also provide guidance on keyboard accessibility, ensuring that individuals who cannot use a mouse can navigate and interact with digital content using only a keyboard. Furthermore, the ADA Accessibility Guidelines require the provision of text alternatives for non-text content like graphs and charts, so that individuals who use screen readers can understand the information being presented. In the context of physical spaces, the guidelines provide specifications for accessible entrances, parking spaces, and restrooms, as well as requirements for proper signage and wayfinding to aid individuals with disabilities in navigating the environment independently. In conclusion, the ADA Accessibility Guidelines are crucial in promoting inclusive and accessible design. By adhering to these guidelines, designers and developers can ensure that their digital content and physical spaces are accessible to all, regardless of their abilities.

ADA Compliance Auditing Services

ADA Compliance Auditing Services refer to a set of assessments and evaluations conducted to determine the compliance of a website or digital platform with the accessibility standards outlined by the Americans with Disabilities Act (ADA). The ADA is a federal law in the United States that ensures equal rights and opportunities for individuals with disabilities. Under Title III of the ADA, businesses and organizations are required to provide accommodations and access to individuals with disabilities, including on their websites and digital platforms. ADA Compliance Auditing Services help organizations assess and address any accessibility barriers that may prevent individuals with disabilities from fully accessing and utilizing their websites or digital platforms.

ADA Compliance Auditing Software

ADA Compliance Auditing Software is a tool used in the field of accessibility design to assess and ensure that digital content and platforms comply with the guidelines set forth by the Americans with Disabilities Act (ADA). The ADA is a federal law in the United States that prohibits discrimination against individuals with disabilities, and it applies to both public and private entities. This software is typically used by web developers, designers, and organizations to evaluate the accessibility of their websites, applications, and digital content. It helps identify any barriers or challenges that might prevent individuals with disabilities from accessing and using these digital platforms effectively. The software analyzes different elements of the digital content, such as text, images, videos, interactive elements, and navigation, to ensure they meet the required accessibility standards.

ADA Compliance Training

ADA Compliance Training refers to a formal education program that aims to provide individuals with the knowledge and skills necessary to ensure that digital content and physical environments are accessible to people with disabilities, in accordance with the standards set forth by the Americans with Disabilities Act (ADA). The ADA is a civil rights law that prohibits discrimination against individuals with disabilities in various aspects of life, including employment, public services, and access to public accommodations. In the context of accessibility design, ADA Compliance Training focuses on equipping individuals with the understanding of how to create inclusive digital platforms and physical spaces that cater to the needs of all users, regardless of their disabilities. The training typically covers a wide range of topics, including but not limited to: 1. Overview of ADA and its applicability to different industries and sectors. 2. Understanding the various types of disabilities and their implications for design and accessibility. 3. Familiarization with the Web Content Accessibility Guidelines (WCAG) and other relevant accessibility standards. 4. Techniques for ensuring accessible digital content, such as web pages, documents, multimedia, and applications. 5. Design considerations for physical spaces, including ramps, doorways, signage, and assistive devices. 6. Testing and evaluation methodologies to assess the accessibility of digital content and physical environments. 7. Strategies for implementing accessibility policies and guidelines within organizations. 8. Best practices for communication and collaboration with individuals with disabilities. ADA Compliance Training is essential for individuals involved in the design and development of websites, applications, and physical spaces, as it enables them to create inclusive experiences that accommodate the needs of diverse user groups. By adhering to ADA standards and guidelines, organizations can not only avoid legal repercussions but also contribute to a more inclusive society that values the rights and dignity of all individuals. In summary, ADA Compliance Training is a formal educational program that equips individuals with the knowledge and skills needed to design accessible digital content and physical environments, in compliance with the Americans with Disabilities Act. It covers a wide range of topics related to accessibility design, aiming to create inclusive experiences for people with disabilities.

ADA Compliance

ADA Compliance, in the context of accessibility design, refers to the adherence of digital content to the standards set forth by the Americans with Disabilities Act (ADA). The ADA is a civil rights law that prohibits discrimination against individuals with disabilities, ensuring they have equal access to public goods and services, including digital platforms. Accessibility is crucial in providing equal opportunities for all users, regardless of their physical or cognitive abilities. ADA Compliance focuses on making websites, applications, and other digital media accessible to individuals with disabilities, including but not limited to visual impairments, hearing impairments, motor impairments, and cognitive disabilities. To ensure ADA Compliance, digital content must be designed and developed in a way that allows individuals with disabilities to perceive, understand, navigate, and interact with the information effectively. This includes considerations such as: 1. Perceptibility: Providing alternatives for non-text content, like images and videos, so that screen readers can convey the information to visually impaired users. This might involve using alt tags for images and captions or transcripts for videos. 2. Operability: Enabling users to interact with the website or application using various input devices, such as a keyboard or voice commands, rather than relying solely on a mouse or touch screen. Additionally, ensuring that any time limits on tasks are adjustable to accommodate individuals who may require more time. 3. Understandability: Using clear and concise language, organizing content in a logical manner, and providing instructions that are accessible and easy to follow. This helps users navigate the digital platform easily and understand the information presented. 4. Robustness: Building digital content using standardized code and using digital technologies that are compatible with different assistive devices and browsers. This ensures that individuals with disabilities can access the information across various devices and platforms. By adhering to these accessibility guidelines, digital content creators can ensure that their websites and applications are ADA Compliant, providing equal opportunities for all users. ADA Compliance is not only legally required in many countries, but it is also essential for promoting inclusivity, reaching a wider audience, and creating a user-friendly experience for everyone.

ARIA (Accessible Rich Internet Applications)

ARIA, which stands for Accessible Rich Internet Applications, is a set of attributes that can be added to HTML elements to improve the accessibility of web content and applications. It provides additional semantic information to assistive technologies, allowing them to interact with web content in a more meaningful way. ARIA is particularly useful in situations where the HTML semantics alone are not sufficient to convey the intended meaning or behavior of an element. For example, it can be used to indicate that a button opens a menu, that a checkbox controls the visibility of a section, or that a slider represents a range of values.

ARIA Roles

In the context of accessibility design, ARIA roles refer to the set of predefined attributes that can be used to define the role or purpose of an HTML element. These roles help assistive technologies, such as screen readers, to better understand and navigate through the content of a web page. ARIA (Accessible Rich Internet Applications) roles provide additional semantic meaning and context to the elements on a web page. They allow web developers to create accessible web content by describing the purpose and behavior of various elements, including interactive components. ARIA roles can be applied to a wide range of HTML elements, such as buttons, links, form elements, headings, and more. By assigning appropriate roles, developers can make sure that assistive technologies interpret the content correctly and convey it to users with disabilities. For example, the "button" role can be used to indicate that an element functions as a button, even if it is not a native HTML button. This helps users who rely on screen readers to understand that the element can be activated or interacted with, just like a traditional button. Similarly, the "heading" role can be used to define the hierarchical structure of headings on a web page. This allows users with visual impairments or cognitive disabilities to navigate through the content more easily, as screen readers can announce the section titles and users can jump directly to the desired section. By using ARIA roles appropriately, developers can create accessible websites that are inclusive to users with disabilities. However, it is important to note that ARIA roles should be used in conjunction with proper HTML elements whenever possible, rather than as a replacement. HTML already provides semantic elements like buttons, links, and headings, which are more robust and accessible by default. In conclusion, ARIA roles play a crucial role in accessibility design by providing additional context and meaning to HTML elements. They help assistive technologies interpret and convey web content accurately to users with disabilities, promoting a more inclusive web experience.

Accessibility Auditing

Accessibility auditing is the process of evaluating and assessing the level of accessibility of a website or application. It involves conducting a comprehensive review to identify any barriers or limitations that may prevent individuals with disabilities from effectively using the digital product. Accessibility auditing focuses on various aspects of the design, layout, and functionality of a website or application to ensure that it meets the needs of people with disabilities. This includes assessing the compatibility with assistive technologies such as screen readers, keyboard navigation, color contrast, font size, and alternative text for images. During an accessibility audit, specific accessibility guidelines and standards are used as a reference point. The most widely recognized standards are the Web Content Accessibility Guidelines (WCAG) developed by the World Wide Web Consortium (W3C). These guidelines provide a set of recommendations and success criteria for making web content accessible to all users, including those with disabilities. Auditing for accessibility involves a combination of automated tools and manual testing. Automated tools scan the website or application for common accessibility issues, such as missing alt attributes or improperly structured headings. Manual testing is essential to evaluate more complex aspects that require human judgment, such as form validation, proper use of ARIA roles, and the overall user experience. The results of an accessibility audit are typically documented in a report, which outlines the findings, identifies areas that do not meet the defined accessibility criteria, and recommends actionable steps for remediation. This report serves as a reference for developers and designers to prioritize accessibility improvements and ensure that the digital product becomes more inclusive and usable for all users. Accessibility auditing plays a crucial role in creating an inclusive digital environment by making websites and applications accessible to people with disabilities. By identifying and addressing accessibility barriers, organizations can provide equal access to information and services, comply with legal requirements, and enhance the overall user experience for everyone. In conclusion, accessibility auditing is the process of evaluating and assessing the level of accessibility of a website or application. It involves reviewing various aspects of design and functionality, utilizing accessibility guidelines, and combining automated tools with manual testing. The results of the audit are documented in a report, which guides the implementation of accessibility improvements to ensure a more inclusive digital experience.

Accessibility Compliance

Accessibility compliance refers to the adherence of design and development practices that ensure equal access to digital content and services for all individuals, regardless of their abilities or disabilities. It is the process of creating and maintaining websites, applications, and other digital platforms in a way that allows people with diverse needs and circumstances to perceive, navigate, and interact with the content effectively. In the context of accessibility design, compliance is achieved by following established guidelines and standards, such as the Web Content Accessibility Guidelines (WCAG) developed by the World Wide Web Consortium (W3C). These guidelines provide a framework for making digital content more accessible, covering various aspects including perceivability, operability, understandability, and robustness. Perceivability focuses on ensuring that content is presented in a way that can be perceived by all users, regardless of their sensory or cognitive abilities. This includes providing alternative text for images, captions for videos, and appropriate color contrast for text and background elements. Operability refers to designing interfaces and interactions that can be operated by users with different input methods and devices. This involves providing keyboard accessibility, avoiding time-based interactions that may be difficult for some users, and ensuring compatibility with assistive technologies. Understandability aims to make content and functionality clear and easy to comprehend for all users. It involves using simple and consistent language, organizing information in a logical manner, and providing meaningful error messages and instructions. Robustness focuses on ensuring that digital content can be interpreted and rendered consistently across different user agents and assistive technologies. This involves using valid HTML, CSS, and other markup languages, and considering compatibility with different browsers and devices.

Accessibility Conformance Documentation Services

Accessibility Conformance Documentation Services refers to the process of documenting the conformance of a website or application to accessibility guidelines and standards. It involves the creation of detailed reports that outline how well a digital product meets the requirements set forth by accessibility guidelines, such as the Web Content Accessibility Guidelines (WCAG). These documentation services typically include an evaluation of the website or application's accessibility features, identifying areas where improvements can be made, and providing recommendations for remediation. The documentation may also include information on the specific guidelines and standards that were considered during the evaluation, as well as any relevant test results or metrics used to assess conformance.

Accessibility Conformance Reporting (ACR)

Accessibility Conformance Reporting (ACR) is a process in the field of accessibility design that involves assessing and documenting the level of compliance of a digital product or service with accessibility standards and guidelines. ACR serves as a means to provide clear and concise information regarding the accessibility features and barriers present in a product or service. It allows organizations and individuals to evaluate and measure the accessibility of their digital offerings, facilitating the identification of areas for improvement and ensuring conformity with accessibility regulations. During the ACR process, a thorough evaluation of the digital product or service is performed to assess its compliance with established accessibility standards, such as the Web Content Accessibility Guidelines (WCAG). This evaluation encompasses a range of criteria, including the perceivability, operability, understandability, and robustness of the product or service. ACR involves conducting various tests and analyses, which may include automated testing tools, manual inspections, user testing, and expert reviews. Once the evaluation is complete, an ACR report is generated, documenting the accessibility status of the digital offering. The report provides detailed information about the accessibility features implemented, as well as any barriers or issues that may hinder access for users with disabilities. It highlights the level of compliance with specific accessibility standards, using a clear and standardized reporting format. The ACR report serves as a valuable resource for developers, designers, and other stakeholders involved in the accessibility design process. It provides them with a comprehensive overview of the product or service's accessibility strengths and weaknesses, enabling them to focus on areas that require improvement. Additionally, the report can be used to showcase the accessibility efforts made by organizations, demonstrating their commitment to inclusivity and compliance with accessibility regulations. In summary, Accessibility Conformance Reporting (ACR) is a vital process in the field of accessibility design, allowing organizations and individuals to assess and report on the level of compliance of their digital offerings with established accessibility standards. It helps foster inclusive design practices and ensures that digital products and services are accessible to all users, regardless of their abilities.

Accessibility Evaluation

An accessibility evaluation refers to the process of assessing and determining the level of accessibility of a website or digital content. It involves analyzing the design, structure, and functionality of the website to ensure that it can be accessed and used by individuals with disabilities or impairments. The evaluation aims to identify any barriers or obstacles that prevent equal access and usability for all users, including those with visual, auditory, motor, or cognitive disabilities. The purpose of conducting an accessibility evaluation is to ensure compliance with accessibility standards and guidelines, such as the Web Content Accessibility Guidelines (WCAG). These guidelines provide a framework for creating accessible websites and digital content that can be easily navigated and understood by individuals with disabilities. By following these guidelines, designers and developers can ensure that their websites are inclusive and accessible to a wide range of users. During the evaluation process, various aspects of the website are assessed, including: 1. Perceivability: This refers to ensuring that all users can perceive and understand the information presented on the website. It involves providing alternative text for images, captions for videos, and clear and concise content that can be easily read by assistive technologies. 2. Operability: Operability focuses on making the website easy to navigate and interact with, even for users with motor impairments. It involves providing keyboard accessibility, clear navigation menus, and consistent and predictable user interfaces. 3. Understandability: This aspect aims to ensure that the information and functionality of the website can be easily understood by all users. It involves using clear and simple language, organizing content in a logical manner, and providing instructions and feedback that are easy to comprehend. 4. Robustness: Robustness refers to the ability of the website to adapt and perform well on different devices and assistive technologies. It involves using standard HTML coding techniques and ensuring compatibility with various browsers and devices. Upon completion of the accessibility evaluation, a report is generated outlining the identified accessibility issues and recommendations for improvements. This helps designers and developers to rectify the barriers and enhance the accessibility of the website for all users, thereby promoting inclusivity and equal access to information and services. Accessibility evaluations are crucial in ensuring that websites meet the needs of individuals with disabilities and provide equal opportunities for all users. By adhering to accessibility standards and guidelines, designers and developers can create digital experiences that are accessible, usable, and enjoyable for everyone.

Accessibility Guidelines

Accessibility guidelines in the context of accessibility design refer to a set of standards and principles that aim to ensure that digital content, websites, and applications are usable and accessible to individuals with disabilities. These guidelines provide a framework for designers and developers to create inclusive and barrier-free digital experiences for all users, regardless of their abilities or impairments. The main objective of accessibility guidelines is to eliminate barriers that can prevent individuals with disabilities from accessing and interacting with digital content. By following these guidelines, designers can improve the user experience for users with disabilities and enable them to fully participate in the digital world.

Accessibility Testing Tools

Accessibility testing tools are software programs or online services that are used to evaluate the accessibility of a website or application. These tools analyze various aspects of a website's design, content, and functionality to determine if it conforms to established accessibility standards and guidelines, such as the Web Content Accessibility Guidelines (WCAG). These tools typically provide automated testing features that can identify common accessibility issues, such as missing alternative text for images, insufficient color contrast, and improperly labeled form elements. They may also include additional functionality to simulate different types of disabilities or assistive technologies, such as screen readers, magnifiers, or keyboard navigation.

Accessible Apps

Accessible apps are applications that are designed and developed with accessibility in mind, aiming to provide equal access and usability for all users, regardless of their abilities or disabilities. These apps prioritize inclusive design principles and employ a range of techniques and features to ensure that individuals with various impairments can fully and independently engage with the app's content and functionality. Accessibility design in apps focuses on addressing barriers that may prevent people with disabilities from using and benefiting from the software. This can include visual, auditory, motor, and cognitive impairments. Accessible apps incorporate a variety of strategies to improve usability and ensure that individuals with disabilities have equal access to information, services, and functionalities.

Accessible Coding

Accessible coding refers to the practice of designing and developing web content that is easily accessible to all users, including those with disabilities. It involves ensuring that websites and web applications can be used and understood by individuals with varying abilities. In the context of accessibility design, accessible coding involves adhering to specific guidelines and standards that aim to provide equal access and usability to all users. This includes following the Web Content Accessibility Guidelines (WCAG), which define the criteria for making web content accessible. Accessible coding involves several key principles, including providing alternative text for non-text content such as images and multimedia, using appropriate headings and descriptive tags to structure content, and ensuring that interactive elements are keyboard accessible. It also involves designing for color contrast to ensure readability for users with visual impairments, avoiding the use of flashing or blinking content that could trigger seizures, and providing accessible forms and tables. By using semantic markup, accessible coding ensures that the structure and meaning of web content are conveyed properly to assistive technologies. This means using HTML elements in a way that reflects the intended purpose rather than relying on visual presentation alone. For example, using semantic headings (such as h1, h2, etc.) to organize content hierarchy, and using lists (ul, ol) for presenting information sequentially. Additionally, accessible coding involves providing clear and concise navigation options that are easily perceivable and understandable. This includes using meaningful link text, providing skip links to bypass repetitive content, and ensuring that form labels are associated with their respective input fields. Accessible coding not only benefits users with disabilities, but also enhances the user experience for all users. By following accessible coding practices, websites and web applications become more inclusive, efficient, and adaptable to different devices and assistive technologies. In conclusion, accessible coding is the process of designing and developing web content that is accessible to users with disabilities. By following guidelines and standards, using semantic markup, and incorporating inclusive design practices, accessible coding ensures that all users can access and interact with web content effectively.

Accessible Color Palettes For Design

An accessible color palette for design refers to a selection of colors that are consistently and effectively distinguishable for people with visual impairments or color vision deficiencies. It ensures that individuals with varying degrees of color blindness or other visual challenges can perceive and comprehend the information presented. In the context of accessibility design, creating an accessible color palette involves carefully choosing colors that have sufficient contrast and are easily distinguishable from one another. This includes considering the contrast ratio between text and background, as well as the contrast between different elements on the same page.

Accessible Color Palettes

Accessible color palettes refer to color combinations that are designed with the goal of being inclusive and accommodating for individuals with visual impairments or color vision deficiencies. These palettes are carefully selected to ensure that the colors used provide sufficient contrast and clarity, allowing all users to easily perceive and distinguish the elements on a webpage or application. The use of accessible color palettes is an essential aspect of inclusive design, as it plays a crucial role in improving the accessibility and usability of digital content. When designing a color palette, designers must consider various factors, such as the contrast ratio between text and background colors, as well as the different types of color blindness that may affect users. Contrast ratio is a key principle in accessible design. It refers to the difference in luminance between two colors, specifically the foreground text color and the background color. A higher contrast ratio ensures that text is legible and easy to read for everyone, including those with visual impairments. Web Content Accessibility Guidelines (WCAG) recommends a minimum contrast ratio of 4.5:1 for normal text and 3:1 for large text. Color blindness is another important consideration. Certain individuals may have difficulties perceiving certain colors or distinguishing between them. The most common types of color blindness are red-green and blue-yellow deficiencies. Designers must select colors that are not only distinguishable for individuals with normal color vision but also for those with common color vision deficiencies. Accessible color palettes often involve using a combination of colors that have been tested and proven to have good contrast ratios and distinguishable shades for individuals with color vision deficiencies. By ensuring that the colors used meet accessibility guidelines and standards, designers can create a more inclusive digital experience for all users. To implement an accessible color palette, designers can use tools and resources that provide color contrast checking and simulation of different types of color blindness. These tools can assist in determining the appropriate color combinations and contrast ratios for a given design. Additionally, designers can refer to WCAG guidelines and color accessibility standards to ensure compliance with accessibility requirements. In conclusion, accessible color palettes are designed to ensure that digital content is easily perceivable and distinguishable for individuals with visual impairments or color vision deficiencies. By considering factors like contrast ratio and color blindness, designers can create more inclusive and accessible user experiences. Implementing accessible color palettes is an essential part of promoting universal accessibility and ensuring that all users can engage with digital content effectively.

Accessible Content

Accessible content refers to information, media, or resources that are designed and developed in a way that ensures equal access and usability for all individuals, regardless of their abilities or disabilities. Accessibility design aims to remove barriers that may hinder people with disabilities from perceiving, understanding, navigating, and interacting with content. It encompasses a range of principles, techniques, and best practices that empower individuals with disabilities to access and engage with digital content, including websites, documents, videos, and more.

Accessible Design Pattern Libraries

An accessible design pattern library is a collection of standardized design components, guidelines, and best practices that are specifically focused on creating inclusive and barrier-free digital experiences for individuals with disabilities. These libraries serve as a valuable resource for designers, developers, and other stakeholders involved in the creation of accessible websites and applications. The primary goal of an accessible design pattern library is to provide a set of reusable and customizable design patterns that have been tested and proven to be accessible to a wide range of users. These patterns may include various user interface elements such as buttons, forms, navigation menus, and content layouts, among others.

Accessible Design Patterns

Accessible design patterns refer to standardized and widely recognized strategies and techniques employed in the creation of digital products and environments, which aim to ensure that individuals with disabilities can access and interact with them effectively. These design patterns are crucial in promoting inclusivity and providing equal access to information and functionalities for all users, regardless of their abilities. Accessibility design patterns focus on various aspects of the user experience, including visual, auditory, motor, and cognitive considerations. They address barriers experienced by individuals with disabilities, such as visual impairments, hearing impairments, limited dexterity, and cognitive or learning disabilities. By implementing these patterns, designers and developers can enhance the usability, navigability, and overall user-friendliness of digital products for everyone. One key aspect of accessible design patterns is ensuring that content is perceivable by all users. This involves offering alternatives to visual content through the use of descriptive text alternatives for images, captions for videos, and transcriptions or synchronizations for audio content. Additionally, implementing proper color contrast ratios and avoiding the use of color as the sole means of conveying information supports individuals with visual impairments. Another important consideration is providing operability for users with physical disabilities. Accessible design patterns include features such as keyboard navigation, which allows individuals who cannot use a mouse to navigate through different elements of a website or application. Tactile feedback and expanded hit areas for interactive elements are also beneficial for individuals with limited dexterity or mobility. Cognitive accessibility is also addressed through design patterns that prioritize simplicity, consistency, and predictability. Designers can help users with cognitive disabilities by minimizing distractions, ensuring clear and concise content, and organizing information in a logical and intuitive manner. Overall, accessible design patterns help ensure that digital products are perceivable, operable, understandable, and robust for all users. They promote inclusivity by accommodating diverse abilities and providing equal access to information and functionalities. By adhering to these patterns, designers and developers can create digital experiences that are inclusive and accessible to everyone. Accessible design patterns refer to standardized and widely recognized strategies and techniques employed in the creation of digital products and environments, which aim to ensure that individuals with disabilities can access and interact with them effectively. These design patterns focus on various aspects of the user experience, including visual, auditory, motor, and cognitive considerations, in order to promote inclusivity and provide equal access to information and functionalities for all users.

Accessible Design Software

Accessible design software refers to computer programs or applications that are specifically developed to enable individuals with disabilities to access and interact with digital content, such as websites, applications, or documents, in an inclusive manner. This type of software aims to remove barriers and enhance the usability of digital platforms, accommodating a wide range of users with diverse needs. Accessible design software typically incorporates various features and functionalities that facilitate accessibility for individuals with disabilities. These features may include: 1. Screen reader compatibility: Accessible design software ensures compatibility with screen reader technology, enabling individuals with visual impairments to navigate and comprehend digital content through auditory feedback. 2. Keyboard navigation: The software allows users to navigate through menus, links, and interactive elements using only keyboard inputs, catering to individuals with mobility impairments or those who rely on alternative input devices. 3. Text-to-speech capabilities: Accessible design software may integrate text-to-speech functionality, converting written content into spoken words. This feature benefits individuals with reading difficulties, cognitive impairments, or visual impairments. 4. Alternative text for images: Images are assigned descriptive alternative text (alt text) that is read aloud by screen readers. This ensures that individuals with visual impairments or those who have disabled images can understand the content conveyed by the images. 5. Color contrast adjustments: The software allows users to modify color contrasts to suit their visual abilities, accommodating individuals with color blindness or low vision. 6. Captioning and transcripts: Accessible design software facilitates the inclusion of captions and transcripts for multimedia content, enhancing access for individuals who are deaf or hard of hearing. 7. Scalable text and layout: The software supports the scaling of text size and layout to enable individuals with visual impairments to read and navigate content comfortably. 8. Logical document structure: Accessible design software encourages the use of proper headings, lists, and other structured elements, which assist individuals using screen readers or other assistive technologies in understanding and navigating content effectively. By implementing accessible design software, designers and developers can ensure that their digital products are inclusive, fostering equal access and usability for users with disabilities.

Accessible Design

Accessible design refers to the practice of designing products, services, and environments that are usable and inclusive for all individuals, including those with disabilities. It involves creating designs that eliminate barriers and provide equal access to information, functionality, and interaction for everyone. When it comes to web design, accessible design aims to ensure that websites and digital content can be accessed and used by individuals with various disabilities, such as visual, auditory, cognitive, and motor disabilities. This involves considering the needs and abilities of these individuals and implementing design principles and techniques that allow them to navigate, perceive, understand, and interact with the website effectively. One important aspect of accessible design is ensuring that web content is perceivable. This means providing alternatives for non-text content, such as images, through the use of alternative text descriptions. It also involves using color contrasts that are readable for individuals with visual impairments and providing captions or transcripts for audio and video content. Another aspect is making web content operable for individuals with disabilities. This includes designing websites that can be easily navigated using keyboards for individuals who cannot use a mouse. It also involves providing clear and consistent navigation menus, headings, and labels that can be easily understood and accessed by individuals using assistive technologies. Accessible design also focuses on making web content understandable. This involves using clear and simple language, avoiding jargon or complex sentence structures that may be difficult for individuals with cognitive disabilities to comprehend. It also includes organizing content in a logical and intuitive manner, ensuring that the user can easily understand the purpose and structure of the website. Finally, accessible design addresses the need for websites to be robust and compatible with a wide range of assistive technologies and user agents. This means designing websites that can be easily interpreted and accessed by screen readers, braille displays, and other assistive devices. It also involves ensuring that the website functions correctly across different web browsers and devices, allowing individuals to access the content regardless of their preferred technology. In conclusion, accessible design is an approach that considers the diverse needs and abilities of individuals with disabilities, aiming to provide equal access and usability for all. By incorporating accessible design principles into web development, designers can create inclusive digital experiences that empower and engage all users.

Accessible Document Conversion Services

Accessible Document Conversion Services:In the context of accessibility design, accessible document conversion services refer to the process of transforming documents into formats that are easily perceivable, navigable, and usable by individuals with disabilities. These services aim to ensure that documents, such as written texts, PDFs, or presentations, can be accessed and understood by people with visual, hearing, cognitive, or motor impairments.

Accessible Document Conversion Software

Accessible document conversion software is a specialized tool designed to convert files and documents into formats that are accessible to individuals with disabilities. It ensures that the content can be read and understood by people with visual impairments, learning disabilities, or other accessibility needs. This software takes various types of documents, such as PDFs, Word documents, or images, and converts them into formats that are compatible with assistive technologies like screen readers or braille displays. It ensures that people with disabilities can access the content and interact with it effectively.

Accessible Documents Software

An accessible documents software, in the context of accessibility design, refers to a specialized tool or application that enables individuals with disabilities to access and interact with digital documents. It is designed to ensure that documents, such as text files, PDFs, or web pages, are structured and presented in a way that can be easily understood and used by people with various impairments. The primary purpose of an accessible documents software is to remove barriers and provide equal access to information for all users, regardless of their abilities or disabilities. It involves implementing a range of techniques and standards to enhance the readability, navigability, and usability of documents, particularly for individuals with visual, auditory, cognitive, or motor impairments. Accessibility features offered by such software include options for adjusting font sizes and styles, enhancing color contrasts, enabling screen reader compatibility, providing alternative text descriptions for images, enabling keyboard navigation, and supporting assistive technologies. By incorporating these accessibility features, the software allows individuals with visual impairments to use screen readers to access and understand text-based content. People with hearing impairments can benefit from captions, transcripts, or sign language interpreters for multimedia elements. Users with cognitive disabilities can benefit from simpler language, clearer headings, and organized content structures. Additionally, individuals with motor impairments can navigate the documents using keyboard-only interactions. Overall, an accessible documents software plays a crucial role in making information universally accessible and ensuring equal opportunities for everyone. It helps organizations and content creators adhere to accessibility standards and guidelines, such as the Web Content Accessibility Guidelines (WCAG), to provide inclusive and barrier-free digital experiences.

Accessible Documents

Accessible documents refer to text-based documents that have been designed with specific features and elements in order to accommodate individuals with disabilities, enabling them to access, navigate, and process the information contained within the document. These documents are created in a way that ensures they can be easily understood and interacted with by individuals with disabilities, such as those with visual impairments, hearing impairments, cognitive disabilities, or mobility limitations. The goal is to eliminate barriers and provide equal access to information for all individuals.

Accessible Formats

Accessible formats refer to the various ways in which information can be presented or displayed to accommodate individuals with disabilities. In the context of accessibility design, it is crucial to provide content in formats that are easily perceivable and understandable for people with different impairments. Accessible formats are particularly important for individuals with visual impairments, hearing loss, cognitive disabilities, or mobility limitations. These formats ensure that everyone, regardless of their abilities, can access and comprehend the content effectively.

Accessible Forms

Accessible Forms are a critical component of web accessibility design, as they ensure that individuals with disabilities can effectively interact with and submit information on web pages. Accessible forms are designed in a way that accommodates various accessibility needs, allowing users with disabilities to complete and submit forms with ease. To create an accessible form, it is important to consider multiple factors. Firstly, labels should be associated with form controls, such as input fields or checkboxes, using the "for" attribute. This enables users with screen readers or other assistive technologies to understand the purpose and function of each form control. Additionally, labels should be descriptive and concise, providing clear instructions to users. Furthermore, it is crucial to provide alternative text for form images or icons, making them perceivable for users who are visually impaired or rely on assistive technologies. The "alt" attribute can be used to provide a brief description of the image or icon. In terms of keyboard navigation, the tabindex attribute can be used to define the order in which form controls can be accessed using the "tab" key. Sequential and logical tab order is key in ensuring users can navigate through the form easily. To enhance readability and comprehension, it is recommended to group related form elements using fieldset and legend elements. This helps users understand the relationship between different form controls and facilitates smoother navigation. Moreover, error handling and validation is an essential aspect of accessible forms. Clear and concise error messages should be provided to users when form submission fails, allowing them to understand and correct any mistakes. ARIA (Accessible Rich Internet Applications) can be leveraged to provide live feedback to users when information is entered incorrectly or incompletely. By considering these various aspects, designers can create accessible forms that ensure equal access and usability for individuals with disabilities. Promoting web accessibility through accessible forms creates a more inclusive online environment, enabling everyone to engage with and submit information on web pages. Accessible Forms are a critical component of web accessibility design, as they ensure that individuals with disabilities can effectively interact with and submit information on web pages. Accessible forms are designed in a way that accommodates various accessibility needs, allowing users with disabilities to complete and submit forms with ease. To create an accessible form, it is important to consider multiple factors. Firstly, labels should be associated with form controls, such as input fields or checkboxes, using the "for" attribute. This enables users with screen readers or other assistive technologies to understand the purpose and function of each form control. Additionally, labels should be descriptive and concise, providing clear instructions to users.

Accessible Games

An accessible game, in the context of accessibility design, refers to a video or digital game that is designed and developed to be playable and enjoyable for a wide range of individuals, including those with various disabilities. Accessibility design aims to ensure that people of all abilities can participate equally in various activities, including gaming. Accessible games take into consideration the needs and preferences of individuals with disabilities, providing them with an inclusive and immersive gaming experience.

Accessible Icon Libraries

Accessible Icon Libraries are collections of graphic symbols that have been specifically designed to depict accessibility-related concepts, ensuring that people with disabilities can easily identify and understand them. These icons aim to enhance inclusivity and improve accessibility in various environments and contexts, such as public spaces, transportation systems, and information materials. The primary purpose of Accessible Icon Libraries is to promote universal accessibility by providing graphic representations that convey vital information to individuals regardless of their abilities. These icons not only serve as visual aids but also act as a means of communication, enabling people with disabilities to navigate and interact with their surroundings more effectively. By incorporating Accessible Icons into design practices, architects, graphic designers, and other stakeholders in accessibility can contribute to a more inclusive society. These icons are typically developed according to recognized accessibility guidelines and standards, ensuring their consistency and usability across different platforms and applications. Accessible Icon Libraries often offer a range of symbols that cover various accessibility-related concepts. These symbols may include depictions of wheelchair accessibility, hearing loops, designated parking spaces, service animals, and other features that promote equal access for all individuals. The icons are usually designed using simple, clear, and easily recognizable graphics, facilitating quick comprehension and reducing the need for text-based explanations. Furthermore, Accessible Icon Libraries can be customized and adapted to specific contexts or requirements. Designers can modify aspects such as colors, sizes, and orientations to suit different applications and environments. This flexibility allows for the integration of Accessible Icons into a wide array of mediums, including signage, websites, apps, and informational materials. In conclusion, Accessible Icon Libraries play a crucial role in promoting inclusivity and accessibility. They provide a standardized set of visual representations that enable individuals with disabilities to understand and engage with their surroundings more effectively. By incorporating these icons into design practices, architects, graphic designers, and other stakeholders can contribute to creating accessible environments and information materials that benefit everyone, regardless of their abilities.

Accessible Icon Project

The Accessible Icon Project is a design initiative focused on creating a more inclusive and accurate representation of people with disabilities, specifically in the context of accessibility design. It aims to challenge the stereotypes and outdated imagery commonly associated with disability, and promote a more universally recognized symbol that portrays individuals with disabilities as active, engaged, and independent members of society. The traditional wheelchair symbol, which has been used for decades to denote accessible facilities and services, features a largely static figure in a wheelchair. This static representation can perpetuate the perception that individuals with disabilities are passive or helpless, reinforcing societal barriers and stigmatization. The Accessible Icon Project seeks to shift this narrative by providing a dynamic portrayal of disability, emphasizing empowerment, autonomy, and inclusion.

Accessible Iconography

Accessible iconography refers to the use of symbols and visual representations that are designed to be easily understood and usable by individuals with disabilities. This approach aims to create inclusive and accessible designs that provide equal opportunities for everyone, regardless of their abilities. In the context of accessibility design, accessible iconography involves the creation and use of symbols that are intuitive and clear, conveying information effectively to people with various disabilities. These symbols are typically simple and concise, using minimal visual elements to convey their meaning. The use of colors, shapes, and illustrative styles is carefully considered to ensure maximum accessibility and comprehension. Accessible iconography plays a vital role in enhancing the accessibility of digital content, user interfaces, signage, and wayfinding systems. By utilizing symbols that are universally recognized and easily understandable, individuals with different disabilities can fully comprehend and engage with the information being conveyed. This promotes independence, inclusion, and equal participation for all users. Designing accessible icons involves adhering to certain principles and guidelines. For instance, icons should have clear outlines and distinct features to improve visibility and legibility. The use of contrasting colors can enhance visibility for individuals with low vision or color blindness. Additionally, icons should be designed in a way that accommodates different magnification levels, ensuring they remain clear and distinguishable at various sizes. When implementing accessible iconography in digital interfaces, it is essential to provide alternative text descriptions for screen readers and assistive technologies. This allows individuals who are blind or have visual impairments to understand and navigate the content effectively. Properly labeling and associating icons with relevant information helps to create meaningful connections and facilitates comprehension. In conclusion, accessible iconography is a crucial aspect of accessibility design that involves creating symbols and visual representations that are easily understood and usable by individuals with disabilities. By following principles of clarity, legibility, and inclusivity, accessible icons contribute to the equal participation and independence of all users in various contexts.

Accessible Infographics

Accessible infographics refer to visual information presented in a format that is designed to be inclusive and usable for individuals with disabilities. Accessibility design in the context of infographics involves creating content that can be easily understood and interacted with by people with diverse abilities, including those with visual impairments, cognitive disabilities, and motor impairments. When designing accessible infographics, there are several key considerations to keep in mind. One important aspect is providing alternative text descriptions, also known as alt text, for images and other visual elements used in the infographic. Alt text is a textual description that is read by screen readers, which are assistive technologies used by people with visual impairments. This allows individuals who cannot see the infographic to still understand the information presented. Another aspect of accessibility in infographics is ensuring that the content is easy to navigate and interact with using assistive technologies. This can include providing clear headings and labels, using appropriate color contrast between text and background, and providing alternative ways to access information, such as providing text transcripts for video or audio content included in the infographic. In addition to addressing visual and cognitive disabilities, accessibility design for infographics also takes into account motor impairments. This involves ensuring that the infographic can be accessed and interacted with using keyboard navigation alone, without the need for a mouse or other pointing device. This includes providing clear focus indicators and ensuring that interactive elements, such as buttons or links, can be easily activated using keyboard commands. In conclusion, accessible infographics are designed to make visual information inclusive and usable for individuals with disabilities. By considering factors such as alt text, clear navigation, and keyboard accessibility, designers can create infographics that are accessible to a wider range of users, allowing everyone to benefit from the information presented.

Accessible Learning Management Systems (LMS)

The term "Accessible Learning Management Systems (LMS)" refers to online educational platforms or software that are designed and developed with accessibility considerations in mind. These systems aim to provide equal access to educational resources and tools for all users, including those with disabilities. Accessibility design in the context of LMS involves ensuring that the platform is usable and navigable by individuals with various disabilities. This includes but is not limited to people with visual, auditory, mobility, and cognitive impairments. Such impairments may require the use of assistive technologies, such as screen readers, keyboard navigation, and captions. Accessible LMS design involves implementing features and functionalities that adhere to established accessibility standards and guidelines. These standards, such as Web Content Accessibility Guidelines (WCAG) 2.0, provide a framework for developers to follow when creating accessible digital content. Key considerations in designing an accessible LMS include providing alternative text descriptions for images and graphics, ensuring proper color contrast for text and background, offering resizable text options, and incorporating keyboard-friendly navigation. The platform should also support closed captions and transcripts for multimedia content, as well as provide audio descriptions for video materials. Moreover, accessible LMS design should prioritize user customization options, allowing individuals to personalize their learning experience according to their specific needs and preferences. This may include the ability to modify font styles, sizes, and colors, as well as adjust playback speed for audio or video content. By incorporating accessibility features, an accessible LMS can empower individuals with disabilities to fully engage in online educational activities. It can help create a more inclusive learning environment where all students have equitable opportunities to access information, participate in discussions, complete assignments, and interact with their peers and instructors. In summary, an accessible Learning Management System (LMS) is an online educational platform that is designed and developed with accessibility considerations in mind. It aims to provide equal access to educational resources, tools, and functionalities for all users, including those with disabilities.

Accessible Learning Materials

Accessible Learning Materials refer to educational materials that are designed and presented in a way that allows individuals with disabilities to access and engage with the content effectively. These materials are created with the aim of ensuring equal learning opportunities for all learners, regardless of their physical, sensory, cognitive, or learning disabilities. The design of Accessible Learning Materials follows the principles of accessibility to ensure that they can be easily understood, navigated, and used by individuals with disabilities. This encompasses various aspects, including but not limited to: 1. Perceivability: Accessible Learning Materials should provide multiple modalities for perceiving and understanding the content. This involves the use of alternative formats such as text-to-speech functionality, closed captions, and audio descriptions for individuals with hearing impairments or visual impairments. Additionally, the materials should have sufficient contrast between the text and background colors, making it easier for individuals with low vision or color blindness to read and comprehend the content. 2. Operability: The materials should be operable by individuals with diverse abilities and disabilities. This includes providing alternative navigation options for individuals who cannot use a mouse or touch screen, such as keyboard shortcuts or voice commands. Interactive elements should be labeled clearly and have sufficient time limits to accommodate individuals who require additional time to process information or respond. 3. Understandability: Accessible Learning Materials should be designed in a way that is clear and easy to understand for individuals with different cognitive abilities. This involves using plain language, providing clear and concise instructions, avoiding jargon or complex terminology, and using visual aids or diagrams to aid comprehension. Overall, the goal of Accessible Learning Materials is to ensure that individuals with disabilities have the same opportunities to access and benefit from educational resources as their peers without disabilities. By following accessibility guidelines and best practices, these materials can help promote inclusive learning environments and empower individuals with disabilities to fully participate in educational activities and achieve their academic goals.

Accessible Learning Platforms For Education

An accessible learning platform is a digital environment that is designed to provide equal access and opportunity to individuals with disabilities, ensuring they can fully participate in educational activities and have an inclusive learning experience. These platforms are developed using principles of accessibility design, which focus on making content and functionalities perceivable, operable, understandable, and robust for all users, including those with disabilities. The goal is to remove barriers and create an inclusive educational environment.

Accessible Learning Platforms

An accessible learning platform refers to an online educational system or software that is designed and developed with accessibility in mind. It aims to provide equal access and opportunities for all learners, regardless of their disabilities or limitations. Accessibility design in the context of learning platforms focuses on eliminating barriers and ensuring that individuals with diverse needs can effectively use and engage with the educational content and tools. Accessible learning platforms prioritize inclusive design principles, incorporating features, functionalities, and design elements that support learners with various disabilities, including visual, hearing, motor, cognitive, and learning impairments. These platforms adhere to international standards and guidelines, such as the Web Content Accessibility Guidelines (WCAG), to ensure compatibility with assistive technologies and optimal accessibility for all users.

Accessible Maps

Accessible Maps refer to digital or physical representations of spatial information that are designed to be accessible to individuals with disabilities. These maps remove barriers to understanding and navigating spatial information by incorporating features that accommodate various types of impairments and disabilities. In the context of accessibility design, accessible maps aim to provide an inclusive and equal experience for all users, regardless of their abilities. They are created with the purpose of ensuring that individuals with disabilities can independently access and interpret spatial information, such as geographic locations, routes, points of interest, and other relevant details.

Accessible Media

Accessible media refers to content that is designed and created in a way that is accessible and inclusive for all individuals, including those with disabilities. It involves the use of various techniques and strategies to ensure that individuals with visual, auditory, cognitive, or physical impairments can perceive, understand, navigate, and interact with the media. In the context of accessibility design, accessible media encompasses various forms of content, such as text, images, audio, and video, that are presented in a format that can be easily accessed and understood by individuals with disabilities. This includes the use of alternative text or captions for images and videos, transcripts for audio content, and properly structured and formatted text for easy readability.

Accessible Navigation Menu Generators

Navigating a website is an essential aspect of the user experience, and accessible navigation menus ensure that individuals with disabilities can easily understand and use a website's navigation features. Accessible navigation menu generators are tools that help developers create navigation menus that conform to accessibility guidelines. These generators provide a user-friendly interface to customize and generate the necessary HTML code for an accessible navigation menu. An accessible navigation menu is designed to be perceivable, operable, understandable, and robust. Perceivability refers to the menu being visually distinguishable, with clear contrast and sufficient color differentiation. People with visual impairments may use screen readers, so it is crucial that the menu structure is properly marked up using semantic HTML elements. Operability means that the menu is easy to use and can be navigated using different input methods, such as keyboard or touch. For individuals with motor disabilities who use assistive devices, the menu should be operable without requiring precise mouse movements. Understandability involves clear and concise labeling of menu items, avoiding ambiguous language and providing additional context when necessary. Finally, the menu should be robust, meaning it works reliably across different browsers and assistive technologies. When using an accessible navigation menu generator, developers can customize various aspects of the menu, such as the layout, styling, and behavior. These generators produce HTML code that adheres to accessibility best practices. The generated code typically includes CSS styles for visual design, JavaScript for interactive behavior, and ARIA (Accessible Rich Internet Applications) attributes for conveying additional accessibility information to assistive technologies. By using an accessible navigation menu generator, developers can save time and effort in implementing accessible navigation menus. These tools streamline the process of creating and implementing menus that meet accessibility requirements. They also help ensure that all users, regardless of their abilities, can effectively navigate and interact with a website. In conclusion, accessible navigation menu generators are valuable tools for creating navigation menus that comply with accessibility guidelines. They simplify the process of generating HTML code for accessible menus, resulting in websites that are inclusive and easy to navigate for individuals with disabilities.

Accessible Navigation Menus

Accessible navigation menus are an essential component of website design that prioritize accessibility for individuals with disabilities. These menus aim to provide an inclusive browsing experience by enabling users to navigate through the website seamlessly, regardless of their abilities or assistive technologies. Accessible navigation menus should adhere to the principles of universal design, ensuring that all users can easily locate and access the content they are looking for. To achieve this, developers need to pay attention to various aspects, such as clear and concise labeling, logical organization, and compatibility with assistive technologies. Clear and concise labeling is fundamental in creating accessible navigation menus. Text labels should accurately and succinctly describe the destination or function of each menu item. Developers should avoid using ambiguous or excessively lengthy labels, as they can confuse users, particularly those with cognitive disabilities. Additionally, providing tooltips or explanatory text can further enhance the understanding of menu items. Logical organization plays a crucial role in helping users navigate efficiently. Menus should be structured in a hierarchical manner, with related items grouped together. This arrangement aids users in understanding the relationship between different sections of the website and locating the desired content or functionality more easily. Developers should avoid cluttering the menu with too many options and strive to strike a balance between inclusiveness and simplicity. Compatibility with assistive technologies is a key consideration when designing accessible navigation menus. Developers should ensure that menu items can be easily accessed and activated using keyboard input alone, without relying on mouse interactions. Designing menus with a focus on keyboard accessibility not only benefits users with motor impairments but also improves overall usability. Furthermore, support for screen readers is vital for individuals with visual impairments. Developers should provide appropriate semantic structure and descriptive text for screen readers to relay essential information about the menu items. A well-designed accessible navigation menu should enable screen reader users to navigate the menu efficiently and understand the context and purpose of each item. In conclusion, accessible navigation menus are an integral part of inclusive website design. By adhering to principles such as clear labeling, logical organization, and compatibility with assistive technologies, developers can ensure that all users, regardless of their abilities, can navigate through websites effortlessly.

Accessible PDF Remediation Software

An accessible PDF remediation software refers to a tool or software application designed to improve the accessibility and usability of PDF documents for individuals with disabilities. The software employs various techniques and features to ensure that PDF documents are accessible to users with disabilities, including those with visual, auditory, cognitive, or motor impairments. Accessible PDF remediation software typically includes a range of functionalities and tools that enable users to modify and enhance PDF files to comply with accessibility standards and guidelines. These tools can perform tasks such as adding alternative text to images, ensuring proper document structure and semantic markup, creating accessible forms, and adding navigational elements to facilitate easy reading and navigation.

Accessible PDF Remediation Tools

An accessible PDF remediation tool is a software or tool that is used to modify or alter a PDF document in order to make it accessible and compliant with accessibility standards. These tools are designed specifically for individuals with disabilities, such as visual impairments or learning disabilities, who may have difficulty accessing or understanding content in a PDF format. By using these tools, designers can modify the PDF document to ensure that it is compatible with assistive technologies, such as screen readers, and provides an inclusive user experience for all users.

Accessible PDF Software

An accessible PDF software refers to a specialized tool or application specifically designed to create and work with PDF documents in a manner that ensures accessibility for individuals with disabilities. This software encompasses features and functionalities that enable the creation, editing, and conversion of PDF files, ensuring that they are perceivable, operable, understandable, and robust for users with disabilities. The purpose of accessible PDF software is to eliminate barriers and provide equal access to information and resources for all users, including those with disabilities. It adheres to accessibility guidelines and standards, such as the Web Content Accessibility Guidelines (WCAG) and the PDF/UA (Universal Accessibility) standard.

Accessible Presentations

Accessible presentations in the context of accessibility design refer to the creation and delivery of content that can be easily understood and consumed by individuals with disabilities. This includes people with visual, hearing, motor, or cognitive impairments, who may face barriers when accessing and comprehending information through traditional presentation formats. To ensure accessibility, presentations must be designed to accommodate different needs and preferences. This can involve various considerations, such as providing alternative formats, using clear and concise language, incorporating appropriate visual elements, and implementing accessible navigation and interaction features. One key aspect of creating accessible presentations is providing alternative formats for individuals who may have difficulty accessing or interpreting the content in its original form. This can include offering text-based transcripts or captions for audio or video components, providing a written outline or summary of the presentation, or using accessible presentation software that can generate accessible versions of the content. Using clear and concise language is also essential in making presentations accessible. Complex or technical jargon should be avoided, and information should be presented in a logical and easy-to-understand manner. Using plain language techniques, such as using simple sentence structures and avoiding unnecessary jargon or acronyms, can enhance the comprehension and usability of the presentation for a wide range of individuals. Incorporating appropriate visual elements is another important aspect of creating accessible presentations. Visual cues, such as images, graphs, or charts, should be used to enhance understanding, but they should also be accompanied by descriptive alternative text (alt text) that can be read by screen readers. Providing sufficient color contrast in visual elements and using large, legible fonts can also improve accessibility for individuals with visual impairments. Furthermore, accessible presentations should include navigation and interaction features that cater to different abilities. This can involve providing clear headings and subheadings, using consistent and intuitive navigation menus, and allowing keyboard navigation for individuals who cannot use a mouse. Providing a transcript or summary of the presentation content can also assist individuals with cognitive impairments in absorbing and comprehending the information. In conclusion, accessible presentations in the context of accessibility design involve creating and delivering content that is inclusive and easy to understand for individuals with disabilities. By incorporating alternative formats, clear language, appropriate visual elements, and accessible navigation and interaction features, presentations can be made accessible to a wider audience, regardless of their abilities.

Accessible Publishing

Accessible publishing refers to the practice of creating and distributing content in a way that ensures it can be accessed and consumed by individuals with disabilities. This approach aims to remove barriers that may prevent people with visual, auditory, cognitive, or physical impairments from accessing information or fully engaging with digital or printed materials. Accessible publishing involves following specific design standards and guidelines to make content inclusive and usable by the widest possible audience. For individuals with visual impairments, it may involve providing alternative text descriptions for images, using clear and readable fonts, and utilizing appropriate color contrast to enhance readability. For those with auditory impairments, it may involve providing captions or transcripts for audio and video content. For individuals with cognitive disabilities, it may involve organizing information in a clear and structured manner, using plain language, and avoiding complex or jargon-filled terminology. For individuals with physical disabilities, it may involve ensuring compatibility with assistive technologies such as screen readers, keyboard navigation, or alternative input devices.

Accessible Symbols

Accessible symbols refer to a set of standardized pictograms or icons that are specifically designed to communicate information quickly and effectively to individuals with disabilities or those who have limited cognitive or language abilities. These symbols are used in various contexts, such as signage, user interfaces, and documentation, to provide concise visual representations of concepts, actions, or objects. Accessibility design strives to create inclusive environments and experiences for all individuals, including those with disabilities. Accessible symbols play a crucial role in this design process by enabling people with diverse abilities to access and understand information, navigate spaces, and interact with technology. By using a universal language of symbols, these designs help bridge communication gaps and remove barriers that may exist for individuals who cannot rely on text-based or verbal communication alone.

Accessible Table Generator Tools

Accessible Table Generator Tools are web-based tools that assist in creating tables that are compliant with accessibility standards and guidelines. These tools are specifically designed to make it easier for designers and developers to create tables that are accessible to all users, including those with disabilities. These tools provide a user-friendly interface that allows users to input data and customize the appearance of the table. They generate the necessary HTML code that ensures the table is accessible. The generated code includes appropriate markup, such as the use of the "caption" element to provide a summary or description of the table, as well as the "th" element for table headers. These tools also generate table cells that are associated with their corresponding headers using the "scope" or "headers" attributes. In addition to generating accessible HTML code, these tools also offer features that enhance the usability and accessibility of the table. They allow users to add alternative text to images and provide descriptions or explanations for complex data. Some tools also provide options for specifying the reading order of the table cells to ensure screen reader users can navigate the table effectively. One of the key advantages of using accessible table generator tools is that they simplify the process of creating accessible tables for web designers and developers. By automating the generation of accessible HTML code, these tools save time and effort, and also help to ensure compliance with accessibility guidelines and standards. They provide a practical solution for those who may not have extensive knowledge of accessibility requirements or HTML coding. Moreover, accessible table generator tools promote inclusion and equal access to information for all users. By creating tables that are accessible to individuals with visual impairments, cognitive disabilities, or other challenges, these tools aid in making the web more inclusive and user-friendly. In conclusion, accessible table generator tools are vital resources for designers and developers who are striving to create accessible and inclusive websites. They simplify the process of creating accessible tables by automatically generating the necessary HTML code and providing additional features for enhancing usability. By using these tools, web professionals can ensure that their tables are accessible to all users, regardless of any disabilities they may have.

Accessible Tables Generator

An accessible tables generator is a tool used in accessibility design to create tables that can be easily understood and navigated by individuals with disabilities. It generates HTML code that follows best practices and standards for table accessibility, ensuring that all users can access and comprehend the information presented in the table. Tables are commonly used to present data in a structured and organized manner. However, for individuals with visual impairments or cognitive disabilities, tables can be challenging to interpret if they are not properly designed and marked up. An accessible tables generator addresses these challenges by generating code that includes necessary elements, attributes, and techniques to enhance table accessibility. When using an accessible tables generator, the resulting HTML code will adhere to accessibility guidelines such as the Web Content Accessibility Guidelines (WCAG) 2.1. This means that the tables will have proper table headers, scope attributes, and related elements to provide context and improve comprehension. Screen readers and assistive technologies can then interpret and present the table data accurately to users with disabilities. By using an accessible tables generator, designers and developers can ensure that their tables are inclusive and usable by a wide range of individuals. The generated code will enhance accessibility by providing clear structure, consistent formatting, and meaningful relationships between table components. This allows users with disabilities to navigate and understand the information within the table effectively. Overall, an accessible tables generator is a valuable tool in accessibility design, as it helps designers and developers create tables that are intuitive, informative, and accessible to all users, regardless of their abilities. By following best practices and incorporating accessibility features into tables, the generator promotes inclusivity and allows individuals with disabilities to access and interact with tabular information on the web.

Accessible Tables

Accessible tables, in the context of accessibility design, refer to tables that are designed and constructed in a way that ensures people with disabilities can access and interact with the table content effectively. To create accessible tables, a number of considerations need to be taken into account. The structure and organization of the table should be clear and logical, allowing users to navigate and understand its content easily. This can be achieved by properly utilizing table headers, captions, and summary attributes, as well as providing meaningful and descriptive table data. Table headers play a crucial role in providing context and helping users understand the relationship between table cells. They should be marked using the `` element and associated with their respective data cells using the `scope` attribute. This enables assistive technologies, such as screen readers, to accurately convey the table structure to users. Additionally, using the `` element allows designers to provide a concise and informative summary of the table's purpose and layout. This not only benefits users who rely on assistive technologies but also improves the overall usability of the table for all users. Providing a summary attribute with the `` tag allows designers to provide additional details about the table's content and purpose. This attribute can be used to describe the rows, columns, or any other relevant information that aids users in understanding the table, particularly when it contains complex or detailed data. Furthermore, the content within each table cell should be meaningful and descriptive. It is important to avoid using vague or ambiguous language, as this can hinder individuals with disabilities from fully understanding the table's content. Designers should also ensure that text alternatives, such as alternative text (alt text) for images within table cells, are provided to accommodate users who are unable to perceive visual content. In conclusion, designing accessible tables involves structuring and organizing table elements in a manner that allows individuals with disabilities to access and comprehend the table content effectively. By following best practices, such as using appropriate headers, captions, summaries, and meaningful content within table cells, designers can ensure that tables are inclusive and usable for all users, irrespective of their abilities.

Accessible Technology Training

Accessible technology training refers to the process of providing individuals with the knowledge and skills needed to effectively use and navigate technology that has been designed with accessibility in mind. This form of training aims to empower individuals with disabilities to independently access and utilize digital tools, platforms, and services. Training in accessible technology encompasses a wide range of subjects and strategies, including but not limited to: understanding assistive technologies, learning how to operate accessible software and hardware, mastering accessible design principles, and acquiring digital literacy skills. The main objective is to bridge the digital divide experienced by individuals with disabilities, ensuring equal opportunities for utilizing technology and participating in the digital world.

Accessible Technology

Accessible technology refers to design principles and practices that aim to make technology usable and accessible to individuals with disabilities. It involves creating, developing, and implementing digital tools and platforms that can be navigated, understood, and operated by people with various disabilities, such as visual, auditory, motor, and cognitive impairments. Accessible technology places a strong emphasis on inclusive design, which involves designing and developing digital products, applications, and websites that can be used by everyone, regardless of their abilities or disabilities. This involves incorporating features and functionalities that are compatible with assistive technologies, such as screen readers, magnifiers, and alternative input devices, allowing individuals with disabilities to interact with technology in a way that suits their needs.

Accessible Text

Accessible Text refers to text content that is designed and structured in a way that makes it easy for all users, especially those with disabilities, to read and understand. It is a fundamental principle of accessibility design, ensuring that information is accessible to everyone, regardless of their abilities or the devices they use to access the content. Accessible Text includes several key elements that help improve the readability and usability of text content. First, it involves using clear and concise language that is easy to comprehend. Complex and jargon-filled sentences should be avoided, and information should be presented in a straightforward and understandable manner. Second, accessible text should be well-structured and organized. This involves using headings, subheadings, and paragraphs to break up the content and provide a logical flow of information. Headings not only aid in navigation but also help users understand the hierarchy and structure of the content. Third, the use of proper text formatting is crucial for accessibility. This includes using appropriate font sizes, line spacing, and contrast to ensure that text is legible for all users, including those with visual impairments. It is important to choose fonts that are easy to read and avoid using decorative or script fonts that may be difficult to decipher. Additionally, accessible text should be inclusive and inclusive language should be used to avoid any bias or discrimination. Neutral and inclusive terms should be used instead of gender-specific or discriminatory language. For example, using "they" instead of "he" or "she" when referring to a generic person. In terms of technical implementation, HTML provides several accessibility features to enhance the accessibility of text. For instance, the proper use of semantic elements such as , , , and can greatly improve the structure and understanding of text content. Adding alternative text descriptions to images using the 'alt' attribute is essential for users who rely on screen readers to understand the context of visual content. In conclusion, accessible text is a vital aspect of accessibility design, ensuring that information is accessible and usable for all users, regardless of their abilities. By following best practices for writing and structuring text content, and utilizing the accessibility features provided by HTML, designers can create inclusive and accessible experiences for all users.

Accessible User Interfaces

An accessible user interface refers to the design and implementation of digital content that allows individuals with disabilities to access and interact with technology effectively.It involves creating a user interface that considers the diverse needs and abilities of users and provides them with equal opportunities to navigate, understand, and interact with the content.

Accessible Videos

Accessible videos refer to video content that is designed and created in a way that ensures it can be easily understood, navigated, and interacted with by individuals of diverse abilities and disabilities. The goal of creating accessible videos is to provide equal access and inclusion to all users, regardless of their physical, sensory, or cognitive capabilities. Accessibility in videos involves various considerations and techniques to make the content perceivable, operable, and understandable for everyone. Some key aspects of accessible videos include: 1. Visual Accessibility: Videos should provide alternatives for individuals with visual impairments. This can be achieved by adding captions or subtitles for dialogue and relevant audio cues, as well as providing audio descriptions of important visual elements or actions. Captions and audio descriptions enable individuals who are deaf, hard of hearing, or blind to access the video's content. 2. Auditory Accessibility: Videos should also be accessible to individuals with hearing impairments. Providing accurate captions or subtitles enables those who are deaf or hard of hearing to understand the dialogue and audio elements of the video. Additionally, providing transcripts of the video's content allows individuals to read the information instead of relying on audio. 3. Navigation and Control: Accessible videos should allow users to navigate and control the playback easily. This includes providing keyboard access so that individuals who cannot use a mouse can still control the video, as well as ensuring that the video player's controls are clearly labeled and intuitive to use. 4. Content and Design: The content and design of the video should also consider accessibility. This involves presenting information in a clear and organized manner, using sufficient color contrast for individuals with low vision, and avoiding flashing or rapid content that could trigger seizures for individuals with photosensitive epilepsy. By incorporating these accessibility considerations into the creation of video content, individuals with disabilities can fully participate in and benefit from the information, education, and entertainment that videos provide. Accessibility in videos not only promotes inclusivity but also aligns with legal requirements and international standards such as the Web Content Accessibility Guidelines (WCAG), ensuring that content creators meet the needs of all users.

Accessible Web Design

Accessible Web Design refers to the practice of designing and developing websites that are inclusive and usable by individuals with disabilities. It involves creating web content using techniques that ensure equal access and equal opportunity to people with diverse abilities. Accessible Web Design aims to remove barriers that may prevent individuals with disabilities from accessing and navigating websites effectively. This includes considering various disabilities such as visual impairments, hearing impairments, motor disabilities, and cognitive impairments, among others. One aspect of Accessible Web Design involves providing alternative text for images. This allows screen reader users to understand and interpret the content of images, providing them with the same information as sighted users. Additionally, Accessible Web Design involves using appropriate color contrast to ensure that text is legible for individuals with visual impairments. Another aspect of Accessible Web Design is the use of proper heading structures. Headings provide an outline of the content and allow users to navigate through a webpage easily. By using headings correctly, individuals with screen readers can quickly navigate to different sections of a webpage. Accessible Web Design also requires providing captions and transcripts for multimedia content such as videos and audio files. This enables individuals who are deaf or hard of hearing to access the information presented in these formats. Furthermore, accessible web designers should ensure that any time-based media can be paused or stopped, enabling individuals who may require more time to process information to do so without being automatically moved on to the next item. In summary, Accessible Web Design is the practice of creating websites that can be accessed and used by individuals with disabilities. It involves considering the needs of diverse users and implementing design techniques that remove barriers and provide equal access to web content. By following accessible design principles, websites can be more inclusive and ensure that no one is excluded based on their abilities.

Accessible Website Template Providers

Accessible website template providers are platforms or services that offer pre-designed templates or themes for creating accessible websites. These templates are designed to comply with accessibility guidelines and standards, ensuring that the websites created using these templates are accessible and usable by all individuals, including those with disabilities. Creating an accessible website involves following best practices for web design and development, such as providing alternative text for images, using proper heading structure, ensuring color contrast, providing descriptive link text, and ensuring keyboard navigation. Accessible website templates provided by these template providers incorporate these best practices, saving time and effort for web developers and designers. These templates are designed to be flexible and customizable, allowing users to modify and personalize the elements according to their specific needs and brand identity. Template providers often offer a wide range of designs and layouts to choose from, catering to different industries and purposes. Using an accessible website template can be beneficial for various reasons. Firstly, it ensures that the website is inclusive and can be accessed by everyone, regardless of their abilities. This can help businesses or organizations reach a larger audience and provide equal opportunities for engagement. Furthermore, accessible website templates can improve the user experience for all users, not just those with disabilities. By following accessibility guidelines, these templates often prioritize usability and user-friendly design, resulting in intuitive navigation and clear content presentation. Additionally, accessible website templates can save time and resources for web developers and designers. Rather than starting from scratch, these templates provide a solid foundation that complies with accessibility guidelines. Developers can then focus on customizing and adding unique elements to the template, rather than spending time on accessibility considerations from scratch. In conclusion, accessible website template providers offer pre-designed templates that comply with accessibility guidelines and standards. These templates provide a solid foundation for creating accessible websites, saving time and effort for web developers and designers. By using accessible website templates, businesses and organizations can create inclusive websites that provide equal opportunities for engagement and improve the user experience for all users.

Accessible Website Templates

Accessible Website Templates are pre-designed website layouts that are built and structured in a way that ensures equal access and usability for all users, regardless of their abilities or disabilities. These templates follow a set of design principles and guidelines that aim to make web content and functions perceivable, operable, understandable, and robust for everyone. Accessibility in web design focuses on creating websites that can be easily understood and used by individuals with different abilities, including those with visual, auditory, motor, or cognitive impairments. Accessible Website Templates take into consideration various factors to make the content and functionality of a website accessible, including: - Text alternatives: Providing alternative text descriptions for images, videos, and audio files so that people who are unable to see or hear the content can still understand it through assistive technologies such as screen readers. - Descriptive link text: Using clear and descriptive text for hyperlinks rather than generic phrases like "click here" to provide context and make it easier for users to navigate the site. - Keyboard navigation: Ensuring that all functionality on the website can be accessed and controlled using a keyboard alone, as some individuals may have difficulty using a mouse or other pointing devices. - Color contrast: Using sufficient color contrast between foreground and background elements to ensure that text and other important content are easily readable for people with visual impairments. - Structured headings: Organizing content using proper heading tags (h1, h2, etc.) to provide a clear hierarchical structure that aids in easy navigation and comprehension. - Accessible forms: Designing forms in a way that allows users to understand, complete, and submit them with ease, providing clear instructions and error messages. By using Accessible Website Templates, web designers and developers can ensure that the websites they create are inclusive and usable by a wide range of people, regardless of their abilities. These templates serve as a starting point for building accessible websites, saving time and effort in implementing accessibility features from scratch.

Accessible Websites

Accessible websites are designed with the goal of providing equal access and usability to all individuals, regardless of their abilities or disabilities. These websites are designed and developed in a way that ensures everyone can perceive, understand, navigate, and interact with the content easily and efficiently. To achieve accessibility, websites follow various guidelines and principles such as the Web Content Accessibility Guidelines (WCAG) developed by the World Wide Web Consortium (W3C). These guidelines provide a set of recommendations to make web content more accessible to people with disabilities. One important aspect of accessible web design is providing alternative text for non-text content. Alternative text, also known as alt text, describes the purpose or meaning of an image or a visual element for those who cannot see it. This enables individuals using screen readers or assistive technologies to understand the context and the message conveyed by the visual elements on the website. Another essential aspect of accessibility is ensuring proper color contrast. Websites should use colors that have sufficient contrast to improve readability and ensure that content is perceivable for individuals with visual impairments or color blindness. This includes ensuring that text is readable against its background and that important information is not conveyed solely through color. Furthermore, accessible websites provide clear and consistent navigation. This includes using logical headings and organizing content in a structured manner using HTML markup such as headings (h1, h2, etc.) and semantic elements (nav, main, etc.). This helps individuals with screen readers understand the hierarchy and structure of the content, making it easier for them to navigate and locate information. Accessible websites also ensure that the content and functionality of the website can be operated through a keyboard alone. This is crucial for individuals with motor disabilities who may have difficulty using a mouse. By ensuring that all interactive elements and forms are keyboard accessible, individuals can navigate and interact with the website without relying on mouse functionality. Overall, accessible websites aim to remove barriers and provide equal access to information and services for all users, regardless of their abilities. By following accessibility guidelines and principles, websites can ensure that everyone can fully engage with and benefit from the content they provide.

Adaptive Interface Design

Adaptive Interface Design, in the context of accessibility design, refers to the development and implementation of user interfaces that can adapt and accommodate the needs and preferences of a diverse range of users, including those with disabilities. An adaptive interface design aims to provide an inclusive and accessible user experience by allowing users to customize and modify the interface to meet their specific needs. This can include adjusting the layout, color scheme, font size, and other elements of the interface to enhance readability and usability.

Adaptive Technology

Adaptive technology, in the context of accessibility design, refers to the tools, devices, or software solutions that enable individuals with disabilities to access and interact with digital content or physical environments. It is a crucial aspect of inclusive design, as it aims to remove barriers and provide equal opportunities for people with diverse abilities. Adaptive technology encompasses a wide range of aids and assistive devices, including but not limited to screen readers, speech recognition software, alternative input devices (e.g., joysticks or eye-tracking systems), tactile interfaces, and adaptive switches. These technologies help bridge the gap between an individual's abilities and the challenges presented by various digital platforms or physical environments.

Aesthetic-Usability Effect

The Aesthetic-Usability Effect is a cognitive phenomenon that suggests people perceive aesthetically pleasing designs as more usable and effective. In the context of accessibility design, this effect highlights the importance of incorporating visually appealing elements that are accessible to all users. Accessibility design aims to create inclusive experiences for users with disabilities, ensuring that they can access and interact with digital content and interfaces. The Aesthetic-Usability Effect suggests that by enhancing the aesthetic appeal of accessible designs, their usability and effectiveness can be further improved.

Age-Related Disabilities

Age-related disabilities refer to physical or mental impairments that are more likely to occur or become pronounced as individuals age. These disabilities can affect various aspects of a person's daily functioning, leading to challenges in accessing and interacting with the physical environment, technology, and information. In the context of accessibility design, it is essential to address age-related disabilities to ensure equal opportunities and inclusion for the elderly population. Physical disabilities related to aging may include difficulties with vision, hearing, mobility, or dexterity. Visual impairments such as presbyopia or cataracts can make it challenging for older adults to read small text, distinguish between colors, or perceive contrasts. Hearing impairments, commonly associated with presbycusis, can result in difficulties understanding speech or perceiving sounds at certain frequencies. Mobility issues can arise due to conditions like arthritis or osteoporosis, limiting a person's ability to walk, balance, or manipulate objects. Decreased dexterity and fine motor skills may affect tasks like typing, using a mouse, or operating small buttons or touchscreens. Cognitive impairments are also prevalent among aging individuals, including mild cognitive impairment (MCI), dementia, or Alzheimer's disease. These conditions may impact memory, attention, problem-solving, or decision-making skills. It is crucial to consider cognitive disabilities in accessibility design, as they can affect an individual's ability to understand and navigate complex interfaces, follow instructions, or remember information. To enhance accessibility for individuals with age-related disabilities, designers should incorporate various principles into their designs. These include providing clear and legible typography with appropriate font sizes and color contrasts to accommodate visual impairments. Text alternatives should be available for non-text content, ensuring that individuals with vision impairments can understand the information through assistive technologies. Captions and transcripts should be provided for multimedia content to support individuals with hearing impairments. In terms of mobility, designers should ensure that interfaces are responsive and navigable using alternative input methods, such as keyboard or voice commands, for individuals with limited dexterity or mobility. It is also important to consider the size and spacing of interactive elements to accommodate larger touch targets or cursor interactions. For individuals with cognitive disabilities, designers should strive for simplicity and clarity in their interfaces, avoiding complex or cluttered designs. Instructions should be concise and easy to understand, with clear feedback and error messages. Providing predictable and consistent navigation pathways can support individuals with memory or cognitive challenges. By proactively addressing age-related disabilities in accessibility design, designers can create inclusive user experiences that cater to the diverse needs of aging individuals. This ensures that older adults can effectively access and interact with technology, information, and the environment, enabling them to participate fully in today's digital society. Age-related disabilities refer to physical or mental impairments that become more pronounced as individuals age, affecting their daily functioning and ability to access technology and information. In accessibility design, considerations for age-related disabilities include visual, hearing, mobility, and cognitive impairments, which can be addressed through principles such as clear typography, appropriate color contrasts, responsive interfaces, and simplified designs.

Alt Attribute

The alt attribute, short for alternative text, is an attribute used in HTML to provide a textual description of an image or graphic element on a web page. It is primarily used for accessibility purposes, allowing individuals who cannot see or have limited vision to understand the content of an image through screen readers or other assistive technologies. The alt attribute is added to the tag and is enclosed within double quotation marks. When an image fails to load, the alt text is displayed in its place, providing a meaningful description of the image. Additionally, screen readers will read out the alt text to visually impaired users, allowing them to comprehend the image's content. The alt text should be concise, descriptive, and convey the purpose or meaning of the image. It should provide relevant information that conveys the same message as the image, aiding users in understanding the context of the visual content. When writing alt text, consider the following guidelines: 1. Be descriptive: Provide a clear and accurate description of the image, focusing on conveying its essential information. 2. Be concise: Keep the alt text brief and to the point to ensure a smooth and efficient reading experience for screen reader users. 3. Avoid redundancy: If the image's content is already described within the surrounding text, the alt text can be left empty (alt="") to avoid repetition. 4. Context awareness: Consider the surrounding content and ensure the alt text provides enough context to understand the image's purpose within the page. Appropriate alt text examples: - Inappropriate alt text examples: - - By providing meaningful alt text for every image on a webpage, the alt attribute contributes to a more inclusive and accessible web experience. It enables individuals with disabilities to comprehend the visual content and ensures equal access to information, regardless of a user's abilities or limitations.

Alt Tags

Alt tags, short for alternative text, are descriptive attributes used in HTML to provide a textual representation of visual elements, such as images, graphs, or charts. They play a crucial role in making web content accessible to individuals with visual impairments or those using assistive technologies like screen readers. By adding alt tags to HTML elements, web designers ensure that users who cannot see or perceive visual content can still understand its meaning or purpose. Alt tags serve as textual substitutes or equivalents to visual elements, allowing individuals who are blind or have low vision to comprehend the content of a web page. To implement alt tags, the "alt" attribute is used within the relevant HTML element. For example, when inserting an image, the "img" tag includes the alt attribute to provide alternative text. Here's an example: ``` Example of an image with an alt tag: ``` In this case, the alt tag describes the image, conveying the key message or information it contains. It should clearly and concisely describe the visual content, using natural language and avoiding technical jargon. When creating alt tags, it's important to consider the purpose and context of the visual element. The alternative text should convey the same meaning or function as the visual content, allowing users to perceive the content in a comparable manner. For decorative images that do not convey important information, an empty alt attribute, alt="", can be used to indicate that the image is purely aesthetic and doesn't provide substantial content value. Additionally, alt tags should be kept relatively concise, typically within 125 characters or fewer. This ensures that the alternative text is efficiently read by screen readers, preventing long-winded descriptions that can be time-consuming for users with visual impairments. Overall, alt tags are an essential accessibility feature that aids individuals with visual impairments in comprehending web content that incorporates visual elements. By providing descriptive alternative text, web designers can contribute to a more inclusive online experience for all users.

Alt Text Generation Services

Alt text generation services are tools or services that automatically generate alternative text descriptions for images, videos, or other media content in order to make that content accessible to individuals with visual impairments or other disabilities that may affect their ability to consume visual content. Alt text, short for alternative text, is a textual description that is added to the HTML code of a website or webpage to describe the content of an image or media element. This description helps individuals using assistive technologies, such as screen readers, to understand and interpret the visual content that they cannot see or access directly.

Alt Text Generation Tools

Alt text generation tools are software or online resources that assist in the creation of alternative text, also known as alt text or alt tags, for visual content such as images or graphics. Alt text is essential for ensuring accessibility in design, as it provides a text alternative for individuals who are unable to perceive or understand visual information. It is particularly important for people with visual impairments or those who use screen readers, which convert on-screen content into auditory or braille formats. These tools are designed to help content creators, web developers, and designers generate accurate and descriptive alt text that effectively conveys the meaning and context of the visual content to accommodate a diverse range of users. Alt text should be concise yet informative, capturing the key details of the visual element to provide a comprehensive understanding to those who cannot see it.

Alt Text Generators

Alt text generators are tools used in accessibility design to automatically generate alternative text descriptions for images. These descriptions are then read aloud by screen readers, providing visually impaired users with a textual representation of the visual content. The purpose of alt text is to convey the meaning and context of an image to individuals who cannot see it. This ensures that people with visual impairments can fully comprehend and navigate web content that contains images. It also plays a crucial role in search engine optimization, as alt text is a key element for search engines to understand and index images. Alt text generators use artificial intelligence algorithms to analyze the content and context of an image, and then generate a relevant textual description. The generated alt text should accurately describe the visual elements and convey the essential information of the image, while also being concise and user-friendly. By automating the alt text generation process, these tools aim to simplify and speed up the accessibility implementation process for website designers and developers. They eliminate the need for manual creation of alt text, which can be time-consuming and prone to human error. Moreover, alt text generators often provide customization options, allowing users to tailor the generated descriptions to specific requirements or preferences. Users can adjust the length, style, and level of detail in the generated alt text, ensuring that it aligns with the intended user experience and adheres to best practices in accessibility design. However, it is important to note that alt text generators are not infallible and may not always produce accurate or relevant descriptions. While advancements in artificial intelligence have improved their accuracy, there can still be instances where human intervention is necessary to create or refine alt text. In conclusion, alt text generators are valuable tools in accessibility design, simplifying the process of creating alt text for images. They use artificial intelligence algorithms to automatically generate text descriptions, which are crucial for individuals with visual impairments to understand and navigate web content. Although not perfect, alt text generators are an important resource in ensuring that websites are inclusive and accessible for all users.

Alt Text

Alt Text, short for alternative text, is a text description that is added to an HTML element, such as an image, to provide a textual representation of the element's content. It is an essential component of accessibility design as it ensures that individuals with visual impairments or those who use assistive technologies can understand and interact with the content on a web page. The purpose of alt text is to convey the meaning and context of an image or other non-textual elements to users who cannot see or interpret the visual content. When an image cannot be displayed, or its content is not easily understandable without visual cues, the alt text acts as a substitute, describing what the image contains or represents. To create alt text, developers use the "alt" attribute within the HTML tag that corresponds to the non-textual element. The text entered in the alt attribute should accurately represent the purpose or function of the element, while being concise and descriptive enough for users to understand the image's content. For images that are decorative or purely aesthetic, alt text is usually left empty or set to a null value (alt=""). This indicates to screen readers and other assistive technologies that the image is not relevant for conveying information and can be skipped. Additionally, alt text should avoid using overly technical language, abbreviations, or acronyms that might not be universally understood. It is important to remember that alt text is primarily intended for individuals who cannot see the image, so the description should provide a clear understanding of its content and contribute to their overall comprehension of the page. By providing accurate and meaningful alt text, web designers and developers enhance the accessibility of their websites, enabling individuals with visual impairments or other disabilities to access and navigate the content. This inclusive design approach promotes equal access to information and supports a more inclusive and diverse online environment. Conclusion: In conclusion, alt text is a textual description added to non-textual elements in HTML, such as images, to ensure accessibility for individuals with visual impairments. By accurately describing the content and function of these elements, alt text enables users who cannot see the visuals to understand and interact with web pages effectively.

Alternative Input Devices

Alternative input devices, in the context of accessibility design, refer to tools or devices that allow individuals with disabilities to interact with digital systems or devices. These devices are designed to accommodate various disabilities that may affect a person's ability to use traditional input methods such as keyboards or mice. Alternative input devices can include technologies such as touchscreens, voice recognition systems, head or eye tracking devices, sip-and-puff switches, and alternative keyboards. These devices provide alternative means of input, enabling individuals with physical, motor, or cognitive disabilities to access and interact with digital content.

Alternative Text

Alternative Text, also known as alt text, is a brief and succinct description of an image or graphical element that is provided in the HTML code of a webpage. It serves the purpose of conveying the meaning and content of the image to individuals who may not be able to see the image due to visual impairment or other disabilities. The alt text is implemented using the alt attribute within the img tag in HTML. It is added as a text alternative so that screen readers, which are assistive technologies used by individuals with visual impairments, can read out the description to the user. This allows them to understand the context and information presented by the image. The alt text should be concise, yet descriptive enough to provide meaningful context. It should convey the purpose and function of the image accurately, without adding unnecessary details. It is important to strike a balance between providing enough information and avoiding verbosity. The alt text should be no longer than a few sentences and should be focused on the essential content of the image. When writing alt text, it is important to consider the intent of the image. Is it decorative or does it contain important information? If the image is purely decorative and doesn't convey any crucial meaning, an empty alt attribute should be used (alt=""). This informs assistive technologies that the image can be ignored and doesn't add any extra burden for screen reader users. In cases where an image is complex and contains extensive information, it may be more suitable to provide a longer description in the form of a link or detailed caption. This allows screen reader users to access the additional information if needed, without overwhelming them with excessive alt text. In summary, alternative text is a crucial aspect of accessibility design as it provides individuals with disabilities, particularly those with visual impairments, a way to understand and interpret images on webpages. By providing concise and accurate alt text, web designers can ensure that their content is accessible and inclusive to all users.

Aria-Label

The Aria-Label is an attribute in HTML that is used to provide additional descriptive text to non-text content on a web page, specifically for the purpose of accessibility design. It is primarily used to communicate the purpose or function of elements that may not be adequately conveyed by their visual appearance alone, such as icons, images, or form elements. By adding the Aria-Label attribute to an element, developers can ensure that screen readers and other assistive technologies can accurately and effectively convey the meaning and functionality of that element to users with disabilities. This attribute is particularly useful when an element's visual representation is not self-explanatory, or when the element does not have any visible text associated with it.

Assistive Apps

Assistive Apps are software applications designed to enhance accessibility and provide support to individuals with disabilities. These apps are specifically developed to assist people who face challenges in various aspects of their daily lives due to physical, cognitive, visual, or hearing impairments. Assistive Apps aim to promote inclusivity and equal opportunities by leveraging technology to bridge the gap between individuals with disabilities and the digital world. These apps offer a range of features and functionalities to empower users and enable them to perform tasks they may otherwise struggle with. By leveraging the capabilities of smartphones, tablets, or computers, assistive apps provide customized solutions to cater to the unique needs of each user.

Assistive Keyboard Devices

Assistive keyboard devices are hardware or software tools designed specifically to assist individuals with disabilities in accessing and controlling a computer or other electronic devices. These devices are part of accessibility design, aimed at providing equal opportunities for people with different physical or cognitive abilities to use and navigate digital platforms and technology. Hardware assistive keyboard devices usually feature specialized designs and functions to accommodate various accessibility needs. For example, they may include larger keys or keyguards to assist individuals with motor disabilities or limited dexterity. Some devices may have high contrast or backlit keys to aid individuals with visual impairments or low vision. Others may have built-in scanning or customizable features to cater to individuals with cognitive disabilities who require alternative input methods. Software-based assistive keyboard devices, also known as on-screen keyboards, provide an alternative to physical keyboards. These virtual keyboards are typically displayed on the computer screen and can be operated with a mouse, touchpad, or other pointing devices. They allow individuals with mobility restrictions, such as those who have limited hand movement, to input text and control the computer using a pointing device rather than physical key presses. Assistive keyboard devices are designed to be customizable and adaptable to individual needs. They often offer configuration options such as key remapping, adjustable sensitivity, or programmable macros, enabling users to modify the device's settings to suit their specific requirements and preferences. This flexibility allows individuals with different types and degrees of disabilities to tailor their keyboard experience to maximize their accessibility and usability. In conclusion, assistive keyboard devices play a crucial role in accessibility design, empowering individuals with disabilities to interact with and navigate digital technology. By providing alternative input methods and customizable features, these devices ensure that individuals with physical or cognitive limitations can access and use computers and electronic devices with equal ease and independence.

Assistive Keyboard Manufacturers

An assistive keyboard is a type of keyboard that is specifically designed for individuals with accessibility needs. These keyboards are designed to provide greater usability and functionality for people with physical or cognitive impairments that may make it difficult for them to use a standard keyboard. Assistive keyboards often feature larger and more prominent keys to help individuals with limited dexterity or vision. These keys may also be color-coded or have tactile indicators to assist individuals with visual impairments. Some keyboards even offer customizable key layouts, allowing users to redefine the functions of specific keys to better suit their needs. In addition to physical adaptations, assistive keyboards may also incorporate advanced technologies to enhance accessibility. For example, some keyboards utilize adaptive scanning, where the keys are scanned sequentially and the user activates a key by selecting it during the scanning process. This can help individuals with limited mobility to input text or commands more easily. Other assistive keyboards may include features such as word prediction, which suggests words or phrases as the user types, reducing the need for extensive manual input. This can be especially beneficial for individuals with cognitive impairments or communication disorders that may affect their ability to type quickly or accurately. Manufacturers of assistive keyboards play a crucial role in designing and producing these specialized keyboards. These manufacturers collaborate with accessibility experts, researchers, and individuals with disabilities to ensure that their products meet the specific needs and preferences of users. They may also conduct usability studies and field tests to gather feedback and make continuous improvements to the design and functionality of their keyboards. The ultimate goal of assistive keyboard manufacturers is to empower individuals with accessibility needs by providing them with tools that enable greater independence and participation in various activities, such as communication, education, and work. Through their efforts, these manufacturers contribute to creating a more inclusive society where everyone can fully engage and contribute, regardless of their abilities.

Assistive Listening Devices (ALDs)

Assistive Listening Devices (ALDs) are specialized devices designed to enhance accessibility for individuals with hearing impairments. They provide assistive technology solutions that allow people with hearing difficulties to overcome communication barriers and participate fully in various activities and environments. ALDs work by amplifying sound, reducing background noise, and improving speech intelligibility. These devices are particularly helpful in scenarios where the speaker's voice needs to be amplified, such as in classrooms, lecture halls, theaters, places of worship, and public events.

Assistive Listening Devices

Assistive Listening Devices (ALDs) are specialized tools designed to enhance hearing and improve accessibility for individuals with hearing impairments. ALDs are commonly used in various settings, such as schools, theaters, lecture halls, and public spaces, to help people better understand and engage with auditory information. ALDs work by reducing background noise, amplifying sound, or transmitting audio directly to the listener. These devices can be used alongside or in place of hearing aids or cochlear implants, depending on the individual's specific needs and preferences. ALDs come in various forms and can be tailored to address different types and degrees of hearing loss.

Assistive Listening Systems

Assistive Listening Systems (ALS) refer to a range of technological solutions designed to enhance the auditory experience for individuals with hearing impairments and improve accessibility in various settings. These systems aim to provide assistance to individuals who may have difficulties in hearing or understanding speech due to factors such as distance, background noise, or their personal hearing capabilities. ALS typically consist of three primary components: a microphone or sound source, a transmission system, and a receiver. The microphone or sound source captures the audio signals, such as speech, music, or other sounds, and converts them into electrical signals. The transmission system then sends these signals wirelessly or via direct connection to the receiver. The receiver, which is worn or held by the user, converts the electrical signals back into sound and delivers them directly to the individual's ears, bypassing the ambient noise and distance challenges. These systems can be utilized in a variety of environments, including educational institutions, public venues, workplaces, and entertainment settings. ALS solutions can include hearing loop systems, infrared systems, frequency modulation (FM) systems, and Bluetooth-based systems, among others. Each system has its own unique advantages and may be more suitable for specific contexts or user requirements. For example, hearing loop systems utilize electromagnetic fields to transmit audio signals directly to hearing aids equipped with telecoil receivers. These systems are particularly beneficial for individuals with telecoil-compatible hearing aids, as they can seamlessly connect to the sound source without the need for additional receivers. Infrared systems, on the other hand, use infrared light to transmit audio signals and require individuals to wear a receiver with an infrared sensor to receive the sound. Overall, Assistive Listening Systems play a vital role in ensuring equal access to information and improving communication opportunities for individuals with hearing impairments. By reducing the impact of environmental noise and distance on their ability to hear and understand sounds, ALS solutions can significantly enhance the overall accessibility and inclusion of individuals with hearing disabilities.

Assistive Listening

Assistive Listening refers to a system or technology designed to enhance the auditory experience of individuals with hearing impairments. It is an integral part of accessibility design, aimed at providing equal access to information and communication for all individuals, regardless of their hearing abilities. This technology typically consists of a transmitter and a receiver. The transmitter captures sound signals from a source such as a microphone, television, or public address system, and transmits them wirelessly to the receiver. The receiver is equipped with a compatible earpiece or hearing aid that allows the individual to listen to the amplified sound directly in their ears, compensating for any hearing loss or difficulty. The purpose of assistive listening systems is to mitigate the challenges faced by individuals with hearing impairments in various settings, including public spaces, educational institutions, workplaces, and entertainment venues. By amplifying and clarifying sound, these systems ensure that individuals with hearing loss can fully participate and engage in a variety of activities, from listening to lectures and attending meetings to watching movies and enjoying live performances. Assistive Listening is governed by various standards and regulations to ensure its effectiveness and compatibility. These standards cover areas such as audio frequency range, signal-to-noise ratio, and wireless transmission technologies. The goal is to provide high-quality sound reproduction that is clear, intelligible, and free from interference, enabling individuals with hearing impairments to fully grasp and comprehend the intended audio content. Furthermore, assistive listening systems are designed to be flexible and adaptable, accommodating different hearing aids and devices. They often include features such as volume controls, tone adjustments, and compatibility with telecoil-equipped hearing aids. This versatility allows individuals to personalize their listening experience based on their specific needs and preferences. In conclusion, assistive listening is a crucial component of accessibility design that empowers individuals with hearing impairments to access and participate in auditory information and communication. By utilizing wireless technologies and compatible devices, assistive listening systems enhance sound perception, ensuring equal opportunities for individuals with hearing loss in various environments.

Assistive Technology Act

The Assistive Technology Act refers to a legislation that aims to promote the accessibility and usability of technology for individuals with disabilities. This Act provides funding grants to states in order to establish programs and services that assist individuals with disabilities in accessing and using assistive technology devices and services. Under the Assistive Technology Act, states are required to develop and maintain comprehensive programs that address the needs of individuals with disabilities across the lifespan. These programs are responsible for increasing awareness and understanding of assistive technology, providing training and technical assistance to individuals with disabilities, their families, and professionals, and facilitating access to assistive technology devices and services.

Assistive Technology

Audio Description (AD)

Audio Description (AD) is a form of accessibility design that aims to provide individuals with visual impairments or blindness with a comprehensive audio narration of visual elements, such as actions, gestures, scene changes, and other crucial visual details. AD supplements the existing soundtrack of a media content, making it accessible to a wider audience. The purpose of Audio Description is to allow people who are blind or visually impaired to fully understand and engage with various forms of media, including movies, television shows, live performances, exhibitions, and digital content. AD enhances their overall viewing experience by providing vital information that is not conveyed through dialogue or sound effects alone. When implementing Audio Description, trained describers or professionals create detailed verbal descriptions that carefully articulate the visual elements, ensuring that each detail is delivered in a clear and concise manner. These descriptions are interwoven between the existing audio content, allowing individuals with visual impairments to follow the storyline, understand the character dynamics, and visualize the visual elements within the media content. Audio Description can be conveyed through various formats, such as live verbal descriptions during performances, pre-recorded narration in movies or television shows, or through dedicated audio streams or separate tracks. The narration typically aims to convey important visual cues, including facial expressions, body language, costume details, and other significant visual information essential for understanding the content. By providing access to visual information through audio narration, Audio Description bridges the communication gap for individuals with visual impairments and enables them to have a more inclusive and engaging media experience. It allows them to fully participate in cultural events, keep up with ongoing storylines, and be active consumers of visual media. In conclusion, Audio Description is a vital accessibility design element that ensures individuals with visual impairments or blindness can fully understand and enjoy various forms of visual media content. Its implementation aims to make content accessible to a wider audience, facilitating inclusivity and equal access to information and entertainment.

Audio Description Services

Audio Description Services refer to a form of accessibility design that aims to make audiovisual content accessible to individuals with visual impairments or other cognitive disabilities. This service involves providing a detailed verbal description of key visual elements present in a video, film, or live performance that cannot be fully understood through dialogue alone. Audio Description Services primarily focus on describing the non-verbal audio cues and visual details, including actions, gestures, facial expressions, costumes, sets, and scene changes, providing a comprehensive understanding of the visual content to individuals who are blind or visually impaired. These descriptions are carefully crafted and inserted into natural pauses in the original audio, ensuring that they do not interfere with the dialogue or sound effects of the original content.

Audio Description

Audio description is a form of accessibility design that allows individuals who are visually impaired or blind to access and understand visual content. It provides a separate audio track that describes the key visual elements, actions, and scene changes in a movie, TV show, play, or other visual media. This audio track is synchronized with the original audio track of the content, allowing individuals to hear the descriptions during pauses in the dialogue or audio elements. The goal of audio description is to provide a comprehensive and objective description of the visual content that enables individuals to form a mental picture of what is happening on the screen or stage.

Audio Descriptions For Movies

Audio descriptions for movies are a form of accessibility design that provides individuals who are blind or visually impaired with a detailed verbal description of the visual elements in a film or television program. These descriptions serve as a means to bridge the gap between what can be seen on the screen and what cannot be perceived through visual means alone. Audio descriptions are typically narrated by a voice-over artist and are inserted into the gaps in dialogue or sound effects during natural pauses in the film. The descriptions aim to convey the key visual elements of the scene, such as actions, facial expressions, body language, gestures, as well as important visual details, settings, and scene changes. They are carefully scripted and timed to provide a coherent and immersive experience for the listener, without interfering with the original audio of the film.

Auditory Disabilities

Auditory disabilities refer to a range of impairments affecting an individual's ability to perceive, process, or interpret sounds. These disabilities can manifest in various ways, such as hearing loss, deafness, or difficulty in understanding speech or other auditory stimuli. In the context of accessibility design, it is crucial to consider the needs of individuals with auditory disabilities in order to provide equal access and inclusivity in digital environments. Designing for individuals with auditory disabilities involves implementing strategies and features that enhance their ability to receive and comprehend auditory information. One fundamental approach is through the provision of captioning or transcripts for audio content, which enables users with hearing impairments to read the text equivalent of what is being spoken or played. This allows them to access and understand the information presented in videos, podcasts, or other audio formats. Captions and transcripts can be presented in a synchronized manner with the audio, ensuring a cohesive experience.

Augmentative And Alternative Communication (AAC)

Augmentative and Alternative Communication (AAC) refers to a set of methods, tools, strategies, and techniques designed to enhance or replace natural speech for individuals with communication impairments or limitations. It is primarily used to assist people who have difficulty producing or understanding spoken language, either temporarily or permanently. AAC is an essential component of accessibility design, as it plays a pivotal role in ensuring effective communication and inclusion for individuals with disabilities. The goal of AAC is to provide individuals with a means to express themselves, participate in social interactions, and access vital information, thereby promoting their independence and overall quality of life.

Automated Captioning Solutions

Automated Captioning Solutions are software or technological solutions that are designed and implemented to automatically generate captions or subtitles for audio or video content. These solutions use various algorithms, machine learning techniques, and speech recognition technology to convert spoken words into written text. The primary objective of automated captioning solutions is to make audio or video content accessible to individuals with hearing impairments or those who may have difficulty understanding or comprehending spoken language. By providing accurate and synchronized captions, these solutions enable individuals who are deaf or hard of hearing to understand and follow the content being presented. Automated captioning solutions typically involve a two-step process: audio transcription and caption synchronization. In the audio transcription step, the software analyzes the audio content and converts it into written text. This task is achieved using sophisticated speech recognition algorithms that are trained to identify and interpret spoken words. The accuracy of the transcription depends on the quality of the audio, the clarity of the speech, and the effectiveness of the speech recognition technology. Once the audio transcription is complete, the text is then synchronized with the corresponding portions of the audio or video content. This synchronization is essential to ensure that the captions appear at the appropriate times, enabling users to read the captions while simultaneously watching or listening to the content. The automated captioning solutions also offer various customization options, such as font size, color, and position, to enhance the readability and usability of the captions. Automated captioning solutions have become increasingly popular in recent years due to their effectiveness, cost-efficiency, and scalability. These solutions can handle large volumes of content and provide captions quickly and accurately. They also eliminate the need for manual captioning, which can be time-consuming and expensive. By automating the captioning process, organizations can ensure that their audio and video content is accessible to a wider range of individuals, thereby promoting inclusivity and compliance with accessibility regulations. In conclusion, automated captioning solutions play a critical role in making audio and video content accessible to individuals with hearing impairments. By leveraging advanced technologies like speech recognition and machine learning, these solutions provide accurate and synchronized captions, enhancing the overall accessibility and user experience of the content.

Automated Captioning Tools

Automated Captioning Tools are software programs designed to generate captions for audio and video content in order to improve accessibility for individuals with hearing impairments. These tools utilize speech recognition technology to automatically transcribe spoken words into written text, which is then displayed as captions that can be read by viewers. By providing captions for audio and video content, automated captioning tools enable individuals with hearing impairments to fully comprehend and engage with the information being presented. Captions are especially helpful for individuals who are deaf or hard of hearing, as they allow them to read the dialogue, sound effects, and other audio elements that may be critical for understanding the content. Additionally, automated captioning tools can benefit individuals who are non-native speakers or have difficulty understanding certain accents or speech patterns.

Automatic Speech Recognition (ASR)

Automatic Speech Recognition (ASR) refers to the technological process of converting spoken language into written text. It is specifically designed for individuals with accessibility needs, such as those who are hearing impaired or have difficulty understanding spoken language. ASR technology utilizes a combination of algorithms, linguistic models, and machine learning techniques to accurately transcribe spoken words into written form. In terms of accessibility design, ASR plays a crucial role in facilitating effective communication and information access for individuals who rely on written text as their main medium of understanding. By transcribing spoken language into text, ASR allows these individuals to participate in verbal conversations, engage with multimedia content, and access information that is primarily delivered through spoken communication.

Barrier-Free Design

Barrier-Free Design refers to the approach of creating spaces, products, and services that can be accessed, used, and enjoyed by individuals with diverse abilities, including those with disabilities. It focuses on removing physical, sensory, and cognitive barriers, to ensure equal and independent participation for everyone. In the context of accessibility design, Barrier-Free Design aims to eliminate obstacles that hinder individuals with disabilities from freely navigating and utilizing their environment. This approach promotes inclusive environments that accommodate all individuals, regardless of their physical or cognitive capabilities.

Braille Displays For Computers

A braille display for computers is a type of assistive technology designed for individuals who are blind or have low vision. It is a device that allows users to access and read digital content on a computer using braille characters. The braille display consists of a series of small, refreshable braille cells that are connected to a computer. Each braille cell typically consists of six or eight small pins, or dots, that can be raised or lowered to represent a braille character. These dots can be felt by users as they read the displayed braille content with their fingertips.

Braille Displays

A Braille display, in the context of accessibility design, refers to a hardware device that allows individuals who are blind or have low vision to access digital information through tactile feedback in the form of Braille characters. Braille displays serve as an interface between a computer or mobile device and the user, providing them with a means to read and navigate content such as text documents, emails, web pages, and more. The display consists of a series of small rounded pins arranged in a rectangular grid, with each pin representing a Braille character.

Braille Embossers

Braille Embossers are assistive devices that convert electronic text into Braille, a tactile writing system used by people who are blind or visually impaired. These devices play a crucial role in promoting accessibility and inclusion for individuals with visual impairments, allowing them to access printed materials, interact with digital content, and participate in various activities that rely on written information. The main function of a Braille Embosser is to emboss or print Braille characters onto a physical medium such as paper or plastic. This process involves translating electronic text into Braille code and then creating raised dots on the output medium to represent each Braille character. The resulting embossed Braille can be read by touch, enabling individuals with visual impairments to comprehend and navigate the content.

Braille Keyboards

A braille keyboard is a specialized input device designed for individuals with visual impairments, specifically those who read and write in braille. It allows them to input text and navigate through digital devices, such as computers and smartphones, using the braille writing system. The braille writing system consists of raised dots on a grid, where each dot represents a different letter or symbol. Braille keyboards are designed to mimic this grid, providing a tactile surface with small concave keys that correspond to the braille dots. Each key represents a specific braille character, allowing users to type in braille by pressing the appropriate combination of keys. Accessibility is a fundamental aspect of design, ensuring that products and services are usable and inclusive for individuals with disabilities. Braille keyboards play a crucial role in accessibility design as they enable individuals who are blind or have low vision to access and interact with digital technology. By providing an alternative input method, braille keyboards allow users to communicate, navigate, and perform various tasks independently. Braille keyboards can connect to devices via USB, Bluetooth, or other wireless technologies, allowing users to easily integrate them into their existing assistive technology setups. In addition to providing braille input, some keyboards may also offer additional functionality, such as speech feedback, haptic feedback, or auditory cues, to further enhance the user experience. These keyboards are particularly beneficial in educational, professional, and personal settings, where individuals with visual impairments rely on digital communication and information access. By using a braille keyboard, users can compose and edit text, send emails, browse the internet, engage in social media, use productivity applications, and perform a wide range of tasks that are essential in today's digital world. Overall, braille keyboards are instrumental tools in promoting accessibility and empowering individuals with visual impairments. By providing a means to communicate and interact with digital devices through the braille writing system, these keyboards enhance independence, participation, and inclusion for users with visual disabilities.

Braille Software

Braille software is a highly essential tool designed to enhance accessibility for visually impaired individuals. It is a computer program specifically developed to convert digital information into Braille code, facilitating the inclusive use of technology for people with visual impairments. This software plays a crucial role in ensuring equal access to information, education, employment opportunities, and various digital functionalities.By utilizing Braille software, visually impaired individuals can effectively navigate and interact with digital content. This software utilizes specialized algorithms that translate text, graphics, and other visual elements into Braille characters, allowing users to read, comprehend, and interact with digital information autonomously. It converts information displayed on a computer screen, digital documents, or other electronic sources into Braille format, which can be easily interpreted through tactile touch or by Braille display devices.

Braille Translation Software

Braille translation software is a specialized tool designed to convert electronic documents or text into braille, a tactile writing system used by individuals with visual impairments. This software plays a crucial role in ensuring accessibility for visually impaired individuals by enabling them to access and comprehend written information through touch. The software applies a systematic approach to convert textual content, such as documents, web pages, or e-books, into the braille representation. It first analyzes the input material, identifying characters, words, and formatting elements. Then, it maps these elements to their corresponding braille equivalents, following the rules and conventions of the braille code. Braille translation software offers several key features and functionalities to support effective braille conversion. It provides compatible input options, allowing users to import various file formats, such as plain text, rich text, PDF, or HTML, thereby accommodating different sources of electronic content. The software also incorporates multiple braille codes, such as Grade 1 and Grade 2 braille, as well as language-specific codes, to ensure accurate and contextually appropriate translations. To enhance readability and legibility for braille readers, the software considers formatting elements, including headings, paragraph breaks, lists, tables, and emphasis. It accurately represents these elements in braille form, enabling visually impaired individuals to navigate through the converted content with ease. Furthermore, the software includes options for adjusting the braille output's formatting, including line spacing, character spacing, and representation of graphics or images as tactile illustrations. Braille translation software often integrates with complementary assistive technologies or braille display devices, facilitating direct output from the software to a braille display unit. This integration allows for real-time, dynamic interaction with the translated content, enabling visually impaired individuals to read and navigate through the information efficiently. In summary, braille translation software serves as a vital tool in the field of accessibility design, converting electronic texts into braille representation for visually impaired individuals. It ensures equal access to information, enabling individuals with visual impairments to read and comprehend written content effectively through touch.

Braille Translation Tools

Braille Translation Tools refer to a set of software or hardware applications specifically designed to convert text or visual information into Braille, a writing system used by people who are blind or visually impaired. These tools play a crucial role in improving accessibility for individuals with visual disabilities by enabling them to access and comprehend written content. The primary function of Braille Translation Tools is to convert text-based information into Braille characters, allowing blind individuals to read and understand the content through tactile perception. With the help of these tools, documents, books, educational materials, signs, and other written texts can be efficiently translated into Braille, making them accessible to people who rely on this tactile writing system. Braille Translation Tools may come in the form of software applications, which can be installed on computers or mobile devices, or as specialized hardware devices that connect to a computer or other electronic devices. These tools utilize advanced algorithms and language processing techniques to analyze the input text and generate the corresponding Braille characters, which are then outputted either visually on a screen or through a tactile display. Some Braille Translation Tools also offer additional functionalities to enhance usability and customization. For example, they may provide options to adjust the speed and intensity of the outputted Braille, allowing users to adapt the reading experience to their preferences. Other tools may offer interactive features, such as real-time translation or speech synthesis, to further support individuals with varying degrees of visual impairment. Overall, Braille Translation Tools serve as essential components of accessibility design, facilitating the inclusion and independence of individuals with visual disabilities. By providing the means for converting text and visual information into Braille, these tools empower blind and visually impaired individuals to access and engage with written content, fostering equal opportunities for education, employment, and social integration.

Braille

Braille is a tactile writing system that enables individuals with visual impairments to read and write. It consists of raised dots arranged in a specific pattern, allowing users to feel and interpret the information using their sense of touch. Developed by Louis Braille in the early 19th century, Braille has become a crucial tool in promoting accessibility and inclusion for blind and visually impaired individuals. The Braille system is based on a grid of six dots, which can be arranged in 63 different combinations. Each combination represents a specific letter, number, punctuation mark, or even a whole word or contraction. By feeling these combinations, individuals can quickly and efficiently comprehend written information, including books, documents, and signage.

Browser Accessibility Extension

A Browser Accessibility Extension is a tool that can be installed in a web browser to enhance the accessibility and usability of websites for individuals with disabilities. It is designed to address the specific needs of users who have visual, auditory, cognitive, or motor impairments, enabling them to navigate and interact with online content more effectively and independently. The main purpose of a Browser Accessibility Extension is to provide additional accessibility features and functionalities that may not be available by default in a web browser or on specific websites. These extensions often come in the form of browser add-ons or plug-ins and can be installed with just a few clicks.

Captcha

A captcha is a tool used in accessibility design to verify that the user accessing a website or online service is a human and not a robot or automated program. It is a security measure implemented to prevent malicious activities such as spamming, data scraping, and automated attacks. Often presented in the form of a visual or audio challenge, a captcha requires the user to perform a specific task or answer a question that is easy for humans but difficult for machines to solve. This helps ensure that the user interacting with the website is an actual person and not a bot.

Captioned Videos

Captioned Videos refer to video content that includes text transcription of the audio elements, enabling individuals with hearing impairments or language barriers to access and understand the content. Captioning is an essential component of accessibility design as it ensures equal access for all users. Captioned videos can benefit a wide range of users, including the deaf and hard-of-hearing, individuals with cognitive or learning disabilities, and individuals who are non-native speakers or have limited proficiency in the language used in the video. By providing textual representation of the spoken words and other relevant audio cues, captioning allows users to comprehend the content even if they cannot hear or understand the audio track. Captioning involves the process of transcribing the audio components of a video, including speech, sound effects, and music, into text format. The captions are typically displayed on the screen synchronized with the corresponding moments in the video. This enables users to read the text as they watch the video, allowing for a more inclusive and accessible experience. In the context of accessibility design, captioned videos should adhere to certain guidelines to ensure maximum effectiveness. These guidelines include: 1. Accuracy and Synchronization: The captions should accurately reflect the spoken words and other relevant audio elements. They should also be properly synchronized with the video, appearing and disappearing at the appropriate times. 2. Readability: The captions should be displayed in a legible font, with sufficient contrast against the background. The text size should also be adjustable to accommodate users with visual impairments. 3. Clarity and Consistency: The captions should be clear and easy to understand, using simple language and punctuation. They should also be consistent in style and formatting throughout the video. 4. Caption Placement: The captions should be positioned in a location that does not obstruct other important visual elements of the video. It is recommended to place them at the bottom of the screen, following accessibility standards. In conclusion, captioned videos play a crucial role in ensuring equal access to video content for individuals with hearing impairments or language barriers. By providing text transcription of the audio elements, captioning enhances the accessibility and inclusivity of videos, allowing a wider audience to benefit from the content.

Captioning Services

Captioning services refer to the process of providing synchronized text for audio and visual content to ensure accessibility for individuals with hearing impairments. It involves the conversion of spoken dialogue, sound effects, and relevant non-speech elements into written form, enabling individuals who are deaf or hard of hearing to comprehend and engage with audiovisual content.By incorporating captions into multimedia content, including videos, films, television shows, online courses, presentations, and online platforms, captioning services enhance accessibility and inclusivity for diverse audiences.

Captioning Software

Captioning software refers to a type of software tool designed to provide captions or subtitles for various forms of media content, such as videos, movies, and presentations, with the aim of enhancing accessibility for individuals with hearing impairments or those who are deaf. This software is primarily developed to ensure that people with hearing disabilities can have equal access to audio information and enjoy the same level of understanding and engagement as individuals without hearing impairments. The main function of captioning software is to transcribe spoken dialogue or other relevant audio cues into text format, which is then displayed on the screen in synchronization with the corresponding visual content. By offering these text-based representations of the dialogue and audio elements, captioning software allows individuals who are deaf or hard of hearing to follow along with the content more easily and effectively. This promotes inclusivity and equal participation in various educational, entertainment, and professional settings.

Captioning

Captioning, in the context of accessibility design, refers to the process of transcribing and displaying text equivalents of spoken words or sounds in audiovisual content. It aims to improve access to information and comprehension for individuals with hearing impairments or those who prefer to read captions. Implementing captioning involves creating synchronized text captions that accompany audio or video content. These captions provide a visual representation of the spoken words or sounds, allowing viewers to follow along with the content even if they cannot hear or understand the audio. Captioning is particularly vital for people with hearing disabilities, as it ensures they have equal access to information and entertainment that others experience through audio.

Closed Captioning Services

Closed Captioning Services refer to a set of techniques used to provide a text-based representation of audio content in videos, films, TV shows, and other multimedia formats. This accessibility feature aims to assist individuals with hearing impairments, language barriers, or those in noisy environments by providing a visual representation of spoken words and sound effects. When it comes to accessibility design, closed captioning plays a crucial role in ensuring that audiovisual content is inclusive and accessible to a wider audience. By transcribing dialogue, sounds, and other relevant audio elements, closed captions enable individuals with hearing disabilities to understand and follow the content without relying on audio cues.

Closed Captioning Tools

Closed Captioning Tools are assistive technologies that provide access to audio content for individuals who are deaf or hard of hearing. These tools enable the display of synchronized text on a screen, allowing users to read the dialogue, sounds, and other audio elements associated with video content. Closed captioning has become an essential feature in modern media, as it ensures that audiovisual content is accessible to a diverse audience. Closed Captioning Tools are typically used in broadcasting, streaming services, movies, educational videos, and online platforms to provide equal access to everyone, regardless of hearing ability. Closed Captioning Tools consist of various components that work together to deliver inclusive audiovisual experiences. One crucial element is a closed captioning file, which contains the text and timing information that will be displayed on the screen. Different file formats, such as SubRip (.srt) or WebVTT (.vtt), are used to store closed captioning data. These files are created by professionals who transcribe and time-sync the audio content. To display closed captions, a video player or streaming platform must support closed captioning functionality. This can be achieved through the use of specialized software or by integrating closed captioning features directly into the player code. The closed captioning file is loaded alongside the video, and the player renders the text in sync with the audio. Closed Captioning Tools also offer customization options to meet individual accessibility needs. Users often have the ability to choose the font style, size, color, and positioning of the text to optimize readability. Some tools even provide customizable background colors or transparency settings, allowing users to ensure a comfortable viewing experience based on their visual preferences. Moreover, Closed Captioning Tools may include additional features for accessibility, such as the ability to scale or resize the video player window, control the playback speed, or adjust the volume independently from the captions. Such tools take into account the fact that accessibility is not limited to hearing impairment alone, but also includes individuals with visual or cognitive disabilities. In conclusion, Closed Captioning Tools are essential in enabling equal access to audiovisual content for individuals who are deaf or hard of hearing. By displaying synchronized text on the screen, these tools empower users to fully engage with various forms of media. The use of accessible technologies such as Closed Captioning Tools is crucial in promoting inclusivity and ensuring that everyone can enjoy and benefit from multimedia experiences.

Closed Captioning

Closed Captioning is a form of text representation that provides a synchronized transcription of the audio content in a video or media presentation. It is designed to make audio-visual content accessible to individuals who are deaf or hard of hearing, as well as to those who have difficulty understanding the spoken language. Closed captions are typically displayed at the bottom of the screen and include dialogue, sound effects, and other relevant audio information. The main purpose of closed captioning is to ensure that individuals with hearing impairments can fully comprehend and enjoy audio-visual content. By providing a visual representation of the audio content, closed captions allow deaf or hard of hearing individuals to follow the dialogue, understand the storyline, and engage with the media presentation. Closed captions also benefit individuals who speak a different language or have difficulty understanding the spoken language, as they can read the text in their preferred language or adjust the playback speed to accommodate their comprehension level. Implementing closed captioning in the design of multimedia content is essential for achieving accessibility and inclusivity. It ensures that individuals with hearing impairments can access the same information and entertainment as their peers. Closed captioning can be added to various types of media, including movies, TV shows, online videos, and live presentations. Content creators can use professional closed captioning services or employ automated captioning tools to generate accurate transcriptions of the audio content. Closed captioning is governed by accessibility standards and regulations, such as the Web Content Accessibility Guidelines (WCAG) set forth by the World Wide Web Consortium (W3C). These guidelines outline the requirements for captioning quality, timing, presentation, and user control. They emphasize the importance of accurate and well-synchronized captions that do not obstruct the visual experience of the media presentation. Compliance with these guidelines ensures that closed captions are effective and usable for individuals with hearing impairments.

Cognitive Disabilities

Cognitive disabilities refer to impairments that affect a person's cognitive processes, including their ability to think, learn, remember, and understand information. These disabilities can impact various aspects of a person's daily life, such as communication, problem-solving, decision-making, and social interactions. In the context of accessibility design, cognitive disabilities pose unique challenges that need to be addressed to ensure equal access for all individuals. People with cognitive disabilities may have difficulties comprehending and navigating complex information, following instructions, and maintaining focus and attention. Therefore, it is essential to design digital content and interfaces that are easily understandable, organized, and intuitive.

Cognitive Walkthrough

A cognitive walkthrough is a method used in the field of accessibility design to evaluate the usability and effectiveness of a digital interface or product, focusing specifically on how users with different cognitive abilities are able to understand and interact with it. In this process, a team of evaluators, including individuals with expertise in accessibility and cognitive impairments, step through the interface or product as if they were users with varying cognitive abilities. They systematically assess each step, considering factors such as clarity of language, simplicity of instructions, and consistency of design. The evaluators start by familiarizing themselves with the interface and the goals of the user, such as completing a specific task or finding relevant information. They then proceed to evaluate each step, analyzing how well the interface supports the user in achieving their goals. During the cognitive walkthrough, the evaluators assess the interface in terms of its ability to provide clear and concise information, offer meaningful cues, and present options in a logical and manageable way. They evaluate factors such as the visibility and prominence of important elements, the availability of guidance or assistance, and the overall flow and intuitiveness of the interface. By focusing on the cognitive aspects of accessibility, the cognitive walkthrough aims to identify potential barriers or challenges that individuals with cognitive impairments may face when interacting with the interface. This evaluation method helps designers understand how well their interface accommodates different cognitive abilities and provides insights into areas that may require further improvement. Ultimately, the cognitive walkthrough serves as a valuable tool for accessibility design, guiding developers in creating interfaces that are inclusive and accessible to individuals with varying cognitive abilities. A cognitive walkthrough is a method used in the field of accessibility design to evaluate the usability and effectiveness of a digital interface or product, focusing specifically on how users with different cognitive abilities are able to understand and interact with it. The evaluators start by familiarizing themselves with the interface and the goals of the user, such as completing a specific task or finding relevant information. They then proceed to evaluate each step, analyzing how well the interface supports the user in achieving their goals.

Color Blindness Simulator

Color blindness simulator is a tool used in the field of accessibility design to assist individuals in understanding how people with color blindness perceive colors. It aims to create awareness and promote inclusivity by providing a virtual experience of different types of color vision deficiencies. The color blindness simulator uses algorithms to simulate the visual effects of various types of color blindness, including protanopia (red-green color blindness), deuteranopia (also red-green color blindness but in a different form), and tritanopia (blue-yellow color blindness). By altering the colors displayed on a screen, the simulator provides a visual representation of how an individual with color vision deficiency would perceive the colors. In accessibility design, the color blindness simulator serves as a valuable tool for designers, developers, and content creators. It helps them ensure that their digital products, such as websites, applications, and graphics, are accessible to individuals with color vision deficiencies. By employing the simulator, designers can visualize how their color choices might appear to users with different types of color blindness. This allows for the identification and modification of potential issues that may impede the usability and comprehension of content for color vision deficient individuals. For example, a designer may use the color blindness simulator to examine whether there is a sufficient contrast between text colors and background colors for individuals with color vision deficiencies. They can also evaluate the legibility of certain color-coded information or data visualizations. By making adjustments based on the simulated color vision deficiencies, designers can create more accessible experiences for a wider range of users. Additionally, the color blindness simulator encourages empathy and understanding among designers and content creators. It emphasizes the importance of designing with inclusivity in mind, as individuals with color vision deficiencies compose a significant portion of the population. By experiencing how color blindness affects the perception of colors, designers gain insight into the challenges faced by these users and can integrate accessibility into their design processes from the beginning. Using the color blindness simulator in the field of accessibility design leads to more inclusive digital experiences. It helps ensure that individuals with color vision deficiencies can access information, navigate interfaces, and engage with content effectively. By striving for accessibility and implementing the insights gained from the simulator, designers contribute to a more equal and inclusive digital landscape.

Color Contrast Analyzer

Color Contrast Analyzer is a tool used in accessibility design to evaluate the contrast between foreground and background colors in order to ensure that text and graphics are perceptible to all individuals, including those with visual impairments. The Color Contrast Analyzer analyzes the luminosity values of different colors and calculates the contrast ratio between them. The contrast ratio is a quantitative measure that determines how distinguishable the foreground elements are from the background. This ratio is crucial for individuals with low vision, color blindness, or other visual impairments, as it affects their ability to read and understand the content. Ensuring an adequate contrast ratio is essential for meeting accessibility guidelines, such as the Web Content Accessibility Guidelines (WCAG). WCAG provides specific requirements for contrast ratios to ensure that individuals with visual impairments can perceive and interact with digital content effectively. The Color Contrast Analyzer allows designers and developers to input the hexadecimal values or RGB values of the foreground and background colors. It then automatically calculates the contrast ratio and provides a clear indication of whether the colors meet the accessibility standards. If the contrast ratio is too low, indicating poor visibility, the analyzer prompts the user to make adjustments to the colors until the ratio meets the required level. In addition to providing a pass/fail status based on the contrast ratio, the Color Contrast Analyzer often includes additional features to assist designers. These features may include the ability to simulate different types of color blindness, visualize the color contrast with various background patterns or textures, and analyze the accessibility of color combinations for users with specific visual impairments. Using the Color Contrast Analyzer in the design process helps ensure that web content is accessible to a wider range of users, including those with visual impairments. By incorporating accessible color contrast, designers can enhance the readability and usability of their websites, applications, and digital products, ultimately providing a more inclusive user experience for all individuals.

Color Contrast Analyzers

A color contrast analyzer is a tool used in the context of accessibility design to analyze the contrast between two or more colors in order to ensure that content is easily readable and perceptible by individuals with visual impairments, such as color blindness or low vision. It helps designers and developers identify color combinations that may present difficulties for certain users and allows them to make informed decisions to improve the accessibility of their digital products. This tool typically evaluates the contrast ratio between foreground and background colors, which is calculated based on the relative luminance values of the colors. The Web Content Accessibility Guidelines (WCAG) provide specific requirements for minimum contrast ratios for text and images to meet different levels of accessibility. For example, the minimum contrast ratio for standard text (14-point font or larger) is 4.5:1, while large text (18-point font or larger) requires a ratio of 3:1.

Color Contrast

Color contrast in the context of accessibility design refers to the distinction and visibility of text or graphical elements against their background colors. It is an essential consideration for ensuring that individuals with visual impairments or color blindness can perceive and comprehend content effectively. The contrast ratio between the foreground (text or graphic) and background colors is measured to assess the accessibility of a design. This ratio is expressed as a numerical value, where higher values indicate better contrast and improved readability. To determine the contrast ratio, the relative luminance of the foreground and background colors is calculated. Relative luminance is a measure of the perceived brightness of a color and is expressed on a scale from 0 to 1, where 0 is black and 1 is white. The contrast ratio is then obtained by dividing the higher relative luminance value by the lower one. The Web Content Accessibility Guidelines (WCAG) provide specific recommendations for minimum contrast ratios to ensure accessibility. The minimum contrast ratio for text and images of text is 4.5:1, except for large-scale text, which requires a contrast ratio of at least 3:1. Adequate color contrast is crucial for individuals with visual impairments, including those with low vision or color blindness. Insufficient contrast can make it difficult or impossible for these individuals to read or understand content. It may also cause eye strain or fatigue for users with visual sensitivities. Developers and designers can enhance color contrast by carefully selecting appropriate foreground and background colors. Dark text on a light background is generally considered more accessible than light text on a dark background. Additionally, avoiding color combinations with similar relative luminance values can contribute to improved contrast. It is important to note that color alone should not be the sole means of conveying information. Text should always be distinguishable and comprehensible even without relying on color perception. Providing alternative cues such as underlines, icons, or text formatting can further enhance accessibility. Incorporating sufficient color contrast is paramount in creating inclusive and accessible designs. By ensuring that text and graphical elements are distinguishable from their backgrounds, individuals with visual impairments can perceive and engage with digital content more effectively.

Color Vision Deficiency (CVD) Simulator

Color Vision Deficiency (CVD) Simulator is a tool used in the context of accessibility design to simulate how individuals with color vision deficiencies perceive colors. It enables designers and developers to understand and address the challenges faced by people with CVD in perceiving certain colors, allowing them to create more inclusive digital experiences. By replicating the visual perception of individuals with CVD, the simulator helps identify potential issues and allows designers to make appropriate adjustments to color schemes, graphic elements, and text content. It provides insights into how colorblind users may experience websites, applications, or other digital interfaces, thereby promoting equal access and usability for everyone.

Color Vision Deficiency Simulators

Color vision deficiency simulators are tools or software applications designed to simulate the experience of individuals with color vision deficiencies (CVDs) or color blindness. These simulators aim to provide a visual representation of how users with different types of CVDs perceive colors, helping designers and developers to create more accessible digital content and user interfaces. The purpose of color vision deficiency simulators in the context of accessibility design is twofold. Firstly, they allow designers and developers to gain a better understanding of how their content or interfaces may appear to users with color vision deficiencies. By simulating the visual perception of individuals with CVDs, these simulators enable designers to identify potential issues regarding color contrast, color coding, and visual information hierarchy. Secondly, color vision deficiency simulators help designers and developers in making informed decisions about color choices and combinations. By visualizing how certain color combinations may be perceived by users with CVDs, these simulators assist in selecting colors that maintain sufficient contrast and do not cause confusion or misinterpretation. This is particularly important for conveying important information, such as error messages, calls-to-action, or data visualization, where the use of color alone should not be relied upon. Color vision deficiency simulators often provide different modes or filters to simulate specific types of CVDs, such as protanopia (red-green color blindness), deuteranopia (green-red color blindness), and tritanopia (blue-yellow color blindness), among others. These modes allow designers to switch between simulations and observe how different color combinations are perceived by users with varying degrees of color vision deficiencies. By using color vision deficiency simulators during the design and development process, designers and developers can ensure that their digital content and user interfaces are accessible and inclusive to a wider range of users, including those with color vision deficiencies. This is in line with the principles of accessibility design, which aim to make digital experiences usable by all individuals, regardless of their abilities or disabilities. In conclusion, color vision deficiency simulators are valuable tools in the field of accessibility design. Their ability to simulate the visual perception of individuals with color vision deficiencies helps designers and developers create more inclusive and accessible digital content and user interfaces.

Color Vision Deficiency Testing Services

Color Vision Deficiency Testing Services refers to a set of assessments and tools specifically designed to determine if individuals have difficulty perceiving colors accurately. In the context of accessibility design, these services play a crucial role in ensuring that digital content and interfaces are accessible to people with color vision deficiencies, such as red-green or blue-yellow color blindness. Accessibility is a fundamental principle in design that aims to create inclusive experiences for all users, regardless of their abilities or disabilities. Considering that color is often used as a visual cue to convey information and indicate functionality in digital interfaces, it is essential to address the needs of individuals with color vision deficiencies. By utilizing Color Vision Deficiency Testing Services, designers and developers can identify potential issues and make necessary adjustments to ensure accessibility. Color Vision Deficiency Testing Services typically include various tests and simulations that assess an individual's ability to discriminate between colors accurately. These tests often involve presenting color patterns, shapes, or images that can highlight potential difficulties in perceiving specific color combinations. The tests may require participants to identify or differentiate between different colors or patterns, depending on the specific type of color deficiency being assessed. Through the results obtained from color vision deficiency tests, designers can gain insights into potential accessibility barriers within their digital products or interfaces. By identifying problematic color combinations, designers can make informed decisions to modify their designs, such as adjusting color contrasts, using alternative visual cues, or providing additional textual information to ensure that all users can understand and interact with the content effectively. Moreover, Color Vision Deficiency Testing Services can assist in complying with accessibility regulations and guidelines, such as the Web Content Accessibility Guidelines (WCAG). WCAG provides recommendations and standards for creating accessible digital content, and addressing color vision deficiencies is a crucial aspect of meeting these guidelines. In conclusion, Color Vision Deficiency Testing Services play a vital role in accessibility design by allowing designers and developers to identify and address potential barriers for individuals with color vision deficiencies. By utilizing these services, designers can ensure that their digital products and interfaces are inclusive and provide equal access to all users.

Color Vision Deficiency Testing Tools

Color vision deficiency testing tools are tools used in accessibility design to assess whether individuals with color vision deficiencies are able to distinguish between different colors accurately. These tools are important in ensuring that web content and graphic designs can be easily perceived and understood by all users, regardless of their color vision abilities. One commonly used color vision deficiency testing tool is the Ishihara Color Test, which consists of a series of plates containing patterns made up of colored dots. Individuals with color vision deficiencies may have difficulty seeing or distinguishing certain patterns or numbers within the dots on the plates. By determining which plates individuals can or cannot accurately identify, designers can gain insights into their color vision abilities and adjust their designs accordingly. Another color vision deficiency testing tool is the Farnsworth-Munsell 100 Hue Test. This test assesses an individual's ability to order and arrange colored caps according to their hue. Users with color vision deficiencies may struggle to accurately differentiate between hues and may make errors in arranging the caps. By analyzing the results of this test, designers can better understand the specific color deficiencies of individuals and make appropriate design adjustments, such as using alternative color combinations or providing additional visual cues. In addition to these traditional color vision deficiency testing tools, there are also various digital tools and software available for assessing color accessibility. These tools often allow designers to simulate different types of color vision deficiencies, such as protanopia, deuteranopia, or tritanopia, and view their designs as individuals with these deficiencies would perceive them. By using these tools, designers can quickly identify potential issues with color contrasts, readability, or the ability to distinguish important elements within their designs. Overall, color vision deficiency testing tools are essential in the accessibility design process to ensure that digital content and design elements can be easily understood and accessed by individuals with color vision deficiencies. By using these tools, designers can make informed decisions regarding color choices, contrasts, and the overall usability of their designs, thus creating more inclusive and accessible digital experiences for all users.

Color Vision Deficiency Tools

Color Vision Deficiency Tools refer to a set of tools and techniques designed to enhance accessibility for individuals with color vision deficiencies. Color vision deficiency, also known as color blindness, is a condition where individuals have difficulty perceiving certain colors or distinguishing between them. These tools aim to ensure that digital content, such as websites, applications, and documents, is accessible and can be effectively used by individuals with color vision deficiencies. The goal is to provide an inclusive experience for all users, regardless of their visual abilities.

Colorblind-Friendly Design

Colorblind-friendly design refers to creating digital content that is accessible and easily perceivable by individuals with color vision deficiencies. This approach involves the implementation of specific design principles and techniques to ensure that users with colorblindness can comprehend and interact with the content without any difficulties or confusion. To achieve colorblind-friendly design, it is crucial to consider the different types of color vision deficiencies, such as red-green colorblindness and blue-yellow colorblindness. These impairments can affect individuals' ability to differentiate between certain colors, leading to challenges in understanding information conveyed through color alone. One key principle of colorblind-friendly design is to avoid conveying information using color alone. This means that important content or instructions should not solely rely on color coding to be understood. Instead, additional visual cues, such as patterns, shapes, or text labels, should be used to provide alternative methods of conveying information. For example, using different patterns or textures to distinguish between different elements of a chart or graph can ensure that colorblind users can interpret the data effectively. Another important aspect of colorblind-friendly design is to use color combinations that have sufficient contrast. This helps individuals with color vision deficiencies to differentiate between different elements on a webpage or app. Colors that are similar in hue but differ in brightness or saturation can be particularly challenging for colorblind users to distinguish. By choosing color combinations with high contrast, designers can ensure that content remains clear and legible for everyone. In addition to these principles, it is also beneficial to provide users with the ability to customize the color scheme of a website or application. This allows individuals with colorblindness to adjust the interface to their specific needs and preferences. Providing options to switch between different color themes or adjust the hue and saturation can greatly enhance the accessibility of a digital product. Overall, colorblind-friendly design is a crucial aspect of accessibility design as it ensures that individuals with color vision deficiencies can access and interact with digital content without any barriers. By implementing design principles that rely on more than just color coding, using contrasting colors, and offering customization options, designers can create inclusive experiences that cater to a diverse range of users. Colorblind-friendly design refers to creating digital content that is accessible and easily perceivable by individuals with color vision deficiencies. This approach involves the implementation of specific design principles and techniques to ensure that users with colorblindness can comprehend and interact with the content without any difficulties or confusion. To achieve colorblind-friendly design, it is crucial to consider the different types of color vision deficiencies, such as red-green colorblindness and blue-yellow colorblindness. These impairments can affect individuals' ability to differentiate between certain colors, leading to challenges in understanding information conveyed through color alone.

Colorblind-Friendly Tools

Colorblind-Friendly Tools are digital resources, applications, or features designed to accommodate individuals with color vision deficiencies, such as colorblindness. These tools aim to enhance accessibility by providing options or alternatives that improve visibility and comprehension of content for colorblind users. One widely used colorblind-friendly tool is the colorblind mode, which can be found in various software applications, web browsers, and operating systems. When this mode is activated, it modifies the color palette of the interface or content, making it more distinguishable and understandable for colorblind individuals. For example, it may transform red and green elements into shades that are easier to differentiate, such as blue and yellow. By utilizing color palettes that consider color vision deficiencies, colorblind modes prevent confusion or misinterpretation of information due to color distinctions that are not discernible for colorblind individuals. Other colorblind-friendly tools focus on improving the accessibility of charts, graphs, and visual presentations. Such tools provide customizable color schemes, allowing users to select color combinations that are more visible and distinguishable for those with color vision deficiencies. Additionally, these tools may offer alternative representations, such as patterns, textures, or labels, that convey information to colorblind individuals effectively. These alternatives ensure that users with color vision deficiencies can perceive and interpret visual content accurately, avoiding any misunderstandings or misinterpretations caused by reliance on color alone. Colorblind-friendly tools also extend to the realm of web design and development. Web designers can incorporate accessible color schemes, fonts, and contrast ratios to ensure a positive browsing experience for colorblind users. For instance, using high contrast between text and background colors can improve readability, particularly for individuals with color vision deficiencies. Tools and guidelines are available to assist designers in selecting appropriate color palettes and optimizing color contrast, thereby enhancing the accessibility of their websites or applications. In conclusion, colorblind-friendly tools are essential in promoting inclusivity and accessibility for individuals with color vision deficiencies. By employing these tools, content creators, software developers, and web designers can ensure that their products and interfaces are accessible to a wider range of users, including those with colorblindness or other color vision impairments.

Colorblindness

Colorblindness, also known as color vision deficiency, is a visual impairment that affects an individual's ability to perceive and distinguish certain colors. It is a prevalent condition, affecting approximately 8% of men and 0.5% of women globally. For individuals with colorblindness, the retina's cone cells, responsible for detecting different colors, do not function properly. This can result in difficulty distinguishing between certain colors, such as red and green, blue and yellow, or both. There are several types of colorblindness, including protanopia (red insensitivity), deuteranopia (green insensitivity), and tritanopia (blue insensitivity).

Communication Access Real-Time Translation (CART)

Communication Access Real-Time Translation (CART) is an accessibility feature designed to assist individuals with hearing disabilities by providing a real-time text display of spoken communication. CART utilizes advanced technology and human transcribers to convert spoken words into written text, allowing individuals with hearing impairments to follow conversations, lectures, presentations, and other verbal information. Through the use of specialized software and hardware, CART captures the spoken words and instantly displays them on a screen in a clear and easily readable format. The transcriber, often referred to as a CART provider, listens to the audio in real-time and types the words into a computer or stenographic machine. The text is then transmitted to a display device, such as a computer monitor or projection screen, where it can be read by the individual requiring the accommodation. This accessibility solution is particularly valuable in educational settings, where it enables students with hearing impairments to fully participate in classroom discussions and lectures. CART can also be used in meetings, conferences, and other public speaking events, ensuring that individuals with hearing disabilities are included and have equal access to the information being shared. By providing a real-time text display of spoken communication, CART helps bridge the gap between individuals with hearing impairments and their hearing counterparts. It enhances communication and comprehension, allowing individuals with hearing disabilities to actively engage in conversations and fully understand the information being conveyed. CART can be used alongside other assistive technologies, such as hearing aids or cochlear implants, to further enhance accessibility for individuals with hearing impairments. It promotes inclusivity and equal participation in various aspects of life, ranging from educational opportunities to professional environments.

Conformance Testing

Accessibility design is the practice of ensuring that digital content and products are accessible to all users, including those with disabilities. One aspect of accessibility design is conformance testing, which involves evaluating whether a website or application meets the established accessibility standards and guidelines. Conformance testing is a systematic process that aims to determine if the design and functionality of a digital product adhere to the specified accessibility requirements. It identifies any barriers or difficulties that users with disabilities may encounter while using the product. The testing process involves examining different components and aspects of the digital product, such as its content, structure, navigation, forms, and multimedia elements. The goal is to ensure that the product can be comprehended, operated, and interacted with effectively by individuals with diverse abilities. When conducting conformance testing for accessibility design, testers typically refer to established accessibility standards and guidelines, such as the Web Content Accessibility Guidelines (WCAG). These guidelines provide a comprehensive set of recommendations for making digital content more accessible to people with disabilities. Testers evaluate the product against these standards and guidelines, identifying any instances where the product falls short of meeting the recommended accessibility criteria. Conformance testing involves both automated and manual testing techniques. Automated testing tools can help identify potential accessibility issues automatically, such as missing alt text for images, improper use of headings, or inadequate color contrast. Manual testing, on the other hand, involves human evaluation and interaction with the product to determine if it can be used effectively by individuals with disabilities. This may include testing with assistive technologies and simulating various disabilities, such as using screen readers for individuals with visual impairments or testing keyboard navigation for individuals with motor disabilities. The results of conformance testing are used to identify areas where the digital product needs improvement to ensure accessibility. These findings can then be addressed by developers and designers, who can make the necessary adjustments to resolve any accessibility issues. Regular conformance testing is essential to ensure that accessibility standards are maintained throughout the development process and to provide a better user experience for individuals with disabilities. In conclusion, conformance testing in the context of accessibility design is a systematic evaluation process to determine if a digital product meets the established accessibility standards and guidelines. It involves examining various components and aspects of the product and can include both automated and manual testing techniques. Correct implementation of conformance testing can help ensure that digital products are accessible to individuals with disabilities, enhancing their user experience and inclusivity.

Conformance

Conformance in the context of accessibility design refers to the degree to which a website or application adheres to specific standards and guidelines to ensure equal access and usability for all individuals, including those with disabilities. In order to achieve conformance, web developers and designers must follow established accessibility guidelines such as the Web Content Accessibility Guidelines (WCAG). These guidelines provide a framework for creating accessible content by outlining specific success criteria that must be met. Conformance is typically measured on a scale of three levels: A, AA, and AAA. Level A conformance includes the most basic accessibility requirements, while level AA includes a higher level of accessibility and is considered the minimum level needed for most web content. Level AAA represents the highest level of accessibility and includes the most stringent requirements. To achieve conformance, designers and developers must ensure that their website or application meets the required success criteria for the chosen conformance level. This includes aspects such as providing alternative text for images, ensuring proper color contrast, using descriptive headings and labels, implementing keyboard accessibility, and providing captions for multimedia content. Conformance is not a one-time task but an ongoing process. It requires regular reviews and updates to ensure that accessibility standards are maintained as technologies evolve and new guidelines are introduced. In addition, conformance should be tested across different devices, browsers, and assistive technologies to ensure compatibility and usability for all users. Ensuring conformance to accessibility guidelines benefits not only individuals with disabilities but also provides a better user experience for all users. It can increase the reach and usability of a website or application, improve search engine optimization, and help organizations comply with legal requirements and regulations regarding accessibility. In conclusion, conformance in accessibility design refers to adhering to established guidelines and standards to create accessible websites and applications. It involves implementing specific success criteria to ensure equal access and usability for all individuals, regardless of their abilities. Achieving conformance requires ongoing efforts and regular reviews to maintain accessibility standards as technologies evolve.

Content Access

Content access refers to the ability of all individuals, regardless of disabilities, to access and comprehend the information presented on a website, application, or any other digital platform. It involves designing and developing digital content in a way that ensures equal access and usability for everyone, including individuals with visual, motor, auditory, cognitive, or other impairments. Content access is a fundamental principle of accessibility design, which aims to remove barriers and provide equal opportunities for all users. This principle recognizes that individuals with disabilities rely on assistive technologies, such as screen readers, magnifiers, or alternative input devices, to perceive, navigate, and interact with digital content. By making digital content accessible, designers can enhance user experience, inclusivity, and compliance with accessibility standards and regulations.

Content Accessibility Guidelines (CAG)

Content Accessibility Guidelines (CAG) are a set of standards and recommendations that ensure digital content is designed to be accessible to all users, regardless of their abilities or disabilities. These guidelines provide a framework for web designers, developers, and content creators to follow, to make their content more inclusive and usable for individuals with disabilities. CAG focuses on various aspects of accessibility, including visual, auditory, motor, and cognitive impairments. It provides guidelines for designing content that is perceivable, operable, understandable, and robust. By conforming to these guidelines, designers can make their content more accessible to a wider range of users, including those who may rely on assistive technologies such as screen readers or voice command systems. Perceivable: The guidelines in this category ensure that people with visual impairments or other disabilities can perceive the content presented on a website. This includes providing alternatives for non-text content, such as images or videos, so that users using screen readers can understand the information. It also includes ensuring sufficient color contrast to make content readable for users with low vision. Operable: These guidelines focus on making the website easy to navigate and operate for users with motor or mobility impairments. This includes providing keyboard accessibility, so that users who cannot use a mouse can still navigate through the website. It also involves ensuring that interactive elements, such as buttons or links, are large enough and spaced adequately to be easily clickable. Understandable: This category of guidelines emphasizes the need for clear and concise content organization, instructions, and labels. It ensures that users with cognitive impairments can understand the information presented on the website. This involves using plain language, avoiding jargon, and providing consistent navigation and page layouts. Robust: These guidelines aim to ensure that content is compatible with a wide range of assistive technologies and future web technologies. By adhering to these guidelines, designers can future-proof their content and ensure that it remains accessible as technologies evolve and new assistive devices are developed. Overall, following the CAG helps to create content that is accessible to all individuals, regardless of their abilities or disabilities. It promotes equal access to information and services, enabling everyone to fully participate in the digital landscape.

Content Adaptation Services

Content Adaptation Services refer to the process of modifying the content of a website, app, or other digital platform to make it more accessible to individuals with disabilities. These services aim to ensure that people with disabilities can access and navigate digital content, regardless of their impairments. The goal of content adaptation services is to remove barriers that may prevent individuals with disabilities from fully participating in the digital world. This involves making the content compatible with assistive technologies, such as screen readers, keyboard navigation, and voice commands. By adapting the content, it becomes easier for individuals with visual, auditory, cognitive, or motor impairments to interact with digital platforms effectively.

Content Adaptation Solutions

Content adaptation solutions refer to the methods and techniques used to modify or transform digital content in order to make it more accessible to individuals with disabilities. These solutions are designed to ensure that people with various impairments are able to perceive, understand, navigate, and interact with digital content, regardless of the devices or technologies they use. Accessibility design is a crucial aspect of web development and content creation, as it aims to provide equal access to information and services for all users, including those with disabilities. Content adaptation solutions address the diverse needs and requirements of individuals with disabilities, such as visual, auditory, cognitive, and motor impairments.

Content Adaptation Tools

Content adaptation tools are software or systems that are used in the context of accessibility design to modify or transform content to make it more accessible to individuals with disabilities.

These tools are designed to address barriers in accessing and understanding information by people with diverse abilities. Content adaptation tools employ various techniques and methods to modify the content and its presentation. For individuals with visual impairments, these tools can adjust the font size, color contrast, and layout of the content to make it easier to read. They may also provide options for highlighting or magnifying specific portions of the content. Additionally, content adaptation tools can convert text into speech or braille, allowing individuals with visual impairments to access the information through alternative means. In the context of accessibility design, content adaptation tools play a crucial role in ensuring equal access to information for individuals with hearing impairments. These tools can provide captions or subtitles for multimedia content, making it accessible to individuals who are deaf or hard of hearing. They may also offer the ability to convert speech into textual form, enabling individuals with hearing impairments to understand spoken content. Moreover, content adaptation tools can assist individuals with cognitive or learning disabilities by simplifying and clarifying the content. These tools can help in breaking down complex sentences, providing definitions or explanations of unfamiliar terms, and offering alternative formats that cater to different learning styles. They may also offer interactive features and prompts to encourage user engagement and enhance comprehension.

Content Delivery Networks (CDN) For Accessibility

Content Delivery Networks (CDN) for Accessibility are specialized systems designed to improve the accessibility of web content by delivering it quickly and smoothly to users in a more efficient and inclusive way. CDNs are networks of servers distributed globally that work together to store and deliver web content, such as images, videos, scripts, and style sheets. They act as intermediaries between the user's device and the website, retrieving and delivering content from the closest server to the user's location. This reduces the distance the content has to travel, minimizing latency and improving overall website performance.

Content Delivery Networks (CDN) For Accessible Content

A Content Delivery Network (CDN) is a network of geographically distributed servers that work together to deliver accessible content to users quickly and efficiently. CDNs help improve the accessibility and performance of websites and web applications by caching and distributing content to multiple servers located near the end users. When a user requests content from a website or web application, the CDN identifies the server closest to the user's location and delivers the content from that server. By selecting the server with the lowest latency, CDNs reduce the time it takes for the content to reach the user, resulting in faster and more accessible experiences.

Content Inventory Software

Content Inventory Software refers to a digital tool designed to assist in the management and organization of digital content. It serves as a central repository for storing, cataloging, and tracking various types of content, such as web pages, images, documents, and multimedia files. In the context of accessibility design, content inventory software plays a crucial role in ensuring that digital content meets the needs and requirements of all users, including those with disabilities. Accessibility design aims to create digital content that is inclusive and usable by individuals with diverse abilities. This means ensuring that individuals with disabilities can access, navigate, and interact with the content effectively. Content inventory software facilitates the accessibility design process by providing features and functionalities that support the assessment and improvement of content accessibility.

Content Inventory Tools

A content inventory tool is a software application or online platform that is used in the field of accessibility design to organize and analyze the content of a website or digital platform. Its primary purpose is to create a structured inventory of the various types of content present on a site, including text, images, videos, audio files, and interactive elements. By generating a comprehensive list of all the content items, a content inventory tool enables accessibility designers to easily identify and evaluate the accessibility attributes and characteristics of each element. These attributes may include proper alternative text for images, closed captions or transcripts for videos, descriptive labels for interactive elements, and other accessibility considerations.

Content Inventory

A content inventory is a systematic approach used in accessibility design to thoroughly analyze and organize all the content on a website, ensuring it is accessible to all users, including those with disabilities. The process involves compiling a detailed list of all the content elements present on the website, including text, images, videos, audio files, and interactive features. Each element is categorized and described, noting its location, purpose, and any accessibility barriers it may present. The content inventory serves as an essential tool for web designers and developers to assess the accessibility of their website and make necessary improvements. It helps identify any content that may not be perceivable, operable, understandable, or robust for users with disabilities. By conducting a content inventory, designers can identify and address accessibility issues such as missing alternative text for images, inaccessible PDF documents, lack of captions for videos, or complex navigation structures. It also allows them to evaluate the overall organization and structure of the content, ensuring it is intuitive and easy to navigate for all users. In addition, a content inventory helps designers understand the scope and complexity of the website, enabling more effective planning and decision-making throughout the design process. It provides insights into content patterns, duplication, or inconsistencies that may hinder accessibility and user experience. To conduct a content inventory, designers typically use various tools and techniques. They manually review each page of the website, examining the source code and interacting with the elements. The information is then recorded in a spreadsheet or database, allowing for easy categorization, sorting, and analysis. Regularly updating and maintaining the content inventory is crucial to accommodate changes to the website. As content is added, modified, or removed, the inventory should be revised to ensure continued accessibility. In conclusion, a content inventory is a systematic approach used in accessibility design to analyze and organize all the content on a website. It helps to identify and address accessibility barriers, improve the overall user experience, and ensure equal access to information for all users, regardless of their abilities.

Content Management System (CMS) Accessibility

A Content Management System (CMS) Accessibility refers to the design and development practices used to ensure that CMS platforms are inclusive and usable by individuals with disabilities. It involves creating websites or applications that can be accessed and understood by people with varying levels of abilities, regardless of their visual, auditory, physical, or cognitive impairments. Web accessibility is crucial as it allows everyone, including people with disabilities, to access, understand, and interact with digital content without any barriers. CMS platforms play a significant role in enabling accessibility as they provide the tools and functionalities to create, manage, and publish web content effectively.

Content Readability

Content readability refers to the ease with which individuals can understand and navigate through written or digital content. In the context of accessibility design, it involves creating content that is easily comprehensible and accessible for people with various disabilities or impairments. This includes individuals with visual impairments, cognitive disabilities, learning disabilities, or those who use assistive technologies such as screen readers. When designing for content readability, it is essential to consider the following factors: 1. Plain Language: Using simple and concise language helps to make content more readable. Avoiding jargon, technical terms, or complex sentence structures enables a wider audience to understand and engage with the information. 2. Font and Typography: Selecting legible fonts and appropriate typography improves content readability. Using sans-serif fonts, maintaining proper font size, and ensuring sufficient spacing between characters and lines contribute to better readability, especially for individuals with visual impairments. 3. Contrast and Color: Employing sufficient contrast between text and background is crucial for individuals with low vision or color blindness. High contrast enables the text to stand out and enhances readability. Additionally, avoiding overreliance on color as the sole means of conveying essential information is important. 4. Text Structure: Organizing content into sections, headings, subheadings, and paragraphs facilitates comprehension for all users. Utilizing appropriate heading tags (e.g., h1, h2, etc.) and maintaining a logical order helps individuals using assistive technologies to navigate the content more easily. 5. Alternative Text: Providing alternative text descriptions for images helps individuals who cannot see the visuals to understand the context. Screen readers read aloud these alternative texts, enabling visually impaired users to gather information about the images. 6. Simplified Navigation: Creating clear and intuitive navigation menus and links ensures that users can locate and access content easily. Organizing content in a logical manner and providing descriptive links and buttons contribute to a more user-friendly experience. By considering these factors and implementing content readability best practices, accessibility designers can make digital content more inclusive and accessible to a wider range of users, regardless of their abilities or impairments.

Content Structure

Accessibility design refers to the practice of creating digital content and user interfaces that can be easily understood and used by individuals with disabilities. It involves considering the needs of a diverse range of users, including those with visual, auditory, physical, cognitive, and neurological impairments, and ensuring that they can access and interact with the content in an inclusive and equitable manner. Accessibility design encompasses various principles and techniques that aim to remove barriers and provide equal opportunities for individuals with disabilities. This involves considering factors such as color contrast, scalable typography, alternative text for images, clear and concise labeling of elements, use of proper headings and hierarchical structures, and keyboard accessibility. These design choices help individuals with visual impairments, cognitive disabilities, or motor impairments navigate and interact with the content effectively through assistive technologies such as screen readers, magnifiers, and keyboard controls.

Contrast Ratio

The contrast ratio, in the context of accessibility design, refers to the difference in luminance between the foreground text or graphics and the background on a web page. It is an important metric that helps ensure that visually impaired users can perceive and read content effectively. In accessibility design, it is crucial to have sufficient contrast between the text or graphics and the background to ensure readability for individuals with visual impairments, such as low vision or color blindness. The contrast ratio is calculated by comparing the relative luminance of the two elements.

Deaf Culture

Deaf Culture refers to the unique customs, behaviors, beliefs, and practices of individuals who are deaf and communicate using sign language. It encompasses a shared community and identity among deaf individuals, characterized by a visual and tactile language, distinct social norms, arts, literature, history, and traditions. The concept of Deaf Culture recognizes that being deaf is not a disability or a condition that needs to be fixed, but rather an inherent trait that contributes to a rich and diverse cultural heritage. Members of Deaf Culture value and embrace their deafness as a natural and significant part of their identity, and they reject the notion that deafness should be viewed as a deficiency or limitation. In the context of accessibility design, understanding and incorporating Deaf Culture is crucial for creating inclusive and equitable experiences for deaf individuals. Designing with Deaf Culture in mind means ensuring that information and communication are accessible to individuals who primarily use sign language for communication. Accessibility design should strive to provide visual and tactile alternatives to auditory information, such as closed captions, transcripts, and visual cues, to accommodate individuals who are deaf. It should consider the specific needs and preferences of deaf users, such as incorporating sign language videos or animations to enhance understanding and engagement. Moreover, it is important to acknowledge the unique communication styles and preferences within Deaf Culture. Providing options for users to choose their preferred communication modality, whether it be sign language interpretation, speech-to-text technology, or other forms of visual communication, can significantly enhance accessibility and user experience. By embracing Deaf Culture in accessibility design, we can promote inclusivity, equal access, and participation for deaf individuals in various domains, including education, employment, entertainment, and social interactions. It fosters a sense of belonging, respect, and recognition for the cultural diversity and linguistic richness of the deaf community.

Descriptive Links

In the context of accessibility design, descriptive links refer to the practice of using clear and informative link text that accurately conveys the target of the link to users with disabilities or those using assistive technologies. Using descriptive links is crucial in ensuring equal access to web content for all users, including those with visual impairments or cognitive disabilities. By providing meaningful link text, users can understand the purpose and destination of a link without relying solely on visual cues. This enhances the overall user experience and enables individuals with disabilities to navigate and interact with web pages more efficiently. Descriptive links can be achieved by avoiding generic or ambiguous link text such as "click here" or "read more," which do not provide any context or information about the link's destination. Instead, it is recommended to use descriptive phrases or keywords that accurately describe the content or action associated with the link. For example, instead of using "click here for more information," a more descriptive and accessible link could be "learn more about the accessibility guidelines." This provides users with a clear indication of what information they can expect to find by following the link. Furthermore, it is important to ensure that links make sense when read out of context. Screen readers, commonly used by individuals with visual impairments, often allow users to navigate through a web page by listening to a list of links on the page. Therefore, link text should be informative even when read on its own, without the surrounding content. When crafting descriptive links, it is also beneficial to consider the length of the link text. Links that are excessively long can be difficult to understand and navigate for individuals using assistive technologies. Keeping link text concise and to the point helps users quickly determine whether the destination of the link is relevant to their needs. Overall, employing descriptive links in web design plays a crucial role in improving the accessibility and usability of a website. By providing clear and informative link text, individuals with disabilities can effortlessly navigate through content and access the information they need. This inclusive approach fosters equal opportunities for everyone to engage with web content, reinforcing the principles of accessibility design. Descriptive links refer to using clear and informative link text that accurately conveys the target of the link to users with disabilities or those using assistive technologies. It enhances accessibility and usability by allowing users to understand the purpose and destination of a link without relying solely on visual cues.

Descriptive Video Service (DVS)

The Descriptive Video Service (DVS) is an accessibility feature that provides additional audio description to assist individuals who are blind or have low vision in understanding visual elements during television programming, movies, or other audiovisual content. DVS is specifically designed to enhance the accessibility of audiovisual materials by providing an additional narrative track that describes important visual details, actions, and scene changes that might not be clear from the existing audio alone. This audio description is typically inserted into natural pauses in the dialogue or audio track and does not interfere or overlap with the original audio content.

Digital Accessibility Assessment Services

Digital Accessibility Assessment Services refer to the evaluation and analysis of digital products, applications, websites, or software to ensure that they are accessible and inclusive to all users, including those with disabilities. These services focus on examining various aspects of a digital product's design, functionality, and user experience to identify any barriers that may prevent individuals with visual, auditory, physical, cognitive, or neurological impairments from fully utilizing and engaging with the digital content. The ultimate goal of digital accessibility assessment services is to ensure that digital products meet internationally recognized accessibility standards, such as the Web Content Accessibility Guidelines (WCAG). The assessment process involves a combination of automated testing tools, manual testing techniques, and expert analysis to evaluate different components of a digital product's accessibility. During the assessment, the accessibility professionals assess and provide recommendations for improving the following areas: 1. Perceivability: Ensuring that all users, irrespective of their abilities, can perceive and comprehend the information presented on the digital platform. This includes aspects such as providing alternative text for images, captions for videos, and appropriate color contrast for text. 2. Operability: Ensuring that users can easily navigate and interact with the digital product, using a wide range of input devices, including keyboards, mouse, or assistive technologies. This involves assessing keyboard accessibility, focus management, and functionality of interactive elements. 3. Understandability: Ensuring that the content and operation of the digital product are clear and comprehensible to all users. This includes evaluating the organization of content, use of plain language, and clarity in error messages. 4. Robustness: Ensuring that the digital product is capable of being interpreted and accessed by a wide range of user agents, including assistive technologies. This involves assessing the compatibility of the product with different browsers, screen readers, and other assistive technologies. By conducting digital accessibility assessments, organizations can identify and address any accessibility barriers early in the design and development process, leading to a more inclusive and equal digital experience for all users. These assessments not only help organizations comply with legal requirements and regulations related to digital accessibility but also contribute to building a positive brand image, increasing user satisfaction, and expanding the potential user base.

Digital Accessibility Assessment Tools

A digital accessibility assessment tool refers to a software or online application that evaluates and measures the accessibility of digital content, such as websites, applications, or documents. These tools automatically analyze various aspects of the user interface, content structure, and functionality to identify potential barriers for people with disabilities. The primary goal of digital accessibility assessment tools is to ensure that individuals with disabilities have equal access to information and services provided through digital platforms. These tools help organizations and developers comply with accessibility standards, guidelines, and regulations, such as the Web Content Accessibility Guidelines (WCAG).

Digital Accessibility Testing

Digital Accessibility Testing is a process that evaluates the extent to which a digital product, such as a website or mobile application, conforms to accessibility standards and guidelines. The goal of this testing is to ensure that individuals with disabilities are able to access and use the product effectively and without barriers. In the context of accessibility design, digital accessibility testing involves assessing various aspects of a digital product to determine its level of accessibility. This includes evaluating both the functionality and design elements of the product. Functionality testing focuses on the interactive components of the product, such as navigation, forms, and media players, to ensure they can be used with assistive technologies like screen readers or keyboard-only navigation. Design testing, on the other hand, examines the visual aspects of the product to ensure it can be easily perceived and understood by individuals with visual impairments. To conduct digital accessibility testing, specific testing techniques and tools are used. These may include manual testing, where testers simulate the experience of users with disabilities, or automated testing, which relies on software tools to identify accessibility issues. Some common accessibility issues that are evaluated during testing include the presence of alternative text for images, proper semantic structure of the HTML, appropriate use of headings and landmarks, color contrast ratios, and keyboard accessibility. Digital accessibility testing is important as it enables organizations to meet legal requirements and standards, such as the Web Content Accessibility Guidelines (WCAG), and ensures equal access to digital content for all users. By identifying and addressing accessibility issues, products can be made more inclusive and usable for individuals with disabilities. In conclusion, digital accessibility testing is a crucial step in the design and development process of digital products. It ensures that individuals with disabilities are not excluded from accessing and using the product, and helps organizations in creating a more inclusive and user-friendly digital experience.

Digital Accessibility

Digital Accessibility refers to the practice of designing and developing digital content, platforms, and technologies that can be accessed and used by individuals with disabilities. It aims to ensure that people with disabilities, including but not limited to visual, auditory, physical, speech, cognitive, and neurological disabilities, can perceive, understand, navigate, and interact with digital content and technologies in an inclusive and equal manner. The concept of digital accessibility encompasses various aspects of design and development, including but not limited to website structure, layout, colors, fonts, images, multimedia, navigation, interaction, and the use of assistive technologies. By incorporating accessible design principles and guidelines, digital accessibility enables individuals with disabilities to independently access and engage with digital resources, services, and information.

Digital Braille Displays

A digital Braille display, also known as a refreshable Braille display, is an assistive technology device designed to provide access to digital content for individuals who are blind or visually impaired. It is a tactile output device that converts text into Braille characters, allowing users to read electronic information in real-time. Utilizing an array of tiny mechanical or electronic Braille cells, a digital Braille display dynamically changes the pattern of raised dots that represent individual letters, numbers, punctuation marks, and other Braille symbols. These dots are produced and retracted to display different combinations, enabling people with visual disabilities to perceive the content displayed on a screen.

Digital Inclusion

Digital inclusion in the context of accessibility design refers to the practice of ensuring that all individuals, regardless of their abilities or limitations, have equal access to and the ability to use digital technologies and online resources. It is crucial to prioritize digital inclusion in accessibility design to ensure that people with disabilities, older adults, and individuals from marginalized communities are not left behind in the digital era. By promoting digital inclusion, it becomes possible to break down barriers and create a more inclusive and equitable online environment.

Disability Advocacy

Disability advocacy, in the context of accessibility design, refers to the active promotion and support of the rights, needs, and inclusive participation of individuals with disabilities. It involves working towards eliminating barriers and implementing measures that ensure equal access and opportunities for people with disabilities. Disability advocates play a crucial role in advocating for the design of accessible environments, products, services, and technologies that accommodate the diverse needs and abilities of individuals with disabilities. They collaborate with various stakeholders, including policymakers, designers, architects, engineers, and businesses, to develop and implement inclusive practices and standards.

Disability Awareness

Disability Awareness in the context of accessibility design refers to the understanding and recognition of the diverse needs and abilities of individuals with disabilities. It involves creating an inclusive environment and designing products, services, and spaces that can be accessed, understood, and used by people of all abilities. Disability awareness is crucial in the field of accessibility design as it ensures that the needs of individuals with disabilities are considered and accommodated. It involves being mindful of various disabilities, including but not limited to physical, sensory, cognitive, and mental health disabilities. By embracing disability awareness, designers can create more accessible and inclusive spaces that promote equal participation and independence for all individuals.

Disability Compliance

Disability compliance refers to the adherence to regulations and standards in order to ensure that individuals with disabilities have equal access to information, services, and facilities. In the context of accessibility design, disability compliance aims to create inclusive digital experiences that can be accessed and used by everyone, regardless of their abilities or disabilities. This involves taking into consideration the needs of individuals with various disabilities, such as visual, hearing, motor, cognitive, or neurological impairments. Disability compliance requires designers and developers to follow specific guidelines and best practices to remove barriers and provide alternative means of access to information and functionality. In the realm of accessibility design, disability compliance can be achieved by implementing techniques like the use of proper semantic HTML elements, providing text alternatives for non-text content (such as images or multimedia), ensuring page structure and navigation are logical and consistent, maintaining readable text with appropriate color contrasts, and supporting keyboard navigation and focus management. Additionally, disability compliance also includes making web content perceivable, understandable, and operable for individuals with disabilities. This may involve providing captions or transcripts for videos, providing alternative text descriptions for images, using clear and simple language, and avoiding content that may cause seizures or other adverse reactions. By adhering to disability compliance standards and guidelines, designers and developers are working towards breaking down barriers that prevent individuals with disabilities from fully participating in digital experiences. It is about creating an inclusive online environment where everyone can access and interact with information and services effectively. In conclusion, disability compliance in accessibility design is the practice of following regulations and guidelines to ensure that individuals with disabilities have equal access to digital content and functionality. It involves considering the needs of different disabilities and implementing design techniques that remove barriers, provide alternative means of access, and create inclusive digital experiences.

Disability Discrimination Act (DDA)

The Disability Discrimination Act (DDA), in the context of accessibility design, refers to a legislation designed to protect individuals with disabilities from being discriminated against. It requires that reasonable adjustments be made to ensure equal opportunities for people with disabilities in areas such as employment, education, and access to goods, services, and facilities. The DDA aims to eliminate barriers to participation and provide accessibility for individuals with disabilities. This includes physical barriers, such as buildings without ramps or elevators, as well as communication barriers, such as information that is not provided in accessible formats for individuals with visual impairments. In terms of accessibility design, the DDA requires that websites and digital content be accessible to individuals with disabilities. This means that websites should be designed with features that allow people with disabilities to navigate, understand, and interact with the content. Web accessibility guidelines, such as the Web Content Accessibility Guidelines (WCAG), provide specific criteria for designers to follow in order to make their websites accessible. This includes providing alternative text for images, ensuring proper color contrast for individuals with visual impairments, and providing captions and transcripts for multimedia content. By adhering to these guidelines and making their websites accessible, designers can ensure compliance with the DDA and provide equal access to individuals with disabilities. This not only helps to avoid legal issues and potential penalties but also expands the reach of their websites to a wider audience. In conclusion, the Disability Discrimination Act (DDA) is a legislation that prohibits discrimination against individuals with disabilities and requires reasonable adjustments to be made to ensure accessibility. In the context of accessibility design, this includes making websites and digital content accessible to individuals with disabilities. By following web accessibility guidelines, designers can meet the requirements of the DDA and provide equal opportunities for individuals with disabilities.

Disability Discrimination

Disability discrimination refers to the unequal treatment, exclusion, or disadvantage faced by individuals with disabilities in the context of accessibility design. It is the act of treating individuals with disabilities less favorably and denying them equal access to physical spaces, products, services, or information due to their impairment. In the realm of accessibility design, disability discrimination occurs when the needs and requirements of individuals with disabilities are not adequately considered or accommodated. While discrimination can manifest in various forms, it ultimately results in barriers that prevent equal participation and hinder the full inclusion of people with disabilities in society.

Disability Etiquette

Disability etiquette, in the context of accessibility design, refers to a set of guidelines and practices aimed at promoting inclusivity and ensuring equal access to facilities, services, information, and products for individuals with disabilities. It involves considering the unique needs and limitations of people with disabilities when designing and creating physical spaces, digital platforms, and other forms of communication. By following disability etiquette, designers and developers can create an environment that respects the dignity and independence of people with disabilities, allowing them to fully participate in society and access the same opportunities as their non-disabled peers. It goes beyond mere compliance with legal requirements and focuses on fostering an inclusive and welcoming environment for everyone.

Document Accessibility Guidelines

Document Accessibility Guidelines refer to the set of principles and recommendations aimed at ensuring that digital documents, such as text-based files, are accessible to individuals with disabilities. These guidelines focus on making the content of the document perceivable, operable, understandable, and robust for all users, regardless of their abilities. Perceivability is achieved by ensuring that the information in the document is available to all individuals, regardless of their sensory capabilities. This can be accomplished by using alternative text for images, providing captions for multimedia content, and using high contrast colors for text. Additionally, it is important to structure the document in a logical manner, using headings and formatting to enhance comprehension. Operability refers to the ability of individuals to interact with the document using various devices or input methods. It is crucial to make sure that the document can be navigated with a keyboard or assistive technologies such as screen readers. Providing clear and consistent navigation elements, such as headings and links, allows users to easily move through the content. Understanding the content of a document is another key aspect of accessibility. This can be achieved by using clear and concise language, avoiding jargon or complex terms whenever possible. Additionally, it is important to use proper semantics and markup to indicate the structure and meaning of the content. Finally, robustness refers to the ability of the document to be interpreted correctly by different browsers and assistive technologies. It is important to use standards-compliant HTML and CSS code, and to test the document's compatibility with different platforms and devices. By following these guidelines, document accessibility can be significantly improved, allowing individuals with disabilities to access and engage with the content more effectively. This not only promotes inclusivity but also ensures compliance with accessibility laws and regulations, such as the Web Content Accessibility Guidelines (WCAG). In conclusion, Document Accessibility Guidelines provide a framework for designing digital documents that are accessible to individuals with disabilities. These guidelines focus on perceivability, operability, understandability, and robustness to ensure equal access to information for all users.

Document Accessibility Remediation Services

Document accessibility remediation services refer to the processes and techniques used to make digital documents accessible to users with disabilities. These services involve modifying the structure, design, and content of documents to ensure they can be accessed, understood, and interacted with by all individuals, regardless of their disabilities. Accessibility design is a fundamental aspect of inclusive and user-centric design, ensuring that digital content and documents can be accessed by everyone, including individuals with visual, hearing, cognitive, or motor impairments. Document accessibility remediation services aim to remove barriers and provide equal access to information, allowing individuals with disabilities to independently navigate, perceive, and interact with digital documents.

Document Accessibility Remediation Tools

Document Accessibility Remediation Tools are software applications or systems that are designed to address and rectify accessibility issues present in digital documents. These tools are specifically created to ensure that documents are accessible and usable by individuals with disabilities, including those with visual, hearing, cognitive, or motor impairments. These remediation tools encompass a range of functionalities and features that enable designers and developers to modify documents and make them more inclusive and accessible. They provide solutions for various accessibility barriers, such as insufficient color contrast, inaccessible document structures, missing alternative text for images, and lack of compatibility with assistive technologies.

Document Accessibility Software

Document Accessibility Software is a type of software designed to improve the accessibility of digital documents for individuals with disabilities. It includes a range of features and tools that help make documents more inclusive and compatible with assistive technologies, ensuring equal access to information for all users. This software is specifically developed with the principles of accessibility design in mind, aiming to create documents that can be easily navigated, understood, and interacted with by individuals with visual, auditory, cognitive, or motor impairments. It helps organizations and content creators comply with accessibility standards and guidelines, such as the Web Content Accessibility Guidelines (WCAG), to ensure their content is accessible to a wide range of users.

Document Accessibility Standards

Document Accessibility Standards refer to a set of guidelines and specifications that aim to ensure that documents, such as web pages, PDFs, and word documents, are accessible to individuals with disabilities. These standards provide a framework for designers and developers to create content that can be effectively consumed by all users, regardless of their abilities or limitations. Document Accessibility Standards typically address different aspects of accessibility design, including but not limited to: The structural organization of documents: These standards emphasize the importance of proper heading hierarchy, clear and concise titles, and logical document structure. By using appropriate heading levels (h1, h2, etc.), designers can create a clear outline for users with screen readers or those who navigate through a document using assistive technologies. Alternative text for non-text elements: Images, graphs, and charts are common elements in documents that may not be accessible to individuals with visual impairments. Document Accessibility Standards require the use of alternative text descriptions (alt text), which provide a clear and concise explanation of the content of these elements. This allows screen readers to relay the information to users who cannot see the visual representation. Color contrast and legibility: To ensure that documents are readable to individuals with low vision or color blindness, Document Accessibility Standards often define specific requirements for color contrast. These standards help designers select colors that provide enough contrast between the text and background, making it easier for all users to read and understand the content. Proper use of tables and data formats: Tables and data formats can present challenges for individuals with visual or cognitive disabilities. Document Accessibility Standards provide guidelines on creating properly structured tables, including using header cells, summaries, and captions. Additionally, they encourage the use of alternative formats for presenting complex data, such as providing downloadable CSV files alongside visual representations.

Document Accessibility

Document Accessibility refers to the design and development of electronic documents in a manner that enables individuals with disabilities to perceive, understand, navigate, and interact with the content effectively. Document Accessibility is essential to ensure that people with disabilities, including those with visual, auditory, cognitive, or motor impairments, can access and engage with digital information and materials. It involves creating documents that are inclusive and can be accessed by everyone, regardless of their abilities or the tools they use to access content. When designing accessible documents, various factors need to be considered. Firstly, the visual design should be created in a way that allows individuals with low vision or color blindness to read and understand the content easily. This may involve using sufficient color contrast, providing alternative text for images, and ensuring clear and legible fonts. Additionally, auditory accessibility should be taken into account by providing captions or transcripts for audio or video content. This supports individuals who are deaf or hard of hearing to access and understand the information being presented. Moreover, cognitive accessibility considers the readability and simplicity of the document, using plain language to ensure comprehension for individuals with cognitive disabilities. Furthermore, document accessibility involves structuring the content using headings, paragraphs, and lists in a logical and meaningful way. This helps individuals using screen readers or other assistive technologies to navigate through the document efficiently. Providing descriptive links and ensuring proper document organization also contribute to enhancing accessibility. In conclusion, Document Accessibility focuses on creating digital documents that are inclusive and can be accessed by everyone, regardless of their abilities. By considering various aspects such as visual, auditory, cognitive, and structural accessibility, individuals with disabilities can engage with digital content effectively. Prioritizing document accessibility facilitates equal access to information and ensures a more inclusive and diverse digital environment.

Document Remediation Software

Document Remediation Software is a type of software used in the context of accessibility design to ensure that digital documents are accessible to individuals with disabilities. It aims to convert documents into a format that can be easily understood and navigated by people with various impairments. This software takes into account accessibility guidelines and regulations to ensure compliance and equal access for all users. The primary purpose of Document Remediation Software is to enhance the accessibility of digital documents, such as PDFs, Word documents, and web pages. It achieves this by analyzing the structure and content of the documents and applying remediation techniques to improve their accessibility. The software typically includes features such as automated tagging, alternative text generation, and structural adjustments. Automated tagging involves adding descriptive labels to elements in the document, such as headings, tables, images, and form fields, making it easier for assistive technologies to interpret the content. Alternative text generation involves creating textual descriptions for images, allowing people who are visually impaired to understand the visual information conveyed by the images. Structural adjustments involve reorganizing the document's layout and navigation elements, ensuring a logical reading order and easy navigation for individuals who use screen readers or other assistive technologies. Document Remediation Software often includes additional functionality to address specific accessibility requirements. For example, it may have features for improving color contrast, adding captions to videos, or providing audio descriptions for multimedia content. The software may also have built-in accessibility checkers to verify compliance with accessibility standards and guidelines. In summary, Document Remediation Software is an essential tool in the field of accessibility design. It helps ensure that digital documents are accessible to individuals with disabilities by converting them into a format that can be easily understood and navigated by various assistive technologies. By improving the accessibility of digital documents, this software promotes equal access to information and supports inclusive design principles.

Dragon NaturallySpeaking

Dragon NaturallySpeaking is a voice recognition software that is designed to provide accessibility to individuals with physical disabilities or limitations. It allows users to control their computer and perform various tasks through voice commands, eliminating the need for manual typing and mouse control. By using Dragon NaturallySpeaking, individuals with mobility impairments, such as those with paralysis or repetitive strain injuries, can interact with their computer system without relying on traditional input devices. The software converts spoken words into written text, enabling them to compose documents, send emails, surf the internet, and perform other activities that typically require keyboard or mouse input. This accessibility design solution is particularly beneficial for people who have limited or no use of their hands or fingers, as it removes the physical barriers associated with conventional computer usage. With Dragon NaturallySpeaking, individuals can navigate through menus, open applications, and execute commands, all by speaking aloud. Furthermore, Dragon NaturallySpeaking is equipped with advanced natural language processing capabilities, allowing it to understand complex commands and context-based instructions. The software adapts to the user's voice and learns their specific speaking patterns over time, resulting in increased accuracy and efficiency. Accessibility design considerations are integrated into Dragon NaturallySpeaking to ensure that it meets the specific needs of people with disabilities. The software supports a wide range of languages and dialects, making it accessible to individuals from diverse linguistic backgrounds. It also offers customizable voice profiles, allowing users to tailor the software's response and behavior to their individual preferences. Overall, Dragon NaturallySpeaking plays a crucial role in enhancing and promoting accessibility by enabling individuals with physical disabilities to effectively use computers and interact with digital content through voice recognition technology.

Dynamic Braille Display

A Dynamic Braille Display is a tactile device that translates digital text into braille characters, allowing individuals with visual impairments to access written information. The display consists of a series of small mechanical elements, known as braille cells, which can be raised or lowered to form different braille characters. The primary goal of a Dynamic Braille Display is to provide a means for blind and visually impaired individuals to read and interact with digital content in a way that is accessible and comparable to how sighted individuals read printed text. It serves as a crucial assistive technology tool that enhances independence and inclusivity for individuals with visual impairments by enabling them to access and navigate various forms of digital information. The device is typically connected to a computer or mobile device through a wired or wireless connection. Textual information from the computer or mobile device is then transmitted to the Dynamic Braille Display, which converts the text into braille characters that can be felt by the user. This allows the individual to read emails, browse the internet, read documents, access e-books, and engage with various applications. The Dynamic Braille Display provides real-time feedback, as the braille characters can be dynamically changed to match the text being read. It allows users to browse through multiple lines of text, scroll through web pages, and navigate through menus and options using dedicated controls or gestures. Some displays also include additional features, such as a braille keyboard for text input or built-in speech output for auditory feedback. By providing access to digital content, a Dynamic Braille Display helps individuals with visual impairments to participate more fully in educational, professional, and recreational activities. It promotes inclusivity by enabling blind and visually impaired individuals to independently engage with the same information that is readily available to sighted individuals. In conclusion, a Dynamic Braille Display is a vital accessibility design tool that facilitates equitable access to digital information for individuals with visual impairments. Its tactile display of braille characters allows users to interact with digital content in a manner that is both efficient and accessible, empowering them to navigate and engage with various forms of written information.

Dyslexia-Friendly Design Tools

Dyslexia-Friendly Design Tools refer to a set of techniques and strategies used in the field of accessibility design to create digital content, websites, and other forms of media that are easily understandable and accessible to individuals with dyslexia. Dyslexia is a specific learning disability that affects reading and language processing skills. Individuals with dyslexia may struggle with recognizing and decoding letters and words, as well as with comprehension and retention of written information. Dyslexia-Friendly Design Tools aim to address these challenges by implementing various design principles that make text more readable and user-friendly for individuals with dyslexia.

Dyslexia-Friendly Font Generators

Dyslexia-Friendly Font Generators are tools used in the context of accessibility design to create readable and easily comprehensible text for individuals with dyslexia. Dyslexia is a learning disorder that affects a person's ability to read, write, and spell. People with dyslexia often struggle with distinguishing and recognizing letters, numbers, and words. To address this challenge, dyslexia-friendly fonts are specifically designed to enhance the readability and legibility of text for individuals with dyslexia. These fonts incorporate various characteristics and features that can help reduce reading difficulties and improve reading speed and accuracy for people with dyslexia. Dyslexia-friendly fonts typically have the following characteristics: 1. Letter differentiation: These fonts make sure that each letter is distinct from others, avoiding letters that are easily confused, such as "b" and "d," or "p" and "q." By promoting clear distinctions between letters, dyslexic readers can more easily identify and recognize them. 2. Increased spacing: Dyslexia-friendly fonts often feature increased spacing between letters, words, and lines of text. This increased spacing helps prevent the letters from blending together and improves readability. 3. Enlarged ascenders and descenders: Ascenders are parts of letters that rise above the main body, like the top of a lowercase "d" or "b." Descenders, on the other hand, are parts that extend below the main body, like the bottom of a lowercase "y" or "g." Dyslexia-friendly fonts enlarge these ascenders and descenders, making them more noticeable and helping dyslexic readers differentiate between letters. 4. Clear and simple letterforms: Dyslexia-friendly fonts utilize clear and simple letterforms that avoid unnecessary embellishments or complexities. The letters are designed to be straightforward and easily recognizable, reducing visual confusion and cognitive load for dyslexic readers. By utilizing dyslexia-friendly font generators, designers and developers can create accessible content that caters to individuals with dyslexia. These font generators offer various dyslexia-friendly fonts to choose from, ensuring that the text is optimized for readability and understanding. The generated fonts can be used across different mediums, such as websites, documents, and educational materials, to make information more accessible and inclusive for individuals with dyslexia. In conclusion, dyslexia-friendly font generators are valuable tools in the field of accessibility design. By incorporating specific characteristics that enhance readability for people with dyslexia, these font generators play a crucial role in promoting inclusive and accessible design practices.

Dyslexia-Friendly Font Tools

Dyslexia-Friendly Font Tools refer to a set of tools and techniques that are designed to enhance readability and readability for individuals with dyslexia. Dyslexia is a learning disorder that affects a person's ability to read, spell, and process written information. While there is no cure for dyslexia, using dyslexia-friendly fonts can help improve reading fluency and comprehension for individuals with this condition. These font tools utilize specific typographic features and design principles that make text more accessible to dyslexic readers. For example, dyslexia-friendly fonts often have a larger letter spacing, which helps prevent letters from blending together and causing confusion. These fonts may also have unique letterforms that differentiate commonly confused letters, such as "b" and "d." Additionally, they may incorporate other visual aids such as bold or italicized text, increased line spacing, or improved background contrast to make reading easier.

Dyslexia-Friendly Fonts

Dyslexia-Friendly Fonts refer to specific typefaces that have been designed and optimized to improve readability for individuals with dyslexia. Dyslexia is a learning disorder that affects a person's ability to read, write, and spell. People with dyslexia often have difficulties differentiating between letters, processing written information, and recognizing shapes and patterns within words. The design of dyslexia-friendly fonts takes into consideration several factors that can enhance reading experiences for individuals with dyslexia. These typefaces incorporate specific characteristics such as varying letter shapes, increased letter spacing, modified letterforms, and improved overall readability. These features aim to minimize common challenges faced by individuals with dyslexia, such as letter confusion, letter reversals, and difficulty distinguishing between similar letters. The characteristics of dyslexia-friendly fonts are based on research and understanding of the specific reading patterns and visual processing difficulties associated with dyslexia. These fonts are specially designed to support the visual perception and recognition of letters and words, improving reading fluency and reducing errors. In addition to the actual font design, other typographic elements can also contribute to making text more accessible for individuals with dyslexia. Such elements may include increased line spacing to reduce crowded text, larger font sizes to improve legibility, and appropriate contrast between text and background to enhance visibility. By utilizing dyslexia-friendly fonts in design, accessibility professionals and designers can help create more inclusive and supportive environments for individuals with dyslexia. Implementing these fonts in educational materials, websites, and other forms of written communication can greatly enhance the reading experience for individuals with dyslexia, improving their comprehension and overall accessibility to information. In summary, dyslexia-friendly fonts are specifically designed typefaces tailored to support the reading needs of individuals with dyslexia. These fonts incorporate features that enhance letter recognition, reduce confusion, and promote overall readability. By utilizing dyslexia-friendly fonts, designers can contribute to creating more accessible and inclusive experiences for individuals with dyslexia.

Dyslexia

Dyslexia refers to a learning disorder that affects a person's ability to read, spell, write, and comprehend written language, despite having normal intelligence. It is a neurodevelopmental condition that is often diagnosed in childhood and can continue into adulthood. Individuals with dyslexia may have difficulties with phonological processing, which is the ability to identify and manipulate the sounds in spoken language. They may also struggle with decoding words and recognizing word patterns, leading to difficulties in reading fluently and accurately. In the context of accessibility design, dyslexia poses unique challenges that need to be addressed to ensure that people with dyslexia can access digital content and information effectively. To make digital content accessible for individuals with dyslexia, it is important to consider several key principles.

E-Accessibility

E-Accessibility refers to the practice and design of making digital content and technologies accessible to individuals with disabilities. It focuses on ensuring equal access and usability of websites, applications, electronic documents, and other digital platforms for people with visual, hearing, motor, cognitive, or other impairments. The main objective of e-accessibility is to remove barriers and provide inclusive experiences for all users, regardless of their disability. It involves implementing design strategies and employing assistive technologies that enable people with disabilities to access, navigate, understand, and interact with digital content effectively.

E-Text

E-Text refers to electronic versions of textual content that are designed to be accessible to individuals with disabilities. It aims to provide equal access to information for individuals who may have visual impairments, learning disabilities, or other disabilities that affect their ability to read printed text. E-Text can take various forms, including digital text files, eBooks, and web pages that are optimized for accessibility. These accessible formats allow individuals with disabilities to access and navigate the content using assistive technologies, such as screen readers or Braille displays.

Electronic Accessibility

Electronic accessibility refers to the design and development of digital content and technology that can be accessed and used by individuals with disabilities. It involves creating a user-friendly environment that accommodates people with various impairments, such as visual, auditory, physical, cognitive, and neurological disabilities. The goal of electronic accessibility is to ensure that all individuals, regardless of their abilities, can independently and effectively engage with digital platforms and content. This includes websites, applications, documents, videos, and any other form of electronic media. By eliminating barriers and providing equal access, electronic accessibility promotes inclusivity, equality, and diversity in the digital world.

Electronic Braille

Electronic Braille refers to a technology that enables individuals with visual impairments to access and read digital information using a tactile interface. It is designed specifically for individuals who are blind or have low vision, allowing them to engage in various activities that require text-based digital content. With electronic Braille, digital information is converted into Braille characters that can be easily read through touch. This technology utilizes a combination of electronic devices and software to transform text-based content into a format that can be interpreted by individuals proficient in Braille reading.

Electronic Notetaking

Electronic Notetaking is the process of capturing, organizing, and storing information electronically. It involves using digital devices and software applications to take, manage, and retrieve notes, enabling individuals to access and review their notes effortlessly. In the context of accessibility design, electronic notetaking plays a crucial role in facilitating equal access to information for individuals with disabilities. People who are deaf, hard of hearing, or have auditory processing disorders often face challenges in traditional note-taking methods. Electronic notetaking allows them to overcome these barriers by providing alternative ways to access information through written or visual means.

Employment Accessibility

Employment accessibility refers to the inclusive design and availability of employment opportunities for individuals with disabilities or other barriers. It focuses on removing physical, cognitive, and social barriers that may prevent equal participation and integration in the workforce. Accessible employment design encompasses various aspects, such as physical accessibility of workplaces, technology accommodations, inclusive hiring practices, and supportive work environments. It aims to provide equal opportunities for individuals with disabilities to apply for, obtain, and advance in employment. Accessibility design promotes the principles of equality, diversity, and inclusion in the workplace.

Employment Of People With Disabilities

The employment of people with disabilities refers to the practice of providing job opportunities and equal employment rights to individuals who have physical, mental, or sensory impairments.

It involves creating an inclusive and accessible work environment that accommodates the specific needs of these individuals, allowing them to fully participate in the workforce. Accessible design plays a crucial role in promoting the employment of people with disabilities. It focuses on creating environments, products, and services that can be used by individuals of all abilities, without discrimination or barriers. In the context of accessibility design, the employment of people with disabilities entails implementing design strategies and features that ensure equal access and opportunities for these individuals in various workplace settings.

Epilepsy-Friendly Design

Epilepsy-Friendly Design refers to a design approach that aims to create digital content and user interfaces that are accessible and safe for individuals with epilepsy or other photosensitive conditions. This design approach takes into consideration the potential triggers of seizures, such as flashing lights, high contrast patterns, and rapid visual stimuli, and aims to minimize or eliminate these triggers to ensure a positive and safe user experience. In epilepsy-friendly design, visual elements are carefully chosen to minimize the risk of triggering seizures. This includes using subdued colors and avoiding high contrast color combinations, as they can induce visual stress and increase the risk of a seizure. Additionally, animations, transitions, and moving elements are controlled to prevent them from being overly stimulating or rapidly changing, as these can also be seizure triggers. The use of flashing or flickering lights is strongly discouraged in epilepsy-friendly design. If any flashing lights are used, they are designed to meet specific guidelines and safety standards, including adhering to internationally recognized guidelines for photosensitive epilepsy. The aim is to minimize the potential for triggering seizures while still maintaining an effective and engaging user experience. Text and typography are also important considerations in epilepsy-friendly design. Clear and legible fonts are used, avoiding text that is too small, too bold, or with excessive spacing. The contrast between text and background is carefully chosen to ensure readability and reduce visual strain. In addition to visual considerations, epilepsy-friendly design also takes into account other aspects of accessibility, such as providing alternative ways to access content for individuals with cognitive or physical disabilities. This may include options for adjusting the speed of content, providing text alternatives for images and videos, and offering keyboard navigation options. Overall, epilepsy-friendly design aims to create a user experience that is inclusive and safe for individuals with epilepsy or other photosensitive conditions. By considering the potential triggers of seizures and implementing design strategies to minimize these risks, digital content and user interfaces can be made accessible to a wider audience, providing a positive and inclusive user experience.

Ergonomic Keyboards

Ergonomic keyboards are a design solution aimed at improving accessibility and reducing the physical strain caused by traditional keyboard use. These keyboards are specifically engineered to provide a more comfortable and natural typing experience, aligning with the principles of ergonomics. By considering the physical and cognitive needs of individuals with disabilities or impairments, ergonomic keyboards strive to accommodate a wide range of users. They often feature unique shapes, layouts, or modifications that promote proper hand and wrist alignment, alleviate muscle tension, and reduce the risk of repetitive strain injuries (RSIs).

Ergonomic Workspace Assessment Services

Ergonomic workspace assessment services are a type of service offered to individuals with disabilities or limitations that require accommodations in their work environment. These services aim to ensure that the workspace is accessible and optimized for the individual's specific needs, allowing them to perform their tasks comfortably and efficiently. An ergonomic workspace refers to a workspace that is designed to fit the physical, cognitive, and sensory abilities of the individual using it. It takes into consideration factors such as accessibility, comfort, and efficiency. The goal is to create an environment that minimizes physical strain, reduces the risk of injury, and enhances productivity.

Ergonomic Workspace Assessment Tools

Ergonomic workspace assessment tools are tools or instruments used to evaluate and analyze the physical environment of a workspace in terms of its ergonomic design and accessibility. These tools aim to assess and address potential barriers or challenges that may affect individuals with disabilities or limitations, allowing for the creation of an inclusive and accessible workspace. Ergonomic workspace assessment tools involve a comprehensive evaluation of various components of the workspace, including furniture, equipment, layout, lighting, and overall design. The assessments typically consider factors such as the height, reach, and adjustability of workstations, the placement of monitors and keyboards, the availability of adjustable chairs, and the presence of sufficient lighting and ventilation. These assessment tools are crucial for creating accessible workspaces as they help identify potential areas of improvement or modifications needed to accommodate individuals with disabilities or limitations. By conducting these assessments, employers and designers can ensure that work environments are designed in a way that minimizes physical strain, maximizes comfort, and promotes productivity for all employees. Furthermore, ergonomic workspace assessment tools take into account accessibility guidelines and standards, such as the Americans with Disabilities Act (ADA) or the Web Content Accessibility Guidelines (WCAG), to ensure compliance with legal requirements. They address not only the physical environment but also the digital accessibility of workstations, considering factors such as the design of software interfaces, the availability of assistive technologies, and the compatibility of various devices. In conclusion, ergonomic workspace assessment tools play a crucial role in creating inclusive work environments that value and prioritize accessibility. By evaluating and addressing the physical and digital aspects of a workspace, these tools contribute to the overall well-being and inclusion of employees with disabilities or limitations, allowing them to fully participate and thrive in the workplace.

Eye Gaze Interaction

Eye gaze interaction in the context of accessibility design refers to the use of the eyes to control and interact with digital devices and interfaces. It is a form of input method that allows individuals with limited or no physical mobility to navigate, interact, and communicate using their eye movements. Eye gaze interaction typically utilizes specialized hardware and software systems, such as eye-tracking devices and algorithms, to track the user's eye movements accurately. These systems can determine the user's point of gaze on the screen, enabling them to control the cursor, select options, and perform various actions through their eye movements.

Eye-Tracking Devices

Eye-tracking devices are technological tools designed to track and analyze the movement of a person's eyes. These devices use special sensors to detect and track the precise gaze of the user, capturing data that can be used to understand how someone interacts with a digital interface or physical environment. In the context of accessibility design, eye-tracking devices play a crucial role in assisting individuals with disabilities to navigate and interact with technology. People with limited motor functions, such as those with physical impairments or spinal cord injuries, often struggle to use traditional input devices such as a mouse or keyboard. Eye-tracking devices provide an alternative means of control and interaction by allowing users to simply move their eyes. Through the use of eye-tracking technology, individuals with disabilities can operate computers, tablets, smartphones, and other devices without the need for direct physical contact. By tracking the movement and focus of the eyes, these devices can detect when a user is looking at a specific area of the screen, allowing them to issue commands or navigate through menus and options. Eye-tracking devices can also be integrated with assistive technology software and applications. This integration enables individuals with disabilities to control and interact with their environment beyond just operating a computer or mobile device. For example, eye-tracking technology can be used to control lights, adjust room temperature, or operate household appliances, providing individuals with greater independence and autonomy. In addition to accessibility design, eye-tracking devices have various applications in fields such as healthcare, market research, and gaming. In healthcare, eye-tracking technology can be used for diagnosing and monitoring certain medical conditions such as autism, attention deficit hyperactivity disorder (ADHD), and traumatic brain injury. In market research, eye-tracking devices help researchers understand consumer behavior and preferences by analyzing which areas of a product, advertisement, or website attract the most visual attention. In the gaming industry, eye-tracking devices enhance the gaming experience by allowing players to control the game using their eye movements. Overall, eye-tracking devices have revolutionized accessibility design by providing an alternative means of interaction for individuals with disabilities. These devices allow individuals to navigate and control technology by simply moving their eyes, empowering them to access and interact with digital interfaces and physical environments in ways that were previously challenging or impossible.

Eye-Tracking Research Equipment

Eye-tracking research equipment refers to a set of tools and devices that are used to track and analyze eye movements and gaze patterns of individuals. This technology plays a crucial role in the field of accessibility design, as it provides valuable insights into how people with various disabilities interact with digital and physical environments. The primary goal of accessibility design is to create inclusive and barrier-free experiences for all individuals, regardless of their disabilities. Eye-tracking research equipment helps achieve this goal by enabling designers to understand how people with disabilities, such as visual impairments or motor impairments, interact with user interfaces and content. By collecting data on eye movements, gaze patterns, and fixation points, researchers can identify potential design flaws or barriers that hinder accessibility.

Eye-Tracking Research Services

Eye-Tracking Research Services refers to a methodological approach analyzing and evaluating user behavior and interaction with digital interfaces. This research technique utilizes eye-tracking technology to monitor and measure the movement of a user's gaze across a screen, providing valuable insights into the accessibility and user experience (UX) design of websites and applications. Eye-tracking research serves as an important tool in accessibility design, allowing designers to identify potential areas of improvement and ensure that digital interfaces are inclusive and user-friendly for individuals with visual impairments or other accessibility needs. By tracking where users focus their attention, designers can understand how users interact with different elements on a webpage, such as menus, buttons, or content. This research technique enables the evaluation of several key aspects in accessibility design. Firstly, eye-tracking research can identify if users are easily able to locate and engage with important information on a webpage. It helps designers understand if users effectively navigate through the content and if any improvements can be made to enhance the overall accessibility. Secondly, eye-tracking research provides insights into the usability of different elements within the interface. Designers can analyze whether users are drawn to the intended focal points or if any elements cause confusion or lead to visual overload. This helps in designing interfaces that guide users effectively and accommodate their accessibility needs. Moreover, eye-tracking research also aids in optimizing the placement and prioritization of interactive elements, such as buttons or links, ensuring that they are positioned in a way that is easily discoverable for users with visual impairments. Overall, eye-tracking research services offer a valuable approach in the field of accessibility design. By tracking a user's eye movement, designers can gain detailed insights into how individuals with different accessibility needs interact with digital interfaces. This data-driven approach helps in identifying areas for improvement and designing inclusive and accessible interfaces that cater to a wide range of users.

Eye-Tracking Software

Eye-Tracking Software is an integral tool used in the field of accessibility design that allows individuals with physical disabilities to interact with digital devices using only their eyes. It utilizes advanced technology to track and interpret eye movements, allowing users to navigate through various applications, websites, and interfaces. By using eye-tracking software, individuals with limited mobility or dexterity can overcome the physical barriers that prevent them from operating traditional input devices such as a mouse or keyboard. This technology monitors the movement of their eyes and translates it into computer commands, enabling them to control cursor movement, perform clicks, and execute other actions on the screen.

Finger Spelling

Finger spelling refers to a method of communication used by individuals with hearing disabilities or limited speech ability. It involves using the fingers to spell out words or express letters of the alphabet, allowing the person to convey messages and participate in conversations. In the context of accessibility design, finger spelling plays a crucial role in ensuring effective communication and inclusion for individuals with hearing disabilities. By incorporating finger spelling into design practices, websites, applications, and other digital platforms can become more accessible to this specific user group. HTML, as a markup language, can be leveraged to integrate finger spelling into web design. The use of appropriate HTML elements and attributes can enhance the user experience for individuals with hearing disabilities, allowing them to engage more actively with online content. For example, designers can utilize the "abbr" element to provide abbreviations or acronyms and the "longdesc" attribute to provide detailed descriptions of images or videos. Moreover, the "alt" attribute can be used to provide alternative text for images, which is particularly beneficial for individuals who rely on finger spelling for communication. By ensuring that the alt text accurately conveys the content and context of an image, designers can enable these individuals to comprehend and engage with visual elements on the web. The use of semantic HTML elements, such as "header" and "footer," can also enhance the accessibility of finger spelling. These elements help establish the structure and organization of a webpage, allowing users to navigate through the content effectively. Additionally, designers can include appropriate heading levels to clearly delineate sections, making it easier for individuals using finger spelling to locate and understand the information they are seeking. It is important to note that finger spelling is just one aspect of accessibility design, and it should be implemented in conjunction with other accessibility techniques. Ensuring proper color contrast, providing keyboard alternatives, and offering captioning or transcriptions for multimedia content are some additional practices that can enhance accessibility for individuals with hearing disabilities. In conclusion, finger spelling is a method of communication used by individuals with hearing disabilities or limited speech ability. By incorporating finger spelling into the design of digital platforms, such as websites, applications, and documents, designers can contribute to creating a more accessible and inclusive online experience. HTML provides various elements and attributes that can be utilized to enhance the accessibility of finger spelling for individuals with hearing disabilities, enabling them to fully participate in online interactions.

Flashing Content Analyzer

A Flashing Content Analyzer is a tool used in the field of accessibility design to evaluate and analyze content with flashing or blinking elements on a website or digital application. These flashing or blinking elements can be potentially harmful or disruptive to individuals with certain medical conditions such as epilepsy, migraines, or attention disorders. The analyzer works by scanning and analyzing the website or application's code to identify any elements that may be classified as flashing or blinking. It then provides a comprehensive report that highlights these elements, allowing developers and designers to make informed decisions about whether to modify or remove them.

Form Field Labels

Form field labels are an essential element in accessibility design. They provide textual descriptions or instructions for the user to understand the purpose or context of an input field in a form. These labels play a crucial role in ensuring that people with disabilities can navigate and interact with form elements effectively. In HTML, the label element is used to associate a text label with a form field. It helps in creating a strong association between the label text and the input field, aiding screen readers, assistive technologies, and users with visual impairments. By using labels correctly, designers can greatly enhance the accessibility and usability of their forms. To create a label for a form field, we can utilize the tag in HTML. This tag should be placed immediately before the associated input field. For example, if we have a text input field for the user's name, the HTML code would look like this: Name: In the above code, the tag is used to create the label "Name:", followed by the tag with the associated id attribute set to "name". The for attribute of the tag should match the id attribute of the input field to establish a connection between them. It is important to note that screen readers and assistive technologies use these associations to announce or read the label when the user interacts with the input field. This enables users to understand the purpose or expected input for a particular form field. Using form field labels also benefits individuals who may have cognitive impairments or limited understanding of specific input fields. The labels provide clear instructions and context that can help these users complete the form accurately. In conclusion, form field labels are a critical component of accessibility design. By properly associating labels with form fields using the HTML tag, designers can ensure that people with disabilities can navigate, understand, and interact with forms effectively.

Functional Testing

Functional Testing is a systematic and structured approach to evaluating the functionality of a digital product or service, specifically in the context of accessibility design. It focuses on verifying whether the product or service meets the defined accessibility standards and guidelines to ensure that it can be accessed and used by individuals with disabilities. This type of testing involves testing various functionalities and features of the product or service to ensure that they are accessible and usable by individuals with different types and levels of disabilities, including visual, auditory, motor, and cognitive impairments. Functional Testing in accessibility design involves assessing the following aspects: 1. Perceivability: This aspect focuses on testing whether the content and interface of the product or service can be perceived by individuals with different types of disabilities. It includes testing the availability of alternative text for images, the use of descriptive headings and labels, and ensuring proper color contrast to aid users with visual impairments. 2. Operability: This aspect involves testing whether the product or service can be operated and controlled by individuals with different types of disabilities. It includes testing the functionality of keyboard navigation, ensuring proper focus and highlighting of interactive elements, and providing alternative input methods for individuals with motor disabilities. 3. Understandability: This aspect focuses on testing whether the content and interface of the product or service can be understood by individuals with different types and levels of cognitive impairments. It includes testing the clarity and simplicity of language, providing clear instructions and feedback, and ensuring consistent and predictable behavior of interactive elements. 4. Robustness: This aspect involves testing the compatibility of the product or service with assistive technologies and different user agents. It includes testing the compatibility with screen readers, speech recognition software, and other assistive devices and tools used by individuals with disabilities. In conclusion, Functional Testing in the context of accessibility design is a comprehensive evaluation of the functionality and usability of a digital product or service for individuals with disabilities. It assesses various aspects such as perceivability, operability, understandability, and robustness to ensure that the product or service meets the defined accessibility standards and guidelines.

Gestural Interfaces

Gestural Interfaces, in the context of accessibility design, refer to the use of hand and body movements to interact with digital devices or interfaces. These interfaces are designed to provide an alternative or supplementary method of input for individuals who may have difficulty using traditional input devices such as keyboards or mice. Gestural interfaces rely on the recognition and interpretation of specific movements, gestures, or poses made by the user. This recognition is often facilitated through the use of specialized sensors or cameras that capture and analyze the user's movements in real-time. The information gathered from these sensors is then used to control and navigate through the digital interface, allowing users to perform various actions such as selecting options, scrolling, zooming, or even drawing.

Google Accessibility Scanner

Google Accessibility Scanner is a tool specifically designed for accessibility design, aiming to enhance the usability of websites and applications for individuals with disabilities. This powerful tool is developed by Google and offers valuable insights and recommendations to improve the accessibility of digital content. The Google Accessibility Scanner works by scanning the web pages or mobile applications of any platform, identifying accessibility issues and providing developers with actionable steps to address them. It automates the process of accessibility evaluation, saving time and effort for designers and developers.

Guided Access (IOS)

Guided Access is a feature on iOS devices that is designed to improve accessibility for individuals with disabilities or special needs. It allows users to limit the functionality of their device to a single app, preventing them from accidentally exiting the app or accessing other features. By enabling Guided Access, users can effectively turn their device into a dedicated tool for a specific task or application. This can be particularly useful for individuals with cognitive disabilities, attention deficit disorders, or sensory impairments, as it helps to reduce distractions and maintain focus on the intended task. Guided Access offers a range of customizable settings to meet individual needs and preferences. Users can disable specific hardware buttons, such as the home button or volume controls, to prevent accidental interruptions. They can also restrict touch input to certain areas of the screen or disable certain gestures, such as pinch-to-zoom or swipe-to-scroll. In addition to controlling hardware and touch input, Guided Access also allows users to set time limits for app usage. This can be helpful for managing screen time and ensuring that individuals are not spending excessive amounts of time on their devices. To enable Guided Access, users can go to the Accessibility settings on their iOS device and navigate to the Guided Access menu. From there, they can toggle the feature on and configure the desired settings for their accessibility needs. Once enabled, users can start Guided Access mode by triple-clicking the home button or side button (depending on the device). Overall, Guided Access is a valuable accessibility feature that helps individuals with disabilities or special needs to effectively use iOS devices. By limiting access to specific apps and functionality, it promotes focus, reduces distractions, and enhances the overall user experience for those who rely on assistive technology.

HTML Accessibility Checkers

An HTML accessibility checker is a tool or software that evaluates the accessibility of a website or web application. It is specifically designed to identify and highlight any potential accessibility issues or barriers that may affect the usability and inclusivity of the content for individuals with disabilities. These accessibility checkers typically analyze HTML code and evaluate it against established accessibility guidelines, such as the Web Content Accessibility Guidelines (WCAG). They can identify common accessibility issues, such as missing alternative text for images, improper use of headings, lack of keyboard navigation support, or insufficient color contrast between text and background. By running an HTML accessibility checker, web developers and designers can quickly identify and address accessibility issues during the development process, ensuring that their websites or web applications can be accessed and used by individuals with a wide range of disabilities, including visual, auditory, motor, and cognitive impairments. Accessibility checkers often provide a detailed report or a list of identified issues, along with recommendations for remediation. These recommendations may include modifying HTML markup to provide appropriate labels or descriptions, ensuring proper keyboard focus management, providing transcripts or captions for multimedia content, and optimizing color contrast for better readability. Using HTML accessibility checkers is essential for web developers and designers to promote inclusive and accessible design. By identifying and addressing accessibility issues early in the development process, they can ensure that their websites or web applications are accessible to as many people as possible, regardless of their abilities or disabilities.

HTML Accessibility Training Courses

HTML Accessibility Training Courses HTML Accessibility Training Courses refer to educational programs that focus on teaching individuals how to design and develop websites and web content that are accessible to all users, including those with disabilities. These courses provide in-depth instruction on the principles and techniques necessary to create web experiences that can be accessed and used by everyone, regardless of their physical or cognitive abilities. In the context of accessibility design, these courses cover various topics related to creating accessible websites using HTML. Participants are taught how to structure and format web content in a way that is compatible with assistive technologies, such as screen readers, which help visually impaired individuals access web information. They learn how to use HTML elements appropriately to provide meaningful information and enhance the navigability of websites. Additionally, these courses emphasize the importance of incorporating alternative text descriptions for images and multimedia elements, making them accessible to individuals who are unable to see or hear the content directly. HTML Accessibility Training Courses also educate participants on the proper use of semantic markup to structure web pages in a way that allows assistive technologies to accurately interpret and convey the content to users with disabilities. This includes utilizing headings, paragraphs, lists, and other HTML elements to organize information logically and enhance readability for all users. Attendees of these courses also learn about the importance of proper color contrast and the use of clear and concise language to ensure that individuals with low vision or cognitive impairments can easily understand and navigate through web content. Furthermore, these courses often cover techniques for creating accessible forms, tables, and multimedia elements using HTML. Participants learn how to add proper labels and descriptions to form fields, ensuring that individuals who rely on screen readers can correctly interact with and submit form data. They are also taught how to design accessible tables that can be easily navigated by assistive technologies and how to provide alternative methods of accessing audio and video content for individuals who are deaf or hard of hearing. Overall, HTML Accessibility Training Courses play a crucial role in promoting inclusive web design practices. By equipping individuals with the knowledge and skills necessary to create accessible web content, these courses contribute to a more inclusive and equal online experience for all users.

HTML Accessibility Validator Software

An HTML Accessibility Validator Software is a tool designed to analyze and evaluate the accessibility of HTML documents according to web accessibility guidelines. It specifically focuses on identifying any barriers that may prevent people with disabilities from accessing and understanding web content. The software examines the structure, elements, and attributes of an HTML document to ensure it meets the accessibility standards set by organizations such as the World Wide Web Consortium (W3C) and the Web Accessibility Initiative (WAI).

HTML Accessibility Validators

An HTML Accessibility Validator refers to a web accessibility evaluation tool that analyzes the compliance of HTML code with accessibility standards to ensure that websites are inclusive and can be accessed by individuals with disabilities. These validators play a crucial role in the accessibility design process, helping web developers and designers identify and fix potential accessibility barriers. HTML Accessibility Validators examine various aspects of a website's HTML code and provide feedback based on established accessibility guidelines such as the Web Content Accessibility Guidelines (WCAG). They typically check for a wide range of accessibility issues, including proper usage of semantic HTML elements, alternative text for images, keyboard navigation support, and the availability of text equivalents for non-text content like videos or audio files. Validators also assess factors like color contrast ratios, which can impact the readability of content for individuals with visual impairments.

HTML5 Accessibility

HTML5 Accessibility refers to the practice and principles of designing web pages and web applications that are accessible to all users, including those with disabilities. It involves creating web content and functionality that can be perceived, operated, and understood by individuals with a diverse range of abilities and disabilities. HTML5 provides a set of features and techniques that enhance the accessibility of web content. These features include semantic elements, ARIA attributes, and multimedia accessibility. Semantic elements, such as , , and , provide a clear structure to web pages, making it easier for assistive technologies to parse and navigate the content. ARIA attributes, such as aria-label and aria-labelledby, can be used to add additional semantics to HTML elements, making them more accessible to assistive technologies. Multimedia accessibility involves providing alternative text, captions, and transcripts for non-text content, such as images and videos, ensuring that individuals who cannot perceive the content can still understand it. When implementing HTML5 accessibility, it is important to consider various disabilities and assistive technologies. Visual disabilities, such as blindness or low vision, may require the use of screen readers or magnification tools. Hearing disabilities may require captions or transcripts for audio content. Cognitive disabilities may require a simplified layout or clear instructions. By understanding the needs and limitations of different disabilities, web designers and developers can create accessible experiences that cater to a wider audience. HTML5 Accessibility is not only beneficial for individuals with disabilities, but it also improves the usability and user experience for all users. Clear and well-structured web pages are easier to navigate and understand, resulting in a more intuitive and efficient user experience. Additionally, accessible websites are more compatible with different devices and assistive technologies, ensuring that users can access the content on various platforms.

Handwriting Recognition

Handwriting recognition in the context of accessibility design refers to the technology that allows individuals with disabilities, particularly those with fine motor skill impairments or visual impairments, to input text or commands using their own handwriting instead of conventional keyboards or mice. This technology utilizes advanced algorithms and machine learning techniques to analyze and interpret handwritten text or symbols, and convert them into digital format. The main goal of handwriting recognition in accessibility design is to provide an alternative input method that is more natural and user-friendly for individuals who may have difficulty using traditional input devices.

Haptic Feedback Device Manufacturers

Haptic feedback device manufacturers refer to companies or organizations that specialize in the design, development, and production of devices that provide haptic feedback. Haptic feedback refers to the use of tactile sensations or vibrations to stimulate the sense of touch in individuals. These devices are created with the aim of enhancing accessibility for individuals with disabilities or impairments, allowing them to interact with technology and the physical world in a more inclusive and intuitive manner. Manufacturers of haptic feedback devices play a crucial role in the field of accessibility design, as they contribute to the development of products that can assist individuals with various impairments. These devices can be used in a range of applications, including but not limited to assistive technologies, virtual reality systems, gaming peripherals, and medical devices.

Haptic Feedback Device Suppliers

A haptic feedback device is a tool or equipment designed to provide tactile or touch-based communication to individuals with visual impairments or limited mobility. It is used in accessibility design to enhance the user experience and improve the accessibility of various digital or physical environments. Haptic feedback devices are essential for creating inclusive designs that cater to the needs of users who rely on touch to navigate and interact with technology. These devices utilize vibrations, pulses, or other tactile sensations to convey information or simulate the sense of touch. Suppliers of haptic feedback devices play a crucial role in ensuring that these tools are readily available for designers, developers, and organizations that prioritize accessibility. These suppliers offer a range of devices that can be integrated into products or systems to provide haptic feedback. By partnering with haptic feedback device suppliers, accessibility designers can source and incorporate suitable haptic feedback technology into their designs. These suppliers often provide comprehensive information about the features, specifications, and installation requirements of their devices, making it easier for designers to select the appropriate haptic feedback solution. The suppliers also offer support services, including technical assistance and guidance, to assist designers in implementing haptic feedback effectively. They may provide documentation, software development kits (SDKs), or application programming interfaces (APIs) that facilitate the integration of haptic feedback into various applications or platforms. Furthermore, haptic feedback device suppliers may collaborate with accessibility organizations and standards bodies to ensure that their products align with industry best practices. This collaboration helps promote the development and adoption of inclusive designs across different sectors. In conclusion, haptic feedback device suppliers play a vital role in the accessibility design process by providing the necessary tools, support, and expertise to incorporate haptic feedback into digital or physical environments. Their collaboration with designers and organizations contributes to the creation of inclusive products and services that prioritize accessibility for individuals with visual impairments or limited mobility.

Haptic Feedback Devices

Haptic Feedback Devices: Haptic feedback devices are technological tools that provide tactile sensations to users, mainly designed for accessibility purposes in the field of user interface (UI) and user experience (UX) design. These devices aim to enhance the interaction and communication between humans and digital or virtual environments by simulating physical sensations through touch. By incorporating haptic feedback devices into accessible designs, individuals with sensory disabilities or impairments can experience and perceive digital content in a more inclusive and immersive way. These devices can deliver various types of haptic sensations, such as vibrations, pulses, textures, or even temperature changes, depending on their capabilities and the intended use. One common application of haptic feedback devices is in the gaming industry, where they contribute to creating an enhanced gaming experience for players with visual or hearing impairments. For instance, haptic game controllers can provide tactile feedback that corresponds to specific in-game actions, allowing players to feel the game environment and interact with it more effectively. Moreover, haptic feedback devices have proven to be valuable tools in assistive technologies and accessibility features for individuals with visual impairments. For example, tactile displays can convert digital information or graphics into Braille-like text or tactile images, enabling people with visual disabilities to access and comprehend digital content, such as websites, educational material, or even graphical representations of data. In the context of accessibility design, haptic feedback devices offer a means to bridge the gap between digital interfaces and individuals with sensory impairments. They enhance the usability and inclusivity of digital products, services, and applications by providing an additional layer of interaction and sensory information. By incorporating haptic feedback devices into accessible design strategies, developers and designers can ensure that individuals with different abilities can fully engage with and benefit from their creations. Overall, haptic feedback devices play a significant role in accessibility design by facilitating tactile communication and interaction in digital environments. These devices empower users with sensory impairments to access and engage with digital content, bringing them closer to a more inclusive, accessible, and equal user experience.

Head Tracking

Head tracking, in the context of accessibility design, refers to the technology that allows individuals with limited or no use of their limbs to control and interact with a computer or electronic device using only head movements. It is primarily designed to ensure equal access and inclusion for people with physical disabilities, enabling them to effectively navigate digital interfaces, operate software applications, and perform tasks that are otherwise challenging or impossible to accomplish using traditional input methods such as keyboards, mice, or touchscreens. Head tracking systems typically utilize a combination of specialized hardware and software to track and interpret the movements of the user's head. The hardware component may consist of a camera, depth sensors, or infrared sensors, which capture the user's head movements and transmit the data to the software for analysis. The software component, on the other hand, processes the input from the hardware and translates it into on-screen actions or commands. This can involve controlling the cursor movement, selecting objects, activating menus, or triggering specific actions based on predefined gestures or head positions. By employing head tracking technology, individuals with physical disabilities gain the ability to independently interact with digital environments, breaking down barriers and promoting greater accessibility. This technology has proven particularly beneficial for individuals with conditions such as spinal cord injuries, muscular dystrophy, cerebral palsy, or amyotrophic lateral sclerosis (ALS), who may have limited or no control over their limbs. It also facilitates the use of augmentative and alternative communication (AAC) systems, which rely on head movement for non-verbal individuals to communicate through synthesized speech or pre-programmed messages. In the field of accessibility design, head tracking is considered essential for creating inclusive user experiences and ensuring equal opportunities for individuals with physical impairments. It allows them to participate in various activities that require digital interaction, such as browsing the web, using social media, writing emails, playing games, or accessing educational materials. By enabling individuals to use their computers or devices effectively through head movements, head tracking technology empowers them to engage in work, education, and leisure activities that were previously inaccessible or limited. In conclusion, head tracking is a vital technology in accessibility design, allowing individuals with physical disabilities to control and navigate digital interfaces using only head movements. Its implementation in computer systems and electronic devices promotes equal access and inclusion, enabling individuals to independently perform tasks and interact with digital environments.

Hearing Impairment

Hearing impairment, in the context of accessibility design, refers to a condition where an individual has a partial or total inability to hear sounds. It can range from mild to severe, and it can impact a person's ability to communicate, understand speech, and engage with auditory stimuli. Hearing impairment is a diverse condition that can affect individuals of all ages, and it requires specific considerations in accessibility design to ensure equal access and inclusion for all users. When designing for individuals with hearing impairment, it is important to provide alternatives to auditory information. This can be achieved through the use of visual cues, such as captions or subtitles in videos, transcripts for audio content, and visual alerts for important auditory notifications. By providing visual alternatives, individuals with hearing impairment can still access and understand information that would otherwise be conveyed through sound.

High Contrast Mode

High Contrast Mode is an accessibility feature designed to improve the visibility and legibility of digital content for individuals with visual impairments or other visual challenges. This mode enhances the contrast between text, images, and background colors, making it easier for users to navigate and comprehend information on a digital interface. When enabled, High Contrast Mode adjusts the visual display by reducing the range of colors and increasing the contrast levels. Background colors are typically changed to black or white, while text and other elements are displayed in high-contrast colors such as black or yellow. This stark contrast ensures that content stands out distinctly and is more easily distinguishable for users with low vision.

Inclusion

Inclusion, within the context of accessibility design, refers to the practice of creating an environment where individuals of all abilities can fully participate in activities, interactions, and experiences. It involves designing and developing digital content, websites, and applications in a way that ensures equal access and usability for everyone, regardless of their physical, sensory, cognitive, or intellectual abilities. Effective inclusion in accessibility design requires considering diverse user needs and preferences right from the initial stages of the design process. It involves adopting a user-centric approach and implementing inclusive design principles to build products and services that can be accessed and used by the widest range of individuals. This includes addressing barriers and challenges faced by users with disabilities and providing alternative ways to access and interact with digital content. One key aspect of inclusion in accessibility design is making sure that the content is perceivable to all users. This means providing alternatives for non-text content, such as images and videos, for individuals with visual or hearing impairments. It also involves using clear and consistent headings, labels, and instructions to facilitate navigation and understanding for individuals with cognitive or learning disabilities. Another important consideration is making the content operable for all users. This includes providing keyboard alternatives for individuals who cannot use a mouse, ensuring sufficient time for individuals with mobility impairments to complete tasks, and avoiding any design elements that might trigger seizures or other physical reactions. Additionally, inclusive design should strive to be compatible with assistive technologies, such as screen readers and voice recognition software, to enable individuals with disabilities to access and interact with the content   effectively. Inclusion in accessibility design also encompasses making content understandable and robust. This involves using plain language and avoiding jargon or complex terminology that may be difficult to comprehend for individuals with cognitive disabilities. It also requires using standard web technologies and avoiding proprietary formats or practices that may limit access for users of different devices or assistive technologies.

Inclusive Communication

Inclusive communication in the context of accessibility design refers to the practice of creating content and delivering messages in a way that ensures all individuals, regardless of their abilities or disabilities, can understand and engage with the information effectively. It focuses on breaking down barriers to communication and promoting equal access to information for everyone. Inclusive communication involves considering various factors, such as different cognitive abilities, visual impairments, hearing impairments, and language proficiency, when designing and delivering content. It aims to provide alternative formats or channels to accommodate different communication needs and preferences.

Inclusive Design Workshops

Inclusive Design Workshops are interactive sessions or events that aim to promote accessibility and inclusive design practices. These workshops provide a platform for designers, developers, and other stakeholders to come together and learn about designing products, services, and spaces that can be used by people of diverse abilities, including those with disabilities. The primary focus of inclusive design workshops is to raise awareness and understanding about the importance of accessibility in design. Participants are encouraged to explore and discuss various accessibility considerations, such as physical, sensory, cognitive, and technological barriers that can hinder the usability of a product or service. Through engaging activities and discussions, these workshops seek to foster a mindset shift towards more inclusive design practices in the industry.

Inclusive Design

Inclusive design, in the context of accessibility design, refers to the approach of creating products, services, and spaces that can be accessed, understood, and used by a wide range of individuals, regardless of their abilities or disabilities. This design approach aims to remove barriers and provide equal opportunities for everyone, including individuals with physical, sensory, cognitive, or other disabilities. It recognizes the diverse needs and requirements of users and aims to create inclusive experiences that cater to everyone's needs.

Inclusive Education Platforms

Inclusive Education Platforms refer to online platforms or systems that are designed and developed with a primary focus on accessibility and inclusivity. These platforms aim to provide an equal opportunity for all learners, regardless of their abilities or disabilities, to access educational content and participate in learning activities. Inclusive Education Platforms utilize various accessibility features to ensure that individuals with diverse needs can fully engage in the learning process. These features may include alternative formats for content delivery, such as text-to-speech or captioning, to accommodate learners with visual or hearing impairments. Additionally, these platforms may offer adjustable font sizes or contrast settings for learners with visual difficulties. Furthermore, inclusive platforms provide support for learners with cognitive disabilities by incorporating features like simplified language options, clear navigation, and interactive elements that aid comprehension. They also prioritize compatibility with assistive technologies such as screen readers or alternative input devices, enabling learners with physical disabilities to interact with the content effectively. Inclusive Education Platforms also promote collaborative learning by facilitating peer-to-peer interaction and group discussions. They may incorporate features like discussion forums, chat rooms, or collaborative document editing tools that support different modes of communication and participation. Such platforms also emphasize user-centric design principles, ensuring that individuals of all abilities can navigate and interact with the interface easily. Moreover, these platforms often offer customization options, allowing learners to personalize their learning environments based on their individual preferences and needs. This includes options for font styles, color schemes, and layout arrangements, enabling learners to create a visually comfortable and accessible interface. In conclusion, Inclusive Education Platforms are online systems designed with a strong focus on accessibility and inclusivity. By incorporating various accessibility features, these platforms empower learners with diverse abilities to access educational content, actively participate in learning activities, and collaborate with peers on an equal footing, creating a truly inclusive learning experience for all.

Inclusive Education Software

Inclusive Education Software refers to a type of software that is designed to ensure accessibility and inclusivity for individuals with diverse abilities and needs in an educational setting. It is a technological solution that aims to remove barriers to learning and provide equal opportunities for all students, regardless of their disabilities or limitations. This software incorporates various features and functionalities that cater to the diverse needs of learners, including but not limited to visual impairments, hearing impairments, mobility impairments, learning disabilities, and cognitive difficulties. It promotes a barrier-free learning environment by enabling students with disabilities to fully participate in educational activities alongside their peers.

Inclusive Education

Inclusive Education refers to a pedagogical approach that aims to provide equal opportunities for all students, regardless of their individual abilities or disabilities, ethnic backgrounds, gender identities, socioeconomic statuses, or any other diverse characteristics. It is based on the belief that every student has the right to receive quality education in a supportive and inclusive environment.Accessibility design plays a crucial role in ensuring that inclusive education is implemented effectively. It involves creating and modifying learning environments, materials, and instructional methods that address the diverse needs of all learners, helping them to access, participate, and succeed in their educational journey.

Information Accessibility

Information accessibility refers to the design and implementation of digital content and technologies that can be easily understood, navigated, and interacted with by all individuals, including those with disabilities. It ensures that people with visual, auditory, cognitive, and motor impairments can access and use information on websites, applications, and digital platforms without facing any barriers. To achieve information accessibility, several factors need to be considered. First, the content should be perceivable, meaning that it should be presented in a way that allows users to easily see and hear it. This includes providing alternative text descriptions for images and captions for videos, using readable fonts and color contrasts, and avoiding the use of audio or video-only content without transcripts or captions. Second, the content should be operable, allowing users to navigate and interact with it using various inputs such as keyboards, mice, touchscreens, and assistive technologies. This involves providing clear and consistent navigation menus, ensuring that interactive elements are accessible through keyboard focus, and avoiding actions that may cause seizures or require precise timing. Third, the content should be understandable, ensuring that the information and user interface are clear and easy to comprehend. This involves using plain language and avoiding jargon or complex terminologies, organizing content in a logical manner, and providing instructions and feedback that are concise and easily understood. Lastly, the content should be robust, meaning that it should be compatible with a wide range of assistive technologies and devices. This includes using standard markup language and following web accessibility guidelines, ensuring that the content remains accessible even as new technologies emerge. In conclusion, information accessibility is a fundamental aspect of inclusive design that aims to provide equal access to digital information for all individuals, regardless of their abilities or disabilities. It involves considering various factors such as perceivability, operability, understandability, and compatibility with assistive technologies to ensure that everyone can effectively access and use digital content.

Interaction Accessibility

Interaction accessibility refers to the design and implementation of user interfaces that are accessible to all individuals, regardless of their disabilities or limitations in using traditional input methods. It ensures that people with disabilities can effectively navigate and interact with websites, applications, and other digital platforms. Inclusive interaction design requires developers to consider the diverse needs of users, including those with visual, auditory, motor, or cognitive impairments. This involves creating user interfaces that accommodate various input methods, such as keyboard, mouse, touch, or voice, and providing alternatives for non-standard or assistive devices. One key aspect of interaction accessibility is keyboard accessibility. This means that all functionality and navigation options within a webpage or application can be accessed and operated solely using a keyboard. This is crucial for people who rely on keyboard navigation due to motor disabilities or those who use alternative devices like switches or sip-and-puff systems. In addition, developers should ensure that interactive elements, such as buttons, links, and form fields, are properly labeled and provide clear and concise instructions or feedback. This helps individuals with visual impairments who rely on screen readers or other assistive technologies to understand and interact with these elements effectively. Another important consideration is providing visual and auditory alternatives for non-text content. Images, graphs, videos, and audio files should have appropriate alternative text, captions, and transcripts to ensure that people with visual or hearing impairments can access the information conveyed by these media formats. Furthermore, consideration should be given to the timing and sequence of interactive events. Users should have enough time to read and understand content, complete tasks, and navigate through the interface without being rushed or interrupted. Providing options to adjust time limits or pausing and resuming interactions can greatly benefit individuals with cognitive disabilities or those who require more time to process information. In conclusion, interaction accessibility aims to remove barriers that individuals with disabilities may face when interacting with digital interfaces. By considering the diverse needs and limitations of users, developers can create inclusive designs that allow everyone to access and engage with digital content effectively.

Interaction Design For Disabilities

Interaction design for disabilities refers to the process of creating digital products and experiences that are accessible and usable by individuals with disabilities. It focuses on designing inclusive interfaces that accommodate a range of impairments, such as visual, auditory, cognitive, or motor disabilities. The goal of interaction design for disabilities is to eliminate barriers and provide equal access to information, services, and functionality for all users, regardless of their abilities. It aims to ensure that individuals with disabilities can independently navigate, understand, and interact with digital interfaces, enabling them to fully participate in all aspects of society and the digital world. Accessible interaction design involves various considerations, including the use of alternative input methods, such as keyboard navigation, voice commands, or switch devices for individuals with limited mobility. It also entails providing multiple ways to perceive and understand information, such as incorporating captions, transcripts, or audio descriptions for individuals with hearing or visual impairments. Another important aspect of interaction design for disabilities is the creation of clear and consistent user interfaces. This includes using appropriate color contrast ratios, providing sufficient visual cues and affordances, and ensuring the proper organization and structure of content. These design principles help individuals with cognitive or learning disabilities to easily comprehend and navigate through digital interfaces. Furthermore, interaction design for disabilities involves considering the diverse range of assistive technologies and tools that individuals with disabilities may use. This includes screen readers, screen magnifiers, speech recognition software, or alternative input devices. Designing with compatibility and interoperability in mind ensures that the digital product or experience can seamlessly integrate with these assistive technologies, enhancing the overall accessibility and usability for individuals with disabilities. In conclusion, interaction design for disabilities is a vital component of accessibility design that prioritizes the needs and experiences of individuals with disabilities. By incorporating inclusive design practices and considering the diverse range of abilities, this approach strives to create digital products and experiences that are usable, intuitive, and barrier-free for all users.

JAWS Screen Reader

JAWS Screen Reader is a widely used assistive technology tool designed to improve accessibility for individuals with visual impairments. It functions as a software program that converts on-screen text into synthesized speech or Braille output, enabling users to navigate and interact with digital content, applications, and operating systems. As an assistive technology, JAWS Screen Reader plays a crucial role in ensuring equal access and inclusion for individuals who are blind or have low vision. It enhances their ability to engage with various digital platforms, such as websites, software applications, and documents, by converting visual information into auditory or tactile feedback. By doing so, it effectively bridges the accessibility gap and empowers users to independently access and interact with information and technology.

Keyboard Accessibility Testing

Keyboard accessibility testing refers to the process of evaluating and ensuring that a website or application can be fully accessed and navigated using only a keyboard, without the need for a mouse or other pointing device. This type of testing is important for people with motor disabilities, visual impairments, or other conditions that may affect their ability to use a mouse or other pointing device. Keyboard accessibility testing involves verifying that all interactive elements, such as buttons, links, and form fields, can be accessed and activated using keyboard commands. It also includes checking that keyboard focus is clearly visible and that users can easily navigate through the content using the keyboard. Additionally, keyboard accessibility testing examines the behavior of the website or application when the user interacts with it solely through keyboard commands. To conduct keyboard accessibility testing, testers typically use a variety of techniques and tools. This can include manually navigating through the website or application using only the keyboard, as well as using automated testing tools that simulate keyboard commands. Testers may also rely on assistive technologies, such as screen readers or speech recognition software, to evaluate the accessibility of the content. The aim of keyboard accessibility testing is to ensure that people with motor disabilities or other impairments have equal access to the website or application. By testing the accessibility of the interface, designers and developers can identify and address any barriers that may prevent users from interacting effectively with the content. Ensuring keyboard accessibility can greatly enhance the usability and inclusivity of the website or application, allowing a broader range of users to benefit from its features and functionality. Overall, keyboard accessibility testing plays a crucial role in accessibility design, as it helps to ensure that websites and applications are usable and accessible to all users, regardless of their physical abilities or impairments. By providing a way for users to interact with the content solely through the keyboard, designers and developers can create a more inclusive and user-friendly experience.

Keyboard Navigation

Keyboard Shortcuts

Keyboard shortcuts in the context of accessibility design refer to predefined key combinations that allow users to perform certain actions or navigate through a software application, website, or operating system more efficiently, without the need for using a mouse or other pointing device. These shortcuts are designed to provide an alternative method of interaction for individuals with mobility impairments or those who prefer using keyboard-based navigation. Keyboard shortcuts can improve accessibility by enabling users to access features and functionalities quickly, without the need to rely solely on mouse-based interactions. They can help individuals with motor disabilities who may have difficulty manipulating a mouse or performing fine motor movements. Furthermore, keyboard shortcuts can enhance the overall user experience for all users, including those who simply prefer using keyboard navigation or those who may have limitations in using a mouse temporarily, such as due to a broken arm or hand injury. By implementing well-designed keyboard shortcuts, accessibility considerations are taken into account, ensuring that individuals with different abilities can effectively operate a software application, website, or operating system. These shortcuts are usually accompanied by clear and concise documentation or on-screen indicators, allowing users to easily discover, learn, and memorize them. In HTML, developers can enhance the accessibility of their websites by providing keyboard shortcuts for frequently used features or actions. This can be achieved through the "accesskey" attribute, which is used to define a shortcut key for an element. This attribute is typically applied to anchor elements (links), buttons, form fields, or any other interactive element that requires user input. For example, the following HTML code demonstrates how to define a shortcut key using the "accesskey" attribute: The Home page provides an overview of our services. Here, the letter "H" is designated as the keyboard shortcut to activate the "Home" link. When the user presses the associated key (in combination with an activation key that varies with each browser and operating system), the link will be activated, allowing the user to navigate to the home page. In conclusion, keyboard shortcuts play a significant role in improving accessibility by enabling users to navigate through digital interfaces efficiently and effectively. They serve as an alternative method of interaction for individuals with mobility impairments or those who prefer keyboard-based navigation. By incorporating keyboard shortcuts into web design, developers can enhance the accessibility of their websites, benefiting a wider range of users with diverse abilities and preferences.

Keyboard-Only Navigation

Keyboard-Only Navigation refers to the design and implementation of a website or application that allows users to navigate and interact with the interface solely by using a keyboard, without the need for a mouse or other pointing device. In the context of accessibility design, keyboard-only navigation is extremely important as it ensures that individuals with mobility impairments or those who are unable to use a mouse can still fully utilize and access digital content. By providing keyboard-only navigation, designers and developers can ensure that their websites or applications are inclusive and accessible to all users.

Large Cursor

A large cursor in the context of accessibility design refers to a visual aid that enhances the usability of a computer system for individuals with visual impairments or those who struggle with fine motor control. It is a feature that enlarges the size of the cursor, making it more visible and easier to track on the screen. The large cursor aims to address the needs of users with varying degrees of visual impairments, including those with low vision or color blindness. By increasing the size of the cursor, it becomes more prominent and stands out against the background, improving its visibility and making it easier to locate and follow. Furthermore, a large cursor helps individuals with fine motor control issues by providing a bigger target to interact with. This is particularly beneficial for those with conditions such as Parkinson's disease or muscular dystrophy, as it reduces the risk of mistakenly clicking on the wrong elements due to an unsteady hand or finger movements. By offering a larger and more noticeable cursor, the accessibility design of a computer system ensures that users with visual impairments or motor control difficulties can have a more comfortable and efficient user experience. It enables them to navigate through the interface with greater ease, accurately select elements or options, and interact with the system without frustrations or challenges caused by a small, hard-to-see cursor. In conclusion, a large cursor is an accessibility design feature that enhances both visibility and usability for users with visual impairments or fine motor control difficulties. It provides a larger cursor size, making it more prominent and easy to track on the screen, thereby improving the overall user experience.

Large Print Materials

Large Print Materials refer to documents, publications, or any written content that is specifically designed and formatted to be easily readable by individuals with visual impairments or reading difficulties. These materials are created with the intention of maximizing legibility and ensuring that the text is clear and accessible to a wide range of individuals with varying degrees of visual acuity. The purpose of large print materials is to accommodate individuals who have difficulty reading standard-sized text due to vision impairments such as low vision or age-related macular degeneration. Large print materials typically feature an enlarged font size, typically ranging from 16 to 24 points, which is significantly larger than the standard 10-12 point font size used in regular print publications.

Large Text And Font Options

Large text and font options refer to the design features that allow users to increase the size of the text and customize the font type and style for better accessibility. These options are essential for individuals with visual impairments or other reading difficulties, as they enable them to perceive and comprehend the content more effectively. In the context of accessibility design, large text and font options provide alternative ways to present and display information that may be easier for users to read and understand. By offering the ability to enlarge the text size, individuals with low vision or those who struggle with small text can adjust it to a comfortable and legible size. This ensures that the content remains accessible and inclusive for all users, regardless of their visual abilities. Moreover, font options facilitate personalization and customization for users. They allow individuals to select a font style that aligns with their preferences or needs, such as a serif or sans-serif font. Some people with dyslexia, for example, find specific font types easier to read, so providing font options caters to their specific requirements. By offering these choices, designers ensure that individuals can engage with the content in a way that works best for them. These features can be implemented in accessible design through various techniques. CSS can be used to define font families and styles, providing users with a range of options to choose from. Additionally, responsive design principles can be employed, ensuring that the text and font options adapt and adjust smoothly across different devices and screen sizes. Accessible design guidelines, such as those outlined in WCAG 2.0, can be followed to ensure compliance and best practices. Overall, large text and font options are vital elements in accessibility design. By allowing users to customize the size and style of the text, designers create a more inclusive and user-friendly experience. These features enable individuals with visual impairments or reading difficulties to access information more effectively, contributing to a more inclusive and accessible digital landscape.

Learning Disabilities

Learning Disabilities refer to a diverse range of neurological conditions that affect an individual's ability to acquire, process, store, or produce information accurately or efficiently. These disabilities can impact various areas of learning, such as reading, writing, mathematics, and comprehension, making it challenging for individuals to develop skills that are typically developed by their peers. Learning Disabilities can manifest differently in each person and may include difficulties with attention, memory, problem-solving, organization, spatial orientation, or motor skills. These disabilities are not related to intelligence and can affect individuals of all ages, backgrounds, and intellectual abilities. It is important to note that Learning Disabilities are distinct from other conditions, such as intellectual disabilities, sensory impairments, or developmental delays.

Legibility

Legibility in the context of accessibility design refers to the readability and clarity of content, particularly in digital interfaces, with the goal of ensuring equal access for all users, regardless of their abilities or disabilities. It is crucial to consider legibility in the design of websites, applications, and other digital platforms to ensure that the content can be easily understood and consumed by a wide range of users. Legibility encompasses several factors that influence how easily users can read and comprehend the information presented. These factors include font choice, font size, contrast, spacing, and formatting. By carefully considering these elements, designers can create content that is legible to a diverse audience, including users with visual impairments, cognitive disabilities, or other accessibility needs.

Lip Reading

Lip Reading is an accessibility design technique that aims to provide individuals with hearing impairments or deafness the ability to understand spoken language by visually interpreting the movements and shape of the speaker's lips, facial expressions, and other visual cues. To implement Lip Reading as part of an accessibility design, certain considerations need to be taken into account. Firstly, the design should ensure that the speaker's face is clearly visible, with adequate lighting to enhance the visibility of their lips and facial expressions. This can be achieved by positioning the speaker in well-lit environments and avoiding shadows or obstructions on their face. Secondly, the design should provide a clear and unobstructed view of the speaker's mouth and lips. This can be achieved by using appropriate camera angles and zoom levels in video-based communication platforms or by placing the speaker in a visible location during face-to-face interactions. Moreover, it is essential to ensure that the audiovisual quality of the communication is optimized for Lip Reading. This can be achieved by using high-definition capture devices, noise reduction techniques, and audio enhancements to improve the clarity of speech. In video-based platforms, lip-syncing should be synchronized correctly to ensure accurate visual representation of the spoken words. Additionally, supporting graphical or text-based aids may be incorporated into the design to supplement the lip reading experience. For example, providing captions or subtitles that display the spoken words can enhance comprehension for individuals who may struggle with certain phonetic distinctions. Overall, Lip Reading as a part of accessibility design focuses on providing individuals with hearing impairments or deafness the ability to understand spoken language through visual interpretation. By considering factors such as visibility, audiovisual quality, and supporting aids, designers can create inclusive communication experiences that cater to the diverse needs of individuals with hearing-related accessibility challenges.

Low Vision Aid Manufacturers

Low Vision Aid Manufacturers are companies or organizations that produce and develop devices, tools, and products specifically designed to assist individuals with low vision. Low vision refers to a significant visual impairment that cannot be corrected by glasses, contact lenses, medication, or eye surgery. People with low vision often have limited visual acuity, field of vision, or both, making it difficult for them to perform daily tasks such as reading, writing, and navigating their surroundings. The role of Low Vision Aid Manufacturers is to create solutions that enhance the visual abilities of individuals with low vision, helping them overcome the challenges they face in their daily lives. These manufacturers employ a variety of technologies and design principles to develop products that address specific vision impairments and provide practical and effective solutions. The range of low vision aids manufactured by these companies is diverse and can include magnification devices, such as handheld or stand magnifiers, which enlarge text and images to make them easier to see. They may also produce electronic magnifiers, which use cameras and displays to provide adjustable magnification levels for different tasks and visual needs. Additionally, Low Vision Aid Manufacturers often produce specialized reading aids, such as text-to-speech devices or screen reader software, which convert written text into audible speech. These aids enable individuals with low vision to access printed materials, such as books, newspapers, and documents, by listening to the text being read aloud. Other types of low vision aids manufactured by these companies include glare control filters, which reduce the glare and contrast sensitivity experienced by individuals with low vision, and mobility aids, such as white canes and navigation aids, which help individuals safely navigate their environment. By creating and manufacturing these low vision aids, Low Vision Aid Manufacturers play a crucial role in promoting accessibility and inclusivity for individuals with low vision. Their products empower individuals with low vision to maintain independence, improve their quality of life, and participate more fully in everyday activities.

Low Vision Aid Providers

A low vision aid provider is a professional or organization that specializes in assessing, recommending, and providing assistive devices and technologies to individuals with low vision. These providers play a crucial role in ensuring accessibility for people with visual impairments, by offering a range of products and services that can enhance their ability to see, interact with their environment, and perform daily tasks. The primary objective of a low vision aid provider is to help individuals with low vision make the most of their remaining vision, by utilizing various tools and technologies. This may include magnification devices such as handheld magnifiers, portable electronic magnifiers, or video magnifiers, which can enlarge text and images to a size that is readable and understandable for the individual. They may also offer non-optical aids such as large print materials, bold-line paper, or high contrast products, which enhance visibility and make reading or writing easier. Moreover, low vision aid providers may offer assistive technologies designed to facilitate independent living, such as talking watches or clocks, digital voice recorders, or text-to-speech software for computers and mobile devices. These tools enable individuals with low vision to manage their schedules, record important information, and access digital content with ease. In addition to providing assistive devices, low vision aid providers often provide comprehensive assessments and consultations to understand the unique needs and preferences of each individual. They take into consideration factors such as the individual's specific eye condition, their functional vision abilities, and any specific tasks or activities they may need assistance with. This allows the provider to recommend the most appropriate low vision aids that will effectively address the individual's needs and enhance their overall quality of life. Overall, low vision aid providers play a critical role in promoting accessibility and inclusion for individuals with low vision. By offering specialized products, services, and expertise, they empower individuals to overcome the challenges posed by their visual impairments and optimize their independence and participation in various aspects of life.

Low Vision Aids

Low vision aids are assistive devices designed to enhance the vision of individuals with visual impairments. These aids are specifically created to address the unique needs and challenges faced by people with low vision, enabling them to participate more effectively in daily activities and improve their overall quality of life. There are various types of low vision aids available, each catering to different levels of visual impairment and specific requirements. One common category of aids is magnification devices, which help individuals with low vision to see text, images, or objects more clearly. These devices include magnifiers, handheld or stand-mounted, that enlarge the size of the desired object, making it easier to read or view. Another type of aid is the closed-circuit television (CCTV), which uses a camera and monitor system to magnify and display images beyond the capability of traditional magnifiers. Lighting aids are another essential category of low vision aids. They consist of different types of lighting options that help improve visibility and contrast. These aids may include adjustable desk lamps, task lights, or portable lighting devices that can be positioned strategically to enhance illumination on specific tasks. Additionally, these aids may also involve glare-reducing filters or anti-glare coatings on electronic displays or eyewear to minimize discomfort and improve visual clarity. Color enhancement aids are designed to enhance color perception for individuals with low vision. These aids may include specialized eyewear or filters that modify the visual spectrum, making it easier for individuals to differentiate colors and perceive contrasts. Additionally, some aids may offer adjustable color settings on electronic devices, enabling users to customize the display to suit their individual needs and preferences. Moreover, there are also various electronic assistive technologies that cater to individuals with low vision. These include screen-reading software, screen magnifiers, and high-contrast display options that optimize the digital experience for people with visual impairments. Additionally, there are also handheld electronic devices that convert printed text into audio, providing individuals with low vision access to written information in an auditory format. In conclusion, low vision aids play a crucial role in accessibility design, enabling individuals with visual impairments to independently engage in daily activities and tasks. By addressing the specific challenges faced by people with low vision, these aids help improve their visual capabilities, enhance their overall quality of life, and promote inclusivity and equality for all.

Low Vision

Low vision refers to a visual impairment that cannot be fully corrected using conventional eyeglasses, contact lenses, or surgical procedures. It is a condition in which individuals have a significant reduction in visual acuity or field of vision, leading to difficulty in performing everyday tasks. People with low vision may experience a range of visual impairments, such as blurred vision, tunnel vision, blind spots, or reduced contrast sensitivity. Some common causes of low vision include age-related macular degeneration, glaucoma, cataracts, diabetic retinopathy, and genetic conditions. This condition can have a profound impact on an individual's ability to read, write, recognize faces, navigate their surroundings, and perform various activities independently. In the context of accessibility design, it is crucial to consider the needs and challenges faced by individuals with low vision. Designing websites and digital content that cater to the requirements of this user group is essential for promoting inclusivity and ensuring equal access to information and services. Accessibility features for individuals with low vision may include options for adjusting text size, font type, and color contrast. Providing high contrast between text and background can enhance readability for those with reduced contrast sensitivity. Offering alternative text for images and graphics enables individuals using screen readers or assistive technologies to understand the content. Implementing resizable text and responsive layouts ensures that the content adapts to different screen sizes and resolutions. Furthermore, designers should consider incorporating clear and concise language, organizing content in a logical manner, and providing headings and subheadings to aid navigation and comprehension. Avoiding the use of complex visual elements, such as overly decorative fonts or excessive animations, can also improve usability for individuals with low vision. In conclusion, low vision refers to a visual impairment that hinders individuals' ability to see clearly and perform daily tasks. Addressing the needs of individuals with low vision through accessible design practices is crucial for creating inclusive digital experiences and promoting equal access to information and services.

Low-Tech Assistive Devices

Low-Tech Assistive Devices refer to simple and cost-effective tools designed to assist individuals with disabilities in performing daily tasks and activities. These devices are characterized by their simplicity, ease of use, and affordability, making them accessible and practical for a wide range of users. Low-tech assistive devices aim to enhance the independence, mobility, communication, and overall quality of life for individuals with disabilities. They can be used in various settings, including homes, schools, workplaces, and public spaces, to address a range of challenges and barriers faced by people with different abilities. These devices are often designed with universal accessibility in mind, ensuring that they can be easily understood and operated by individuals with varying levels of abilities. They do not require complex technological infrastructure or advanced skills to use, making them suitable for individuals with limited technological literacy or access to technology. Examples of low-tech assistive devices include mobility aids such as canes, walkers, and crutches, which assist individuals with physical limitations in walking and navigating their surroundings. Communication aids such as picture boards, symbol charts, and sign language cards are also commonly used to support individuals with speech or language impairments in expressing themselves effectively. In addition, low-tech devices for daily living tasks include adaptive utensils, grippers, or holders, which enable individuals with dexterity or fine motor skill impairments to eat, drink, or perform various self-care activities independently. Hearing amplifiers, magnifiers, and large-print materials are other examples of low-tech assistive devices that address sensory impairments by enhancing hearing and visual capabilities. Overall, low-tech assistive devices play a critical role in promoting inclusivity and accessibility for individuals with disabilities. By providing simple, affordable, and readily available solutions, these devices empower individuals to overcome barriers and participate fully in everyday activities, improving their overall quality of life and fostering a more inclusive society.

MAGic Screen Magnification

MAGic Screen Magnification is a feature designed for accessibility purposes that allows individuals with visual impairments to enlarge the content displayed on their computer screens. It provides a means for people with low vision to view and interact with digital content with greater ease and clarity. The MAGic Screen Magnification feature works by increasing the size of text, icons, and other visual elements on the screen, making them more visible and easier to discern. This can be especially beneficial for individuals with conditions such as macular degeneration, cataracts, or other vision impairments that affect their ability to see fine details or small text. By enlarging the content on the screen, MAGic Screen Magnification enables users to read text, navigate through menus, and access various applications with improved visibility. It ensures that the information displayed on the computer screen is easily readable and comprehensible for those with low vision. This feature can be adjusted according to the individual's specific needs and preferences. Users can customize the magnification level, font sizes, and other visual settings to suit their requirements. The ability to personalize and fine-tune the magnification settings allows individuals with different visual impairments to optimize their viewing experience and enhance their overall usability. MAGic Screen Magnification also provides additional features to enhance accessibility further. These include color enhancements, contrast adjustments, and cursor enhancements, which can be particularly helpful for individuals with color blindness or other color-related vision impairments. These features contribute to a more inclusive and usable digital environment, ensuring that people with varying degrees of visual impairments can fully participate in digital activities. By enabling individuals with low vision to magnify the on-screen content, MAGic Screen Magnification promotes equal access to digital information and technology. It empowers users with visual impairments to independently use computers, interact with software applications, browse the internet, and perform various tasks that would otherwise be challenging or inaccessible. In conclusion, MAGic Screen Magnification is a valuable accessibility feature that enlarges on-screen content, enhances visual clarity, and enables individuals with low vision to effectively use computers and interact with digital content.

Magnification Software

Magnification software is an assistive technology tool designed to enhance the visibility of digital content for individuals with visual impairments or those experiencing difficulties in reading small text. This software allows users to enlarge the size of text, images, and other visual elements on their computer screens, making them more accessible and easier to perceive. In the context of accessibility design, magnification software plays a crucial role in providing an inclusive digital environment for individuals with low vision. By increasing the size of text and visual elements, it compensates for limitations in visual acuity and empowers users to access and interact with digital content more comfortably.

Manual Testing

Manual testing in the context of accessibility design refers to the process of evaluating the usability and inclusivity of a website or web application for individuals with disabilities. It involves manually inspecting and interacting with the website to identify any accessibility issues that may hinder the user experience for persons with disabilities. The purpose of manual testing in accessibility design is to ensure that all users, regardless of their abilities or disabilities, have equal access to the content and functionalities of a website. By performing manual tests, developers and designers can identify and address accessibility barriers that may prevent individuals with disabilities from fully engaging with the website.

Microsoft Accessibility Checker

The Microsoft Accessibility Checker is a tool designed to promote the principles of accessibility in the realm of digital design. It aims to assist users in creating content that can be easily accessed and understood by individuals with disabilities. Accessibility in design refers to the practice of making digital content inclusive and usable for people with various limitations or impairments. This can include individuals with visual, auditory, cognitive, or motor disabilities, as well as those who use assistive technologies like screen readers or alternative input devices. The Microsoft Accessibility Checker serves as a helpful aid for designers, developers, and content creators to ensure their digital products meet accessibility standards and regulations. It is built into Microsoft Office applications like Word, PowerPoint, and Excel, providing real-time feedback and suggestions on how to improve the accessibility of documents and presentations. When using the Accessibility Checker, the tool scans the content and structure of the document, identifying potential accessibility issues. It then provides step-by-step instructions and suggestions on how to address these issues, making it easier for designers to make the necessary modifications and improvements. For example, the Accessibility Checker may identify a document that lacks alternative text for images, making it difficult for individuals with visual impairments to comprehend the content. In response, the tool would prompt the user to add descriptive alternative text, ensuring that screen readers can convey the meaning and context of the images to users who cannot see them. Through its guidance and recommendations, the Microsoft Accessibility Checker empowers designers and creators to enhance the accessibility of their digital content, promoting inclusivity and equal access for all individuals, regardless of their abilities or disabilities.

Microsoft Narrator

Microsoft Narrator is an assistive technology feature in Microsoft Windows operating systems that provides text-to-speech (TTS) functionality. It is designed to improve accessibility for individuals with visual impairments or reading difficulties by reading text out loud. Narrator can be accessed through the Ease of Access Center in the Control Panel, and it can also be activated using keyboard shortcuts. Once activated, it will read aloud any text on the screen, including menus, dialog boxes, documents, and web pages. Narrator can also be used to navigate through the operating system, allowing users to interact with programs and perform tasks with the assistance of auditory prompts.

Mixed Abilities

Mixed Abilities: In the context of accessibility design, mixed abilities refer to the diverse range of physical, cognitive, sensory, and neurological abilities that individuals possess. This concept recognizes that people have different levels of abilities, limitations, and disabilities, and aims to design environments, products, and services that are inclusive and can be accessed by all individuals, regardless of their abilities. Accessibility plays a crucial role in ensuring that individuals with mixed abilities can fully participate in and interact with the digital world. By considering the needs of individuals with diverse abilities, designers can create inclusive and user-friendly experiences that accommodate a wide range of users. In the realm of web design, creating accessible websites means adhering to guidelines and best practices that enable individuals with mixed abilities to access and navigate online content. This includes considering factors such as visual impairments, hearing impairments, motor impairments, and cognitive impairments. For visually impaired individuals, accessibility design focuses on providing alternatives to visual content. This can include providing descriptive text for images, ensuring proper color contrast for text readability, and using semantic markup to facilitate screen reader navigation. For individuals with hearing impairments, accessibility design involves providing captions or transcripts for audio and video content, as well as ensuring that important information is not conveyed solely through audio. Motor impairments can affect individuals' ability to use a mouse or navigate a website easily. Designing for motor impairments involves implementing keyboard accessibility, allowing users to navigate and interact with a website using only the keyboard. Cognitive impairments may affect individuals' ability to process information, concentrate, or remember certain tasks. To ensure accessibility for individuals with cognitive impairments, designers may use clear and simple language, minimize distractions, provide clear instructions, and ensure consistency throughout the website. In conclusion, mixed abilities in the context of accessibility design refers to considering and accommodating the varying abilities and disabilities of individuals when designing environments, products, and services. By adopting accessibility guidelines and considering the needs of individuals with diverse abilities, designers can create inclusive and user-friendly experiences. This is particularly important in web design, where accessible websites enable individuals with mixed abilities to fully engage with and access online content.

Mobile Accessibility Testing

Mobile accessibility testing refers to the process of evaluating the accessibility of a mobile application or website for users with disabilities. It involves assessing the design, layout, and functionality of the mobile interface to ensure that individuals with visual, hearing, motor, or cognitive impairments can effectively perceive, interact with, and understand the content. Accessibility design aims to make digital products inclusive and usable by all, regardless of their abilities. Conducting mobile accessibility testing ensures that the application or website meets the standards and guidelines set by accessibility regulations, such as the Web Content Accessibility Guidelines (WCAG) 2.1. During the testing process, various aspects are evaluated to ensure that the mobile interface provides a positive user experience for individuals with disabilities. These aspects include: 1. Perceivability: Assessing whether the content, including text, images, and multimedia, can be perceived by individuals with visual impairments. This involves checking for proper color contrast, providing alternative text for images, and ensuring that media is accompanied by captions or audio descriptions. 2. Operability: Examining the mobile interface's ease of use, especially for individuals with motor impairments. This involves assessing the size of interactive elements, such as buttons and links, to ensure they can be easily tapped or clicked. Keyboard accessibility is also evaluated to ensure that users can navigate through the interface without relying solely on touch gestures. 3. Understandability: Checking if the content and navigation are presented in a clear and understandable manner. This involves assessing the language and readability levels used, providing clear instructions and error messages, and organizing content in a logical and predictable manner. 4. Robustness: Verifying the compatibility of the mobile interface across different devices, operating systems, and assistive technologies. This involves testing the application or website on different platforms and devices to ensure consistent accessibility support. Mobile accessibility testing may involve manual evaluation by experts using assistive technologies such as screen readers, magnifiers, or switch devices. It may also include automated testing using tools that scan the code for accessibility errors and provide reports on the identified issues. In conclusion, mobile accessibility testing is a crucial step in the development process to ensure that mobile applications and websites are accessible to individuals with disabilities. By conducting thorough testing and making necessary improvements, designers and developers can create digital experiences that are inclusive and usable for all users.

Mobile Accessibility

Mobile Accessibility refers to the design and development of mobile applications and websites that are inclusive and accessible to users with disabilities or impairments. It ensures that individuals with visual, hearing, motor, or cognitive limitations can navigate, understand, and interact with digital content effectively on mobile devices. To achieve mobile accessibility, designers and developers adhere to established guidelines and standards that promote equal access for all users. These guidelines address various aspects of mobile interface design, such as content structure, navigation, visual presentation, and interaction patterns. By following these guidelines, mobile applications and websites can provide a seamless user experience regardless of the user's abilities. One essential aspect of mobile accessibility is providing alternative text descriptions for non-textual content, such as images, videos, and icons. These descriptions, known as alt text, enable users who are visually impaired or using screen readers to understand the context and function of the visual elements on the mobile interface. Another important consideration is ensuring that mobile interfaces are keyboard navigable. Some users may have difficulties using touch screens, so it is crucial to provide keyboard shortcuts or alternative input methods for efficient navigation and interaction. This ensures that individuals with motor impairments can access and interact with all the functionalities of the mobile application or website. Mobile accessibility also focuses on providing adjustable text size and color contrast options. Users with visual impairments may require larger text sizes or high contrast settings to read content comfortably. By offering customization options, mobile interfaces can accommodate a wide range of user preferences and needs. Furthermore, incorporating closed captions or transcripts for multimedia content, such as videos and audio clips, is crucial for users with hearing impairments. These features provide an alternative way for users to consume the information presented in the media without relying solely on audio. In summary, mobile accessibility is a design approach that ensures mobile applications and websites are usable and inclusive for all users, irrespective of their abilities or impairments. It involves following guidelines and implementing features that address the specific needs of individuals with disabilities, such as alternative text descriptions, keyboard navigation support, customizable text and color options, and accessible multimedia content. By prioritizing mobile accessibility, developers create digital experiences that empower and enable equal access for everyone.

Mobile Screen Reader Apps

A mobile screen reader app is a software application designed for mobile devices that provides auditory or tactile feedback to individuals with visual impairments. These apps use the device's speech synthesis capabilities or vibration function to convey information displayed on the screen, allowing users to navigate and interact with the device's interface and content. Mobile screen reader apps are an essential tool for individuals with visual impairments, as they enable access to mobile devices and the vast array of apps and services available on them. These apps are designed with a strong focus on accessibility, ensuring that individuals with visual impairments can effectively use and interact with their mobile devices.

Mobile Screen Reader Developers

A mobile screen reader is a software application that enables individuals with visual impairments or print disabilities to access and interact with the content displayed on a mobile device. It reads aloud the text and other visual elements on the screen, providing audio feedback and allowing users to navigate through different sections, menus, buttons, and links. Mobile screen readers are essential tools for ensuring accessibility for people who are blind or have low vision, as they provide them with an alternative way to perceive and interact with the digital world. These software solutions use various techniques to analyze and interpret the visual information on the screen, converting it into spoken words or braille output.

Mobile Screen Readers

Mobile screen readers are software applications that provide auditory feedback to individuals with visual impairments or other disabilities that affect their ability to read text on a mobile device. These screen readers convert the visual content on a mobile screen into spoken words, allowing users to access information, navigate through menus, and interact with apps and websites. Screen readers are an essential accessibility tool, as they enable individuals with visual disabilities to independently use mobile devices. By using voice synthesis or Braille output, screen readers read aloud the content displayed on the screen, including text, buttons, icons, and other user interface elements. This auditory feedback enables users to understand the interface, interact with it, and access the information they need. To ensure compatibility with screen readers, developers follow specific design guidelines and best practices. These guidelines include providing descriptive and meaningful textual alternatives for non-text content such as images, graphs, and charts. Screen readers rely on these alternatives to convey the visual information to users. Similarly, using appropriate markup and semantic HTML helps screen readers interpret the structure and hierarchy of the content accurately. Furthermore, developers strive to create mobile interfaces that are keyboard and screen reader accessible. This means that users should be able to navigate through menus, input fields, and interactive elements using only the keyboard, without the need for precise mouse or touch gestures. Providing clear instructions, focus indicators, and logical tab order enhances this accessibility. Screen readers often include advanced features to accommodate different user preferences and needs. For example, users can adjust the speed and volume of the spoken feedback, choose different voices or languages, and customize the navigation and interaction methods. These customization options ensure that individuals with diverse abilities can personalize their screen reading experience according to their specific requirements. In conclusion, mobile screen readers are vital tools for inclusive design, making mobile devices accessible to individuals with visual impairments or other disabilities. By providing auditory feedback and enabling navigation and interaction, screen readers empower users to access information, communicate, and participate in the digital world. Proper accessibility design, including the use of descriptive alternatives and semantic HTML, ensures a seamless experience for screen reader users.

Motor Impairment

Motor impairment is a condition that affects an individual's ability to move or control their muscles or limbs. It can result from various underlying factors, such as neurological disorders, injuries, or genetic conditions. This limitation in motor function can range from mild to severe, impacting different aspects of a person's mobility and coordination. People with motor impairments may experience difficulties in performing activities that require physical movements, such as walking, grasping objects, or using fine motor skills. These limitations can significantly impact their independence and quality of life. In the context of accessibility design, motor impairment is a crucial consideration when developing digital platforms, websites, or products. It is essential to ensure that these designs are inclusive and accessible for individuals with motor impairments. By accommodating their unique needs, we can provide equal opportunities for participation and engagement in the digital realm. Accessibility design for motor impairment involves implementing features and functionalities that facilitate easy navigation and interaction with digital interfaces. This can include, but is not limited to, the following considerations: - Providing alternative input methods: Designing interfaces that allow users to interact through various input devices such as keyboards, switches, or voice recognition software. This ensures that individuals with limited motor control can control and navigate digital content effectively. - Optimizing interface elements: Ensuring that buttons, links, and interactive elements have a sufficiently large size, making it easier to select and activate them. This consideration helps individuals with motor impairments, who may have difficulties with precise movements or gestures. - Offering customizable interaction settings: Allowing users to adjust aspects such as scrolling speed, keyboard sensitivity, or input delays, enabling them to tailor the user experience to their specific needs and abilities. - Providing clear visual feedback: Incorporating visual cues or feedback to indicate the current state or progress of an action to compensate for limited motor control. For example, highlighting selected elements or displaying loading indicators can help users understand the system's response. In summary, motor impairment refers to a condition that affects a person's ability to control their muscles or limbs. In the context of accessibility design, it is crucial to consider the unique needs of individuals with motor impairments and implement inclusive features and functionalities that facilitate easy interaction and navigation through digital interfaces.

Motor Impairments

Motor impairments refer to limitations or difficulties in movement and physical coordination caused by various conditions or disabilities. These impairments can affect a person's ability to perform tasks that require fine motor skills, gross motor skills, or both. In the context of accessibility design, motor impairments can significantly impact a person's interaction with technology and their ability to access and use digital content. Individuals with motor impairments may have difficulties with tasks such as typing, using a mouse or touchscreen, operating physical buttons or switches, or navigating through digital interfaces. These impairments can arise from various conditions, including but not limited to paralysis, muscular dystrophy, cerebral palsy, multiple sclerosis, and Parkinson's disease. The severity and specific limitations associated with motor impairments vary between individuals, ranging from mild to severe.

Multimodal Interaction Research Labs

Multimodal Interaction Research Labs focus on the design, development, and evaluation of interactions between humans and digital systems through multiple modes of communication. This research area primarily aims to improve the accessibility of digital systems by allowing users to interact with them using various input modalities, such as speech, touch, gesture, and gaze, in addition to traditional keyboard and mouse interactions. The goal of multimodal interaction research in the context of accessibility design is to create inclusive digital systems that can be accessed and used by a wide range of individuals, including those with physical, sensory, cognitive, or age-related disabilities. By providing multiple modes of input, these systems enable users to overcome barriers and limitations associated with traditional interaction methods, promoting equal access and usability for everyone.

Multimodal Interaction Research Tools

Multimodal Interaction Research Tools refer to a set of tools that are used in the field of accessibility design to study and improve the interaction between users and multimodal interfaces. These tools enable researchers to investigate and evaluate the effectiveness and usability of multimodal user interfaces, which combine multiple modes of input and output, such as gestures, voice commands, touch, and visual displays. In the context of accessibility design, multimodal interaction research tools play a crucial role in ensuring that digital products and services are accessible to a wide range of users, including those with disabilities. By studying the interaction patterns and preferences of users with diverse abilities, researchers can identify barriers and challenges in the user interface and develop solutions to make these interfaces more inclusive and user-friendly.

Multimodal Interaction Testing

Multimodal Interaction Testing refers to the process of assessing the effectiveness and accessibility of a user interface that integrates multiple modes of interaction, such as speech recognition, touch, gestures, and more. It aims to ensure that individuals with various abilities can interact with digital systems using a combination of input methods. In the context of accessibility design, multimodal interaction testing plays a vital role in evaluating the inclusivity and usability of interfaces for users with diverse needs. It focuses on verifying whether the interface provides alternative options for input and output, making it accessible to individuals with disabilities or limitations. The testing process involves evaluating the different modes of interaction individually and in combination to ensure they function correctly and provide a seamless user experience. It examines whether the system recognizes and interprets input correctly across various modes, such as voice commands or gestures, and responds appropriately. Moreover, multimodal interaction testing also investigates how the interface presents information to the user through different modalities. It checks if the system offers alternative forms of output, such as spoken responses for individuals with visual impairments or tactile feedback for those with hearing impairments. By conducting multimodal interaction testing, accessibility designers can identify and address any barriers or limitations that prevent users from fully engaging with the interface. This testing helps ensure that individuals with disabilities can navigate, interact, and benefit from digital systems in a manner that is equivalent to users without disabilities. In conclusion, multimodal interaction testing in the context of accessibility design involves assessing the effectiveness and inclusivity of interfaces that integrate multiple modes of interaction. It focuses on verifying the correct interpretation of input and providing alternative forms of output for individuals with disabilities. This testing is crucial in promoting universal accessibility and ensuring that digital systems cater to the needs of all users, regardless of their abilities or limitations.

Multimodal Interaction Tools

Multimodal Interaction Tools refer to a set of technologies and techniques that allow individuals with disabilities to interact with digital devices and applications using multiple modes of input and output. These tools aim to provide accessible and inclusive design solutions by enabling users to interact with technology using a combination of gestures, voice commands, touch input, and other sensory modalities. In the context of accessibility design, multimodal interaction tools play a crucial role in ensuring that individuals with varying abilities can effectively use digital devices and applications. These tools recognize the diversity of user capabilities and offer alternative means of interaction beyond traditional keyboard and mouse input. By supporting multiple modes of input and output, they cater to users with mobility, dexterity, vision, hearing, and cognitive impairments.

Multimodal Interaction

Multimodal Interaction, in the context of accessibility design, refers to a method of interactivity between humans and computer systems that utilizes multiple modes of communication and input/output channels. This approach aims to enhance accessibility for individuals with diverse abilities and disabilities, including those with visual, auditory, cognitive, or physical impairments. In multimodal interaction, users are provided with various means of interacting with the system, such as using voice commands, gestures, touch, keyboard input, or a combination of these modalities. By offering multiple options, individuals with disabilities can choose the mode of interaction that best suits their abilities and preferences, ensuring an inclusive and accessible user experience.

Multiple Sensory Channels

In the context of accessibility design, multiple sensory channels refer to the use of various methods of communication and perception to provide information and user experience to individuals with disabilities. This approach recognizes that people have different abilities and preferences when it comes to accessing information and interacting with digital content. By engaging multiple sensory channels, designers aim to make their websites, applications, and digital products more inclusive and accessible to a diverse range of users. This can include incorporating visual, auditory, tactile, and even olfactory stimuli to convey information and enhance the user experience.

Multisensory Design

Multisensory Design is an approach to accessibility design that incorporates various sensory elements to enhance the user experience for individuals with disabilities or impairments. It involves creating environments, products, or services that engage multiple senses, such as touch, sight, hearing, taste, and smell, in order to provide a more inclusive and holistic experience. In the context of accessibility design, multisensory design aims to create experiences that cater to diverse user needs, ensuring that individuals with disabilities can fully engage with and understand their surroundings. This approach recognizes that people have different ways of perceiving and interacting with the world, and strives to accommodate these differences through thoughtful design choices.

NVDA (NonVisual Desktop Access) Screen Reader

NVDA (NonVisual Desktop Access) Screen Reader is a software application designed to provide accessibility to visually impaired individuals by converting visual content on a computer screen into synthesized speech or braille. It allows users to access and navigate through digital content, applications, and operating systems without relying on visual cues. The NVDA Screen Reader is specifically designed to cater to the needs of blind or visually impaired users, enabling them to effectively use computers and access information that would otherwise be inaccessible to them. It provides a non-visual alternative to traditional graphical user interfaces, making it possible for individuals with visual impairments to independently interact with technology.

Non-Visual Interaction

Non-Visual Interaction refers to the design and implementation of user interfaces that allow individuals with visual impairments or who are unable to see the screen to interact with digital content effectively. The goal of non-visual interaction is to ensure inclusivity and accessibility by providing alternative methods for users to perceive and interact with web content without relying on visual cues. Non-visual interaction techniques include, but are not limited to: - Auditory feedback: Provide auditory cues, such as spoken instructions or sound effects, to guide users through the interface and provide feedback on their interactions. This can be achieved through text-to-speech (TTS) technology or audio recordings. - Keyboard navigation: Enable users to navigate through content using keyboard inputs instead of relying on mouse or touch gestures. This involves ensuring proper focus management and providing keyboard shortcuts for essential functions and controls. - Alternative input methods: Allow users to interact with the interface using alternative input devices, such as switch control, head tracking, or speech recognition. This caters to individuals who have limited motor skills or are unable to use traditional input methods. - Text-based alternatives: Provide textual alternatives for visual elements, such as alternative text (alt text) for images, transcripts for videos, and captions for audio content. This allows individuals who cannot see or perceive visual content to access the information it conveys. - Structured content: Use proper HTML semantics and markup to structure and organize content. This helps screen readers and other assistive technologies interpret and present information accurately to users. - Assistive technology compatibility: Ensure that the website or application is compatible with popular assistive technologies, such as screen readers, magnifiers, or braille displays. This involves adhering to accessibility standards and guidelines, testing for compatibility, and addressing any issues that may arise.

OCR (Optical Character Recognition)

OCR (Optical Character Recognition) is a technology designed to convert scanned or printed text into editable and accessible digital format. It involves using specialized software to analyze and interpret the shapes and patterns of text characters from an image or document. OCR plays a crucial role in the field of accessibility design as it enables individuals with visual impairments or other print disabilities to access and interact with written content more effectively. By converting text into a format that can be read by screen readers or other assistive technologies, OCR helps to bridge the gap between printed information and individuals who rely on technology to access materials.

On-Screen Keyboard

An on-screen keyboard, in the context of accessibility design, refers to a graphical user interface (GUI) tool that allows users to input text and commands using a virtual keyboard displayed on the screen. It is primarily designed for individuals who have difficulty using a physical keyboard, such as those with mobility or dexterity impairments. The on-screen keyboard provides an alternative means of input for users who may have limited hand function or are unable to use a traditional keyboard due to physical constraints. It enables them to access and interact with computers, digital devices, and software applications by selecting keys or characters through various input methods. The on-screen keyboard typically consists of a virtual representation of a standard physical keyboard, with keys displayed on the screen. Users can interact with the virtual keyboard by either touching the keys directly if using a touch-enabled device or by using alternative input devices such as a mouse, joystick, or switch. To input text or commands, users interact with the on-screen keyboard by selecting keys, which then generate the corresponding characters or commands on the screen. The selected keys can be displayed within a text box or text area, allowing users to see and edit the entered text easily. Besides the basic alphanumeric keys, on-screen keyboards often provide additional functionalities such as modifier keys (e.g., shift, control) and special function keys (e.g., backspace, enter). These additional keys allow users to perform various actions like navigating through the text, accessing menus, and executing commands. On-screen keyboards offer customization options to cater to individual user needs. Users can often personalize the appearance and layout of the virtual keyboard according to their preferences. This customization may include options for resizing the keyboard, changing the key layout or color scheme, and even rearranging the keys based on frequency of use. Overall, the on-screen keyboard serves as an essential accessibility feature, ensuring that individuals with physical disabilities or limitations can effectively utilize computers and digital devices. It provides an alternative means of inputting text and commands, thereby enabling inclusivity and accessibility for all users.

On-Screen Keyboards

On-Screen Keyboards are virtual input devices that provide an alternative means for individuals with physical disabilities or limitations to input text and perform keyboard functions using a computer or other electronic devices. These keyboards are designed to improve accessibility by enabling users with mobility impairments, such as limited hand dexterity or the inability to use a physical keyboard, to interact with digital interfaces. On-Screen Keyboards are typically displayed as a graphical representation of a standard keyboard on the computer screen or touch-enabled devices. They feature a set of keys, including alphabets, numbers, symbols, and function keys, which can be activated either by clicking or tapping on the keys using a mouse or stylus, or by using alternative input methods like touch gestures or eye movement tracking. The main purpose of On-Screen Keyboards is to provide an inclusive computing experience for individuals who may have difficulty using a physical keyboard due to various reasons, such as spinal cord injuries, muscular dystrophy, or temporary mobility restrictions. These tools allow users to input text, access software applications, browse the web, and perform other computer-based tasks. In terms of accessibility design, On-Screen Keyboards are crucial as they remove barriers to digital communication and interaction for people with physical disabilities. By offering an alternative input method, they ensure that individuals who cannot use a traditional keyboard can still participate in online activities, access information, and communicate effectively. Furthermore, On-Screen Keyboards can be customized and adapted to suit the specific needs and preferences of different users. Features such as key size, layout, color contrast, and auto-completion can be adjusted to enhance usability and accommodate varying motor abilities. Additionally, the integration of assistive technologies like predictive text input, word prediction, and voice input further enhances the usability and efficiency of On-Screen Keyboards. In conclusion, On-Screen Keyboards are virtual input devices that provide accessible means for individuals with physical disabilities or limitations to input text and perform keyboard functions. These tools play a crucial role in inclusive design by enabling individuals with mobility impairments to interact with digital interfaces and participate fully in online activities. Customizable features and integration with assistive technologies further enhance usability and efficiency, ensuring an inclusive computing experience for all users.

Operable Keyboard

An operable keyboard, in the context of accessibility design, refers to a type of keyboard that is specifically designed to be functional and usable by individuals with physical disabilities or impairments. This type of keyboard is an essential tool for those who may have difficulty operating standard keyboards due to limitations in mobility, dexterity, or strength. An operable keyboard typically features larger keys or buttons that are spaced further apart, allowing for easier finger movement and reducing the risk of accidental key presses. The keys may also have specific shapes, textures, or tactile feedback to assist individuals with visual impairments in locating and distinguishing between different keys.

Orientation-Detection Software

Orientation-Detection Software refers to a specialized tool used in accessibility design to identify the orientation of a user's device or display screen. It plays a crucial role in ensuring that digital content is presented in a user-friendly and accessible manner across different devices and orientations. This software utilizes various sensors and algorithms to detect and determine the orientation of a device, such as smartphones, tablets, or desktop monitors. By accurately identifying whether a device is in portrait, landscape, or any other orientation, it allows developers to optimize the layout, formatting, and interaction of digital content accordingly.

Orthopedic Impairments

An orthopedic impairment, in the context of accessibility design, refers to a physical disability that affects the musculoskeletal system, including bones, joints, muscles, ligaments, and tendons. It can result in functional limitations or difficulties in movement, strength, posture, or coordination. Individuals with orthopedic impairments may have conditions such as cerebral palsy, muscular dystrophy, spina bifida, or amputations. These impairments can vary in severity and can be congenital or acquired due to injuries, diseases, or medical conditions.

PDF Accessibility Checker Tools

A PDF Accessibility Checker (PAC) tool, also known as an accessibility validation tool or an accessibility checker, is an application or software specifically designed to assess and evaluate the accessibility features of PDF documents. Its primary purpose is to identify and highlight potential barriers that may hinder individuals with disabilities from accessing and comprehending the content within these documents. PAC tools utilize a variety of techniques and algorithms to analyze the structure and content of PDF files. These tools typically perform automated inspections and conduct various tests to ensure adherence to accessibility standards, such as the Web Content Accessibility Guidelines (WCAG) or the PDF/UA (Universal Accessibility) standard. PDF Accessibility Checkers help in identifying different types of accessibility issues, such as: Missing or inadequate alternative text for images, charts, or graphs Inaccessible forms or form fields Lack of proper headings, nesting, or document structure Insufficient color contrast for text content Inconsistent or inappropriate reading order Improper use of tags or semantic elements Unreliable or insufficient bookmarks Inaccessibility of tables and data Incomplete or non-descriptive links PAC tools present the results of their analysis through detailed reports or accessibility checklists. These reports provide a comprehensive overview of the identified issues, including their severity, location, and advice for remediation. The tools may offer suggestions or automated fixes for certain issues, helping authors or designers to make necessary modifications and improvements to enhance the accessibility of their PDF documents. In summary, PDF Accessibility Checker tools are invaluable in the accessibility design process as they enable designers, authors, and content creators to evaluate and rectify potential accessibility barriers in their PDF documents. By using these tools, individuals and organizations can ensure that their documents are accessible to a wide range of users, including those with visual impairments, cognitive disabilities, and other disabilities that may affect their ability to access information through traditional means.

PDF Accessibility Checkers

PDF Accessibility Checkers are tools or software programs that are used to evaluate the accessibility of PDF documents for individuals with disabilities. These checkers are specifically designed to identify any barriers or difficulties that may prevent people with disabilities from accessing and understanding the content within a PDF file. A PDF document is considered accessible when it is designed in such a way that ensures people with disabilities, such as visual impairments or cognitive disabilities, can effectively read, navigate, and understand its contents. PDF Accessibility Checkers help in achieving this accessibility by scanning the document and providing feedback on its conformance to accessibility standards, such as the Web Content Accessibility Guidelines (WCAG) 2.0 or PDF/UA (Universal Accessibility). The main purpose of using a PDF Accessibility Checker is to ensure that the document can be accessed and understood by people who utilize assistive technologies, such as screen readers or text-to-speech software. These assistive technologies rely on structured markup and other accessibility features within the PDF file to interpret and convey the content to users. By identifying any accessibility issues or non-compliant elements within the PDF, the checker allows designers and developers to make the necessary modifications to improve accessibility. PDF Accessibility Checkers perform various checks on a PDF document, evaluating elements such as document structure, tagging, alternative text for images, color contrast, heading hierarchy, and navigation. They generate reports highlighting any accessibility violations or issues that need to be addressed. The reports often provide recommendations on how to fix these problems and make the document more accessible. When using a PDF Accessibility Checker, it is important to choose a reliable and up-to-date tool that is regularly updated to reflect the latest accessibility standards and guidelines. Additionally, it is essential to manually review and test the document by users with disabilities to ensure its accessibility. While PDF Accessibility Checkers are powerful tools in evaluating the accessibility of a document, they should be used as aids and not as a sole indicator of accessibility. In conclusion, PDF Accessibility Checkers are valuable tools used in the design and evaluation of accessible PDF documents. They help identify and address barriers that may hinder people with disabilities from accessing and understanding the content within a PDF file. By making use of these checkers, designers and developers can create inclusive and accessible PDFs that cater to a wider audience.

PDF Accessibility Consulting Services

PDF Accessibility Consulting Services refers to a professional service that focuses on ensuring that PDF documents are designed and created in a way that makes them accessible to individuals with disabilities. The goal of PDF Accessibility Consulting Services is to ensure that PDF documents can be easily used and understood by all users, regardless of their abilities or the assistive technologies they may rely on. PDF documents are widely used to share information and content online. However, they can present barriers to accessibility for individuals with disabilities, such as visual impairments or cognitive limitations. PDF Accessibility Consulting Services aim to address these barriers and make PDF documents accessible to all users.

PDF Accessibility

PDF accessibility refers to the design and implementation of PDF documents in a way that ensures they can be accessed, understood, and navigated by individuals with disabilities. It involves following specific guidelines and techniques to make PDF files inclusive and usable for people with various impairments, such as visual, auditory, cognitive, and motor disabilities. Creating accessible PDFs involves several considerations. One crucial aspect is ensuring the document's content is perceivable by all users, irrespective of their disabilities. This includes providing alternative text descriptions for images, charts, and graphs, so that individuals who cannot see them can understand the information conveyed. It also involves using proper color contrast to ensure that text and other visual elements are legible for individuals with low vision or color blindness. Another important aspect of PDF accessibility is making the document navigable. This means including a logical and consistent structure that allows users to navigate through the document using assistive technologies, such as screen readers or keyboard navigation. Proper heading hierarchy, lists, and table structure enable individuals with disabilities to locate and understand the content more efficiently. PDFs should also be designed in a way that accommodates individuals with cognitive disabilities. This can involve using plain language, short sentences, and clear instructions to ensure the content is easily understood. Additionally, providing summaries, highlights, or other forms of content organization can assist users in grasping the main points and structure of the document. Furthermore, PDF accessibility extends to ensuring compatibility with assistive technologies. This involves utilizing proper tagging and metadata to provide additional information about the document's structure, language, and other properties. It also entails providing meaningful link text and ensuring proper document reflow, so that individuals using assistive technologies can navigate and understand the content in a seamless manner.

PDF Remediation

PDF remediation, in the context of accessibility design, refers to the process of making PDF documents accessible to individuals with disabilities. Accessibility design aims to ensure that digital content, including PDFs, can be easily accessed and understood by all users, including those with visual, auditory, cognitive, or motor impairments. PDF documents are popular for sharing and distributing information due to their consistent appearance across different devices and platforms. However, PDFs often pose accessibility challenges, as they are not inherently accessible. Many PDFs lack appropriate structure, navigation, and alternative text, making them inaccessible to individuals using assistive technology, such as screen readers, screen magnifiers, or voice recognition software. PDF remediation involves modifying the existing PDF document to enhance its accessibility. This process generally includes adding structural elements such as headings, lists, and tables, ensuring the proper reading order, providing alternative text for images, and adding interactive form fields. By incorporating these accessibility features, individuals with disabilities can more effectively navigate, comprehend, and interact with the PDF content. During PDF remediation, specific techniques and tools are used to improve accessibility. These may include the use of Adobe Acrobat Pro, a widely used software for PDF editing, which allows for adding alternative text to images and creating accessible forms. Other tools may be used to perform OCR (Optical Character Recognition) on scanned PDFs, converting them into selectable and searchable text. PDF remediation also involves adhering to accessibility standards, such as the Web Content Accessibility Guidelines (WCAG). These guidelines provide a set of recommendations for web accessibility, which can be applied to PDF documents to ensure their compatibility with assistive technologies and user needs. In conclusion, PDF remediation is the process of modifying PDF documents to make them accessible to individuals with disabilities. By enhancing the structure, navigation, and content of PDFs, individuals using assistive technology can access, understand, and interact with the information contained within the document. This process follows accessibility standards and incorporates various techniques and tools to improve the overall accessibility of PDFs. Provided answer: PDF remediation, in the context of accessibility design, refers to the process of making PDF documents accessible to individuals with disabilities. PDF remediation involves modifying the existing PDF document to enhance its accessibility, including adding structural elements, ensuring proper reading order, providing alternative text for images, and adding interactive form fields. This process adheres to accessibility standards and uses various techniques and tools to improve the overall accessibility of PDFs.

PDF/UA (PDF/Universal Accessibility)

PDF/UA (PDF/Universal Accessibility) is a standard established by the International Organization for Standardization (ISO) to ensure that PDF documents are accessible to individuals with disabilities. This standard focuses on the design and structure of PDF files, making them more accessible for people with visual impairments, cognitive disabilities, or other accessibility needs. PDF/UA provides guidelines and requirements for creating accessible PDF documents. It emphasizes the use of proper document structure, text alternatives, and interactive features that allow assistive technologies to access and navigate the content effectively. In terms of document structure, PDF/UA encourages using tags to convey the semantic structure of the document. These tags allow screen readers and other assistive technologies to interpret and convey the content accurately. It also specifies requirements for headings, paragraphs, lists, tables, images, and other elements to ensure proper accessibility. Text alternatives play a crucial role in making PDF documents accessible. PDF/UA requires providing alternative text for images, form fields, and other non-text elements, ensuring that users with visual impairments can understand the content. This includes concise descriptions that convey the essential information conveyed by the visual element without redundant details. PDF/UA also addresses the use of color in PDF documents. As color alone may not be perceivable by individuals with color blindness or other visual impairments, PDF/UA guidelines recommend providing text alternatives or other means of conveying information that is reliant on color cues. Furthermore, interactive features and form fields in PDF/UA-compliant documents need to be designed with accessibility in mind. This includes providing adequate keyboard navigation, clear instructions, and error messages for form fields, ensuring that individuals with mobility or cognitive disabilities can interact with these features effectively. By adhering to the PDF/UA standard, organizations and individuals can create PDF documents that are accessible to a broader range of users. This promotes inclusivity and ensures that people with disabilities can access and comprehend information presented in PDF format. In conclusion, PDF/UA (PDF/Universal Accessibility) is a standard established by the ISO to improve the accessibility of PDF documents. It provides guidelines for document structure, text alternatives, color usage, and interactive features, enabling individuals with disabilities to access and understand PDF content effectively.

Password Management

Password management refers to the process of securely storing and organizing passwords in order to enhance accessibility and user experience for individuals with disabilities. It involves the implementation of effective strategies and tools that facilitate the creation, storage, retrieval, and customization of passwords for users with diverse accessibility needs. A well-designed password management system ensures that individuals with disabilities can easily and independently manage their passwords while maintaining a high level of security. It takes into account the unique challenges faced by users with disabilities, such as cognitive, visual, or physical impairments, and aims to provide an inclusive and accessible experience for all users.

Pause, Stop, Hide

The terms "Pause," "Stop," and "Hide" refer to accessibility design principles aimed at improving user experience and ensuring equal access to digital content for individuals with disabilities. Pause: In the context of accessibility design, 'Pause' refers to providing users the ability to temporarily halt or suspend auto-updating or auto-playing content. This allows individuals with cognitive or physical disabilities to have control over the pace of the content consumption. For example, a website with a sliding carousel should include a pause button that allows users to pause the carousel to allow for easier reading or interaction with the content. Stop: 'Stop' in the context of accessibility design means offering users the ability to completely halt auto-updating or auto-playing content. This goes a step further than 'Pause' by giving the users the option to stop the content permanently. Users may have slower internet speeds or may simply prefer manual control over content updates. For instance, an online news website should provide a 'Stop' button to disable auto-refreshing and avoid interrupting the reading experience. Hide: 'Hide' within accessibility design pertains to giving users the option to hide or remove certain elements from the user interface. This feature is particularly helpful for individuals with cognitive disabilities or visual impairments who may find cluttered interfaces overwhelming. For instance, a website with multiple sidebars might include a 'Hide Sidebars' option that allows users to hide the sidebars and focus solely on the main content area.

Physical Accessibility

Physical Accessibility refers to the design and provision of environments, products, services, and technologies that are inclusively designed and usable by individuals with disabilities or limited mobility. It is a concept that aims to eliminate barriers and create equal opportunities, allowing individuals with disabilities to fully participate in activities and access all aspects of society. In the context of accessibility design, physical accessibility involves making sure that the physical environment or infrastructure is designed and constructed in a way that allows people with disabilities to navigate, use, and access it independently and safely. This includes considering various factors such as wheelchair accessibility, auditory and visual impairments, mobility limitations, and cognitive disabilities. The design of physical spaces should provide an inclusive environment for everyone, regardless of their physical abilities. This includes ensuring that buildings have ramps, elevators, and accessible entrances for individuals using wheelchairs or other mobility aids. It also includes providing accessible parking spaces, accessible restrooms, and adequate signage that is easy to read and understand. Moreover, physical accessibility extends beyond buildings and also encompasses outdoor spaces and transportation systems. It involves creating accessible pathways and sidewalks, installing tactile paving for individuals with visual impairments, and providing accessible public transportation options such as ramps or lifts on buses and trains. Additionally, physical accessibility also involves considering the design and usability of products and technologies. This includes designing user-friendly interfaces for individuals with limited dexterity, providing alternative formats for individuals with visual impairments, and ensuring the compatibility of assistive technologies with mainstream products and services. In conclusion, physical accessibility is an essential aspect of accessibility design as it aims to create an inclusive and equal environment for individuals with disabilities. By considering the needs and requirements of people with disabilities, physical accessibility ensures that everyone can independently access and participate in various activities, thereby promoting equality and inclusion in society.

Physical Impairment Aids

Physical impairment aids refer to devices, tools, or modifications that are designed to assist individuals with physical disabilities in accessing and interacting with their environment. These aids aim to enhance mobility, communication, and independence for people with various physical impairments. One category of physical impairment aids is mobility aids. These include devices such as crutches, canes, walkers, and wheelchairs, which provide support and assistance for individuals with difficulties in walking or maintaining balance. Mobility aids help improve the ability to move around and perform daily activities. Another type of physical impairment aid is assistive technology. This includes devices such as prosthetic limbs, braces, or orthotic devices, which support and augment the function of impaired body parts. Assistive technology also encompasses specialized equipment such as environmental control systems, voice recognition software, or alternative input devices (e.g., modified keyboards or switches) that enable individuals with limited mobility to operate computers, access electronic devices, and control their surroundings. Communication aids are also an essential category of physical impairment aids. These aids assist individuals with speech impairments or limited vocal capabilities in communicating effectively. Examples include augmentative and alternative communication (AAC) devices, which can be analog or digital and can range from simple picture boards to sophisticated speech-generating devices. AAC aids provide alternative means of communication for individuals who are unable to rely solely on spoken language. Sensory aids are designed to assist individuals with sensory impairments, such as hearing or vision loss. Hearing aids amplify sound for individuals with hearing impairment, while cochlear implants provide individuals with severe or profound hearing loss the ability to perceive sound. Visual aids, on the other hand, encompass a variety of devices such as glasses, magnifiers, or screen readers, which enhance visual perception and accessibility for individuals with visual impairments. In the context of accessibility design, physical impairment aids play a crucial role in making the built environment, communication systems, and digital platforms more accessible and inclusive for all individuals. They empower individuals with physical disabilities to engage in various activities, participate fully in society, and enhance their overall quality of life. Accessible design principles should consider the diverse needs of individuals with physical impairments and incorporate the use of appropriate aids to ensure equal access and opportunities for all.

Physical Impairments

Physical impairments, in the context of accessibility design, refer to conditions or disabilities that affect a person's physical abilities and limit their mobility or dexterity. These impairments can include but are not limited to limitations in movement, sensation, coordination, or strength. Individuals with physical impairments may face challenges in accessing and using products, environments, or digital interfaces that are not designed to accommodate their needs. Therefore, when creating accessible designs, it is crucial to consider the diverse range of physical impairments that users may have and provide inclusive solutions.

Plain Language Guidelines

Plain Language Guidelines are a set of principles and recommendations that aim to improve the accessibility and understandability of written content, particularly for individuals with disabilities or limited literacy skills. In the context of accessibility design, these guidelines provide direction on how to create digital content that is clear, concise, and easily comprehensible for a diverse range of users. The use of Plain Language Guidelines is crucial in ensuring that information is accessible to all individuals, regardless of their cognitive abilities or literacy levels. By following these guidelines, designers can remove barriers and improve the user experience for people with disabilities. One key aspect of Plain Language Guidelines is to use simple and straightforward language. This includes avoiding jargon, technical terms, and complex sentence structures. Instead, designers should opt for everyday language that is commonly understood by a wide range of individuals. Additionally, it is important to organize content in a logical and structured manner. This involves using headings and subheadings to break up text and make it easier to navigate. Designers should also use paragraphs to group related information and ensure that each paragraph focuses on a single topic. To enhance readability, designers should aim for a consistent writing style throughout the content. This includes using a conversational tone, active voice, and avoiding excessive use of passive voice or complex phrasing. By maintaining a consistent style, users can easily follow the flow of information and understand the intended message. Furthermore, Plain Language Guidelines emphasize the importance of using visual aids, such as images, charts, and infographics, to enhance comprehension. However, it is crucial to provide alternative text descriptions for these visuals, ensuring that individuals with visual impairments can still understand the content. In conclusion, Plain Language Guidelines are a set of recommendations that aim to improve the accessibility and understandability of written content. By following these guidelines, designers can create digital content that is clear, concise, and easily comprehensible for all users, regardless of their cognitive abilities or literacy levels. Plain Language Guidelines are a set of principles and recommendations used in accessibility design to create clear and understandable written content. These guidelines emphasize the use of simple language, logical organization, and consistent writing style to ensure that information is accessible to individuals with disabilities or limited literacy skills.

Plain Language Tools

Plain Language Tools are techniques and strategies used in the field of accessibility design to ensure that information is presented in a clear and understandable manner to a wide range of users, including those with disabilities. In the context of accessibility design, Plain Language Tools aim to remove unnecessary complexity and barriers in communication, making information more accessible to individuals with various cognitive, language, and learning disabilities. These tools focus on simplifying language, organizing information effectively, and using appropriate formatting techniques. One plain language tool commonly used is simplifying vocabulary and sentence structures. By avoiding jargon, technical terms, or complex grammar, information can be easily understood by a broader audience. Additionally, using shorter sentences and active voice helps to convey messages more efficiently. Another tool is organizing information in a logical and structured manner. Breaking down content into shorter sections with clear headings and subheadings allows users to navigate and locate information more easily. Providing summaries or key points at the beginning of a document or section also helps users to quickly grasp the main ideas. Using appropriate formatting techniques is crucial for accessibility design. This includes using consistent font styles, adequate spacing between lines and paragraphs, and appropriate font sizes. The use of headings, bullet points, and numbered lists can also enhance readability and understanding. Visual aids, such as images, diagrams, and charts, can be effective tools for conveying information. However, it is important to provide alternative text descriptions (alt text) for these visuals, allowing individuals using screen readers or those with visual impairments to understand the information. In summary, Plain Language Tools are strategies employed in accessibility design to ensure that information is presented in a clear, concise, and organized manner. By simplifying language, organizing content effectively, and considering appropriate formatting techniques, these tools help to enhance the accessibility of information for all users, including those with disabilities.

Plain Language Training Programs

Plain Language Training Programs are educational programs that aim to teach individuals the principles and techniques of creating accessible written content. These programs focus on teaching participants how to communicate effectively and clearly in their writing, making their content more inclusive and easily understandable by a wide range of people, including those with cognitive or literacy challenges. The goal of Plain Language Training Programs is to bridge the gap between complex or technical information and the average reader's comprehension level. By simplifying language, removing jargon, and using clear and concise sentences, individuals can create written materials that are more accessible to various audiences. Plain Language Training Programs often provide training materials, workshops, or online courses that cover topics such as clear writing techniques, plain language standards, and content testing methods.

Plain Language Training Resources

Plain Language Training Resources are educational materials aimed at promoting inclusive and accessible communication practices to improve the understanding and usability of information for all individuals, including those with disabilities. In the context of accessibility design, Plain Language Training Resources focus on helping content creators and communicators develop written materials that are clear, concise, and easy to comprehend. These resources provide guidance on using plain language techniques, eliminating jargon, and organizing information in a logical manner. Plain Language Training Resources are particularly important for individuals with cognitive or language disabilities, as well as those with low literacy skills. By following the principles and best practices outlined in these resources, organizations can enhance the accessibility of their content and ensure that it can be understood by a diverse range of users. These training materials typically include guidelines, tips, and examples that illustrate how to simplify complex concepts, structure sentences and paragraphs effectively, and use visuals and other supportive elements to enhance comprehension. They may also cover strategies for presenting numerical data, using active voice, and avoiding vague or ambiguous language. Plain Language Training Resources often emphasize the importance of user testing and feedback to ensure that the information provided is truly accessible and inclusive. They may provide guidance on conducting usability studies, gathering input from individuals with disabilities, and incorporating their perspectives into content development. Furthermore, these resources may address the legal and regulatory aspects of plain language accessibility requirements, particularly in industries such as healthcare, finance, and government. They may provide information on specific standards, guidelines, or legislation that organizations need to comply with to ensure equal access to information. Overall, Plain Language Training Resources play a crucial role in promoting inclusivity and ensuring equal access to information for individuals with disabilities. By equipping content creators and communicators with the knowledge and tools to create clear and understandable materials, these resources contribute to the overall goal of designing for accessibility and fostering an inclusive digital environment. Plain Language Training Resources enable content creators to communicate information in a way that is understandable and accessible to all individuals, regardless of their cognitive abilities or literacy skills.

Plain Language

Accessibility design refers to the practice of creating digital products and environments that can be easily used and accessed by all individuals, regardless of their abilities or disabilities. It involves incorporating design elements, features, and functionalities that make it possible for people with disabilities to perceive, navigate, interact with, and understand the content and functionality of a website or application. This can include providing alternatives for visual content, such as text descriptions for images and captions for videos, to ensure that individuals who are blind or have low vision can still understand the information being conveyed. For individuals who are deaf or hard of hearing, accessibility design may involve providing transcripts or captions for audio content. Additionally, accessibility design aims to ensure that individuals with cognitive or learning disabilities can easily comprehend and navigate through a website or application by using clear and simple language, predictable navigation structures, and consistent user interfaces.

PowerMapper

PowerMapper is a software tool that aids in the creation of accessible designs for websites and applications. It provides valuable insights and analysis to ensure that the digital content is inclusive and usable by individuals with disabilities. With its comprehensive features, PowerMapper allows designers to evaluate the accessibility of their designs and identify areas that may pose challenges for users with disabilities. It enables the detection of various accessibility issues, such as improper document structure, non-descriptive links, missing alternative text for images, and insufficient color contrast. By highlighting these potential obstacles, PowerMapper empowers designers to make necessary adjustments and enhancements to improve accessibility.

Print Disabilities

Print Disabilities refer to a range of visual, physical, cognitive, and learning impairments that hinder individuals from accessing or comprehending printed material in its original form. People with print disabilities may encounter difficulties in reading or understanding text-based information due to their condition. These disabilities can include but are not limited to blindness or low vision, dyslexia, dysgraphia, and physical limitations that affect manual dexterity. In the context of accessibility design, it is crucial to consider the needs of individuals with print disabilities to ensure equal access to information and content. The goal is to create inclusive digital experiences that accommodate these users, allowing them to have the same level of access as those without print disabilities.

Proximity Sensing

Proximity sensing, in the context of accessibility design, refers to the technology and techniques used to detect the presence or movement of individuals within a certain range or proximity of an object or device. It enables individuals with mobility or sensory impairments to interact with their environment more easily and independently. Proximity sensors utilize various methods to detect the proximity of an individual, such as infrared, ultrasound, or capacitive sensing. These sensors can be integrated into various devices and objects, including assistive technology devices, smartphones, automatic doors, or elevators, to name a few.

Punctuation And Spelling Checker

The Punctuation and Spelling Checker is a tool used in accessibility design to ensure that written content is free of errors in punctuation and spelling. This tool can be particularly helpful for individuals with visual impairments or learning disabilities, as it assists in providing a clear and easy-to-read experience. The primary purpose of the Punctuation and Spelling Checker is to identify and correct mistakes in punctuation and spelling within a given text. This includes errors such as missing or misplaced punctuation marks, incorrect capitalization, and misspelled words. By alerting the user to these errors and providing suggested corrections, the tool supports the creation of content that is grammatically correct and properly spelled.

Readability

Readability in the context of accessibility design refers to the ease with which users can perceive, understand, and absorb the content on a website or any digital interface. It focuses on presenting information in a clear and concise manner, ensuring that it can be easily read and comprehended by a wide range of users, including those with visual, cognitive, or learning disabilities. Enhancing readability involves implementing various design principles and techniques to improve the legibility and clarity of content. This includes using appropriate fonts, font sizes, and contrasting colors to ensure that text is easily distinguishable from the background. Additionally, proper line spacing and adequate paragraph spacing help prevent the content from appearing cluttered, making it easier for users to read and navigate. To enhance readability, designers should consider the use of plain language and avoid complex jargon or technical terms whenever possible. Using simple and concise sentences helps users quickly understand the message being conveyed. Breaking up long paragraphs into shorter ones and organizing content with headings, subheadings, and bullet points can further aid readability by improving content scannability and organization. Incorporating appropriate text formatting techniques can also contribute to readability. It is important to use headings and subheadings to structure the content and guide users through the information. By using semantic HTML tags properly, such as for main headings and for subheadings, assistive technologies can accurately convey the hierarchical structure of the content to users with disabilities. In summary, readability in the context of accessibility design involves presenting content in a way that makes it easy for users to read and understand. This includes using appropriate fonts, colors, and spacing, employing plain language, and structuring the content with headings and subheadings. By optimizing readability, digital interfaces can ensure that all users can access and comprehend the information provided, regardless of their abilities or limitations. Readability in the context of accessibility design refers to the ease with which users can perceive, understand, and absorb the content on a website or any digital interface. It focuses on presenting information in a clear and concise manner, ensuring that it can be easily read and comprehended by a wide range of users, including those with disabilities.

Reading Comprehension Tools

Reading Comprehension Tools, in the context of accessibility design, refer to a set of techniques, methods, or tools that aim to enhance the understanding and accessibility of written content for individuals with various cognitive abilities and disabilities. These tools enable people with visual impairments, reading difficulties, or cognitive impairments to effectively comprehend and interact with textual information. Reading comprehension tools strive to eliminate barriers that may hinder the access to and understanding of written content. They empower users by providing alternative formats, adjusted reading settings, or additional support. Reading comprehension tools may include features such as text-to-speech converters, screen readers, and alternative text formats. Text-to-speech converters enable users to hear the content being read out loud, enhancing comprehension for those who struggle with reading or have visual impairments. Screen readers help individuals who are visually impaired by audibly rendering the content of a web page or document. Alternative text formats, such as large print or accessible PDFs, provide users with different reading needs an option to access the information in a format that suits them best. Furthermore, these tools commonly offer customizable reading settings. Users can adjust the font size, color contrast, spacing, and other visual aspects of the text to ensure optimal readability. These settings accommodate various visual impairments or reading difficulties, allowing individuals to optimize their reading experience. By employing reading comprehension tools, individuals with different cognitive abilities and disabilities can access and comprehend written content effectively. These tools promote inclusivity, enabling equal opportunities for individuals with diverse needs to engage with information, learn, and participate in various activities online. In conclusion, reading comprehension tools in the field of accessibility design are essential resources that aim to make written content accessible to individuals with cognitive impairments or disabilities. They provide alternative formats, adjust reading settings, and offer support features to enhance comprehension and ensure equal access to information.

Real User Monitoring (RUM)

Real User Monitoring (RUM), in the context of accessibility design, refers to the process of measuring and analyzing the performance and user experience of a website or web application from the perspective of real users with diverse abilities and disabilities. RUM provides valuable insights into the accessibility of a website, helping to identify and address any barriers that may impede users with disabilities from accessing and navigating the content effectively. RUM involves implementing tracking scripts or code snippets on the website, which collect and analyze data on user interactions, such as page loads, clicks, and form submissions. This data is then used to generate reports and metrics that reflect the actual experience of users with disabilities, enabling website owners and developers to make informed decisions to improve accessibility. Through RUM, it becomes possible to measure and evaluate different aspects of accessibility, including the performance and responsiveness of the website, as well as the usability and effectiveness of the user interface. For example, RUM can provide information on the time it takes for a page to load, the functionality of interactive elements, like dropdown menus or carousels, and the ease of navigating through the website using assistive technologies such as screen readers or keyboard-only interactions. By monitoring and analyzing real user data, RUM helps to uncover accessibility issues that may go unnoticed during development or automated testing. It provides a holistic view of how users with disabilities interact with the website, enabling designers and developers to identify and prioritize areas for improvement. For instance, RUM may reveal instances where certain user groups experience longer loading times or encounter difficulties utilizing specific features, highlighting the need for optimization or alternative solutions. Furthermore, RUM allows for ongoing monitoring and tracking of accessibility performance over time. Regularly analyzing and comparing the data can help identify trends, track improvements, and ensure that accessibility efforts remain effective. It enables website owners to measure the impact of accessibility enhancements and assess overall compliance with accessibility standards and guidelines. Overall, Real User Monitoring (RUM) is a vital tool in the field of accessibility design, providing valuable insights into how users with disabilities interact with websites or web applications. By measuring and analyzing real user data, RUM helps identify and address accessibility barriers, ensuring that websites are inclusive and accessible to all users, regardless of their abilities or disabilities.

Relay Services

Relay Services, in the context of accessibility design, refer to a telecommunications service that enables people with hearing or speech disabilities to communicate with others through the use of a relay operator. The service acts as a bridge between individuals using different communication modes, allowing effective and inclusive communication. Relay Services typically involve relay operators who facilitate the conversation between the parties involved. The process involves the relay operator receiving messages from one party, transcribing them, and relaying them to the other party in real-time. This allows individuals with hearing or speech impairments to participate in telephone calls, video calls, or video conferences, bridging the communication gap.

Responsive Design

Responsive Design refers to the approach of designing and developing a website or web application that adapts and responds to the user's device and screen size, providing an optimal viewing experience. It aims to ensure that the website's content, images, and functionalities are accessible and usable on a variety of devices, from desktop computers to smartphones and tablets. In the context of accessibility design, responsive design plays a crucial role in creating an inclusive and user-friendly experience for individuals with disabilities. By allowing the website to adjust its layout and content based on the user's device, responsive design enables individuals with visual impairments or other disabilities to access the website's information efficiently.

Responsive Web Design

Responsive web design refers to the practice of creating websites that adapt and respond to different device sizes and screen resolutions, in order to provide an optimal viewing experience for all users, regardless of their device. It is a key principle in accessibility design, as it ensures that individuals with disabilities can access and navigate websites easily, regardless of their assistive technology or device specifications. Responsive web design involves using fluid grids, flexible images, and CSS media queries to dynamically adjust the layout and content of a website, depending on the screen size and orientation of the device. This means that the website will automatically resize, reposition, or hide certain elements, to ensure that they are easily viewable and usable on any device, whether it is a desktop computer, a tablet, or a smartphone.

Role Attribute

Role Attribute is an important component in the field of accessibility design, specifically in the context of web development using HTML. It is a HTML attribute that allows developers to define the role or purpose of an element on a web page, providing additional information to assistive technologies such as screen readers in interpreting and understanding the content. The role attribute can be applied to any HTML element, and it helps in clarifying the intended function or meaning of an element, especially in cases where the default HTML semantics may not accurately convey this information. This is particularly useful for non-standard or custom elements that may not have well-defined roles by default.

Screen Enlargement Software

Screen enlargement software is a type of assistive technology designed to improve accessibility for individuals with visual impairments. It allows users with low vision or other visual challenges to enlarge the content displayed on their computer screens, making it easier to read and interact with digital content. This software works by magnifying the display of text, images, icons, and other on-screen elements, giving users the ability to adjust the size to their specific needs. By increasing the size of the content, screen enlargement software enhances visibility and reduces eye strain for individuals with visual disabilities.

Screen Magnification Software

Screen magnification software is a type of assistive technology designed to help individuals with visual impairments by enlarging the content displayed on a computer screen. This software allows users to adjust the size of text, images, and other visual elements, making them more visible and accessible. Screen magnification software works by capturing the content displayed on the screen and then magnifying it to a desired level. This can be particularly useful for individuals with low vision or other visual impairments that make it difficult to read small text or discern detailed images. By increasing the size of the content, screen magnification software enables these individuals to more easily navigate and interact with digital content.

Screen Magnification

Screen Magnification refers to a feature in accessibility design that allows users with visual impairments to enlarge the content displayed on their computer screens. This feature is particularly beneficial for individuals with low vision or those who have difficulty seeing small text or images. Screen Magnification works by scaling up the content on the screen, making it appear larger and more visible to the user. It can be adjusted to suit the individual's specific needs, allowing them to zoom in or out as desired. This magnification can be applied to all elements on the screen, including text, images, icons, and interface elements. By using Screen Magnification, users with visual impairments can comfortably view and interact with the digital content displayed on their screens. It enables them to read text, view images, navigate menus, and manipulate interface elements effectively. The magnification feature compensates for their reduced visual acuity, helping them access digital information and perform tasks with ease. In the context of accessibility design, implementing Screen Magnification is crucial in order to ensure an inclusive user experience. It enables individuals with visual impairments to have equal access to digital content and empowers them to participate fully in various activities, such as web browsing, reading documents, using applications, and engaging in online communication. HTML provides essential support for implementing Screen Magnification in web design. By utilizing appropriate CSS properties, web developers can easily enable users to adjust the magnification level of web pages to their preferences. This allows individuals with visual impairments to read and interact with web content comfortably, without compromising the overall design and functionality of the webpage. In conclusion, Screen Magnification is a vital feature in accessibility design that enhances the usability of digital content for individuals with visual impairments. By enabling users to enlarge the content displayed on their screens, it ensures equal access to information, promotes inclusivity, and empowers individuals with low vision to seamlessly navigate and engage with digital interfaces.

Screen Magnifier Software Providers

Screen magnifier software providers are companies or organizations that develop and offer software solutions designed to enhance accessibility for individuals with visual impairments. These software tools are specifically designed to enlarge the content displayed on a computer or mobile device screen, making it easier for visually impaired individuals to read or navigate the digital content. Screen magnifier software providers typically offer a range of features and customization options to meet the diverse needs of visually impaired users. These may include adjustable magnification levels, various color and contrast settings, and the ability to track and magnify the cursor or active area of focus. Some software providers also incorporate additional accessibility features, such as speech output or screen reader compatibility, to further enhance usability for individuals with vision loss.

Screen Magnifier

A screen magnifier is an accessibility feature used to enlarge the content displayed on a computer screen for individuals with visual impairments or difficulty in reading small text. It provides a useful solution by increasing the size of the on-screen text, images, and other elements, allowing users to see and interact with the content more effectively. Screen magnifiers work by displaying a portion of the screen at a larger size or by zooming in on specific elements. Users can control the magnification level, choose the portion of the screen to enlarge, and navigate within the magnified view. The magnified content is dynamically updated as the user interacts with the screen, ensuring a real-time display of the enlarged information. In terms of accessibility design, a screen magnifier is an essential component to ensure that individuals with visual impairments can access digital content and perform tasks on a computer. By enlarging the screen, it enables users to read text, view images, navigate menus, and interact with user interfaces more comfortably and accurately. To implement a screen magnifier, developers can incorporate accessibility APIs provided by modern web browsers or operating systems. These APIs enable the programmatic control of the screen magnification feature. By utilizing these

APIs, the web application can offer users the ability to control the magnification level, navigate within the enlarged view, and customize other options according to their specific needs. Web developers can also incorporate responsive design techniques to ensure that the screen magnifier works seamlessly across different screen sizes and resolutions. This involves utilizing relative units for text and element sizes, allowing the screen magnifier to adjust the content proportionally without causing any layout inconsistencies or readability issues. Overall, a screen magnifier plays a crucial role in making digital content accessible to individuals with visual impairments. By enlarging the screen and offering customizable options, it enables users to comfortably view and interact with digital content, ensuring an inclusive and user-friendly experience.

Screen Magnifiers

Screen magnifiers are assistive technology tools used to enlarge the content displayed on a computer screen or mobile device, making it easier for individuals with visual impairments or low vision to view and interact with digital content. They are designed to improve accessibility and provide an inclusive user experience for individuals who have difficulty seeing or reading text, graphics, or other visual elements on a screen. Screen magnifiers function by zooming in on a particular area of the screen, usually following the movement of the user's cursor or finger. When the user moves the cursor or touches the screen, the magnified view adjusts accordingly, allowing them to see the enlarged content in real-time. The magnification level is adjustable and can be set according to the user's preferences and visual requirements. Screen magnifiers are highly customizable, offering a range of options to enhance the viewing experience. Users can modify the magnification level, color contrast, brightness, and other display settings to suit their specific needs. Some screen magnifiers also include additional features like text-to-speech functionality, which enables the conversion of on-screen text into spoken words, further assisting individuals with reading difficulties. In terms of implementation, screen magnifiers can be either hardware or software-based. Hardware-based screen magnifiers typically consist of a separate monitor or display unit, dedicated to magnifying the content from the primary screen. They are often used in conjunction with other accessibility tools and devices. Software-based screen magnifiers, on the other hand, are applications or programs that can be installed on a computer or mobile device. They utilize the existing hardware capabilities of the device, such as the graphics card, to provide the magnification functionality. Overall, screen magnifiers play a crucial role in making digital content accessible to individuals with visual impairments or low vision. By enlarging the content and providing customizable options, they enable users to interact with digital interfaces and consume information with ease. By incorporating screen magnifiers in the design of websites, applications, and other digital platforms, developers can ensure that their products are inclusive and usable for a wider range of users.

Screen Reader Software Developers

Screen Reader Software Developers are professionals who specialize in designing and developing software that enables individuals with visual impairments to access and interact with digital content. These developers play a crucial role in ensuring that websites, applications, and other digital platforms are fully accessible to people with disabilities, particularly those who are blind or have low vision. Screen reader software is a type of assistive technology that converts text and other visual elements into synthesized speech or a braille output, allowing individuals with visual impairments to navigate and understand content on a computer or mobile device. Screen Reader Software Developers are responsible for creating and optimizing these software programs, ensuring they are compatible with different operating systems and digital platforms. The primary goal of screen reader software is to provide individuals with visual impairments equal access to information and resources on the internet, as well as other digital content. These software programs utilize various techniques to convert visual elements into an audio or braille format, such as scanning the screen, interpreting the underlying code, and using optical character recognition (OCR). Screen Reader Software Developers must have a deep understanding of accessibility standards and guidelines, including the Web Content Accessibility Guidelines (WCAG), to ensure their software complies with best practices. They collaborate with other professionals, including designers and user experience specialists, to implement accessible design principles into their software. In addition to enabling individuals with visual impairments to access digital content, screen reader software may also provide other features to enhance usability and customization. This may include options to adjust the reading speed, change the voice or language for text-to-speech output, navigate different types of content (e.g., tables or forms), and customize keyboard shortcuts or gestures. Overall, Screen Reader Software Developers play a crucial role in the field of accessibility design by creating software that empowers individuals with visual impairments to independently access and engage with digital content. Their expertise and dedication contribute to a more inclusive digital landscape, where everyone has equal opportunities to participate in the digital age, regardless of their abilities.

Screen Reader

A screen reader is a type of technology designed to assist individuals with visual impairments in accessing and interacting with digital content. Screen readers are software programs that use synthesized speech or Braille output to read aloud the text displayed on a computer screen. They provide audio feedback, enabling individuals who are blind or visually impaired to navigate websites, applications, and other digital interfaces. When a screen reader is active, it interprets the structural elements and content of the web page or application and converts them into audible or tactile information. This allows users to understand the layout, interact with buttons, links, forms, and access the textual content displayed on the screen. Screen readers typically have configurable settings that allow users to customize the reading speed, voice, pitch, and other preferences. They also offer navigation options to help users move through headings, paragraphs, tables, lists, landmarks, and other elements within the content. To ensure compatibility with screen readers, developers and designers need to adhere to accessibility guidelines and best practices. This involves using semantic HTML markup to provide appropriate heading structure, labeling form inputs, providing alternative text for images, and writing clear and concise content. Additionally, designers should avoid using visual-only cues to convey important information, as screen readers cannot interpret visual elements such as color or graphical icons. Instead, alternative textual descriptions or ARIA (Accessible Rich Internet Applications) attributes should be used to convey the same information to screen reader users. Screen readers play a crucial role in making digital content accessible to individuals with visual impairments. By enabling them to independently navigate and interact with websites and applications, screen readers empower users to access information, communicate, and participate in the digital world on an equal basis with others. In conclusion, screen readers are essential accessibility tools that facilitate access to digital content for individuals with visual impairments. Through synthesized speech or Braille output, they convert the visual information on computer screens into audible or tactile form, allowing people who are blind or visually impaired to navigate and interact with websites and applications. By following accessibility guidelines and best practices, developers and designers can ensure compatibility with screen readers, thus creating a more inclusive and accessible digital environment.

Screen Reading Software

A screen reading software is an assistive technology tool designed to enhance accessibility for individuals with visual impairments. It serves as a vital tool for people with blindness or low vision by providing them with audible information about the content displayed on a computer screen or mobile device. Screen reading software utilizes advanced text-to-speech (TTS) technology to convert text into spoken words. It works by scanning the screen and converting the displayed text into synthesized speech which can be heard through speakers or headphones. Additionally, some screen readers also provide braille output, converting the text into braille patterns for users who are proficient in braille. The primary purpose of screen reading software is to enable individuals with visual impairments to access and interact with digital content. It allows them to read and navigate through websites, documents, emails, and various applications independently. The software is typically customizable, allowing users to adjust the reading speed, voice, and other preferences to suit their needs. To ensure optimal accessibility, screen reading software relies on a hierarchical structure of the content. It recognizes headings, paragraphs, lists, and other elements present in a web page or document and provides users with the ability to navigate through these elements with ease. For instance, a screen reader can announce the presence of headings and allow users to jump directly to a specific section of a document by selecting the desired heading. Moreover, screen reading software often includes additional features such as keyboard shortcuts, voice commands, and auditory feedback to enhance the user experience. These features enable individuals with visual impairments to perform various actions, such as filling out forms, submitting online transactions, and interacting with multimedia elements. In conclusion, screen reading software plays a pivotal role in enhancing digital accessibility for individuals with visual impairments. It provides them with the means to access and interact with digital content through synthesized speech or braille output. By converting text into audible or tactile formats, screen reading software empowers users to navigate websites, read documents, and use various applications independently.

Screen Reading Tools

Screen reading tools are assistive technologies designed to provide accessibility for individuals with visual impairments or reading difficulties. These tools are specifically developed to convert text-based content into synthesized speech or braille output, enabling users to access and comprehend digital information. Screen reading tools rely on text-to-speech (TTS) technology to convert written content into audible speech. They parse and interpret the text displayed on the screen, including web pages, documents, emails, and other digital content. By analyzing the structure and semantics of the text, these tools generate spoken output that accurately represents the original content. Users can adjust the speed, volume, and pitch of the synthesized speech to suit their preferences. In addition to converting text to speech, screen reading tools often include other features for enhanced accessibility. For instance, they provide navigation options to help users navigate through different elements of a document or web page. This allows users to quickly jump to headings, links, tables, or other important components of the content. Users can also interact with the content using keyboard shortcuts or gestures specific to the screen reading tool. Screen reading tools also offer support for reading braille. In conjunction with refreshable braille displays, these tools can convert the digital text into braille output. This enables individuals with visual impairments to read and comprehend the content through touch. Moreover, screen reading tools may include OCR (optical character recognition) functionality. This allows users to access scanned documents or images containing textual information. The tool processes the images and extracts the text, which can then be read aloud or displayed in braille. The significance of screen reading tools in accessibility design cannot be overstated. They empower individuals with visual impairments or reading difficulties by providing equal access to information and enabling them to participate in various activities such as education, employment, and communication. By converting visual content into auditory or tactile formats, these tools bridge the accessibility gap, promoting inclusivity and independence. In conclusion, screen reading tools are essential assistive technologies that convert text-based content into speech or braille output, making it accessible for individuals with visual impairments or reading difficulties. These tools play a crucial role in providing equal access to digital information and fostering inclusivity in the digital age.

Section 504

A Section 504 refers to a provision in the Rehabilitation Act of 1973 that prohibits discrimination against individuals with disabilities in programs and activities that receive federal financial assistance. In the context of accessibility design, Section 504 requires that websites, software applications, and electronic documents be accessible to individuals with disabilities. To comply with Section 504, accessibility design encompasses various elements that ensure individuals with disabilities can access and use digital content. This includes providing alternatives for non-text content such as images, videos, and audio, through the use of alt text or captions. Additionally, accessibility design involves making sure that the layout and structure of web pages and electronic documents are logically organized and can be navigated using assistive technologies such as screen readers.

Section 508

Section 508 refers to a set of accessibility guidelines and standards that promote equal access to information and technology for individuals with disabilities. These guidelines were enacted as part of the Rehabilitation Act of 1973 and apply to all Federal agencies, as well as organizations receiving Federal funding. In the context of accessibility design, Section 508 requires that websites and digital content be designed and developed in a way that ensures individuals with disabilities can access and interact with the information. This includes individuals who may have visual, auditory, motor, or cognitive impairments. Section 508 covers a wide range of requirements, including but not limited to: 1. Text Equivalents: Websites should provide text equivalents for non-text content such as images, videos, and audio files. This ensures that individuals who cannot perceive these elements can still access the information they convey. 2. Keyboard Accessibility: Websites should be navigable using only a keyboard, as some individuals may have mobility impairments that prevent them from using a mouse or other pointing device. 3. Color Contrast: Websites should have sufficient color contrast between background and foreground elements to ensure readability for individuals with low vision or color blindness. 4. Multimedia Accessibility: Websites with multimedia elements should provide captions and audio descriptions to make the content accessible to individuals with hearing impairments or visual impairments. 5. Focus Indicators: Websites should clearly indicate which element has keyboard focus, ensuring that individuals who rely on keyboard navigation can easily identify their location on the page. 6. Compatibility with Assistive Technologies: Websites should be designed in a way that is compatible with assistive technologies such as screen readers, screen magnifiers, and alternative input devices. Overall, Section 508 aims to remove barriers to information and technology for individuals with disabilities, ensuring equal access to digital content. By following these accessibility guidelines, organizations can create inclusive and usable websites that benefit all users, regardless of their abilities. Section 508 refers to a set of accessibility guidelines and standards that promote equal access to information and technology for individuals with disabilities. In the context of accessibility design, Section 508 requires that websites and digital content be designed and developed in a way that ensures individuals with disabilities can access and interact with the information.

Self-Voicing Applications

Self-voicing applications are software programs or applications that are designed with built-in text-to-speech functionality, allowing users with visual impairments or reading difficulties to access digital content by hearing it read aloud. These applications can be especially valuable for individuals who are blind or have low vision, as well as those with learning disabilities such as dyslexia. Self-voicing applications typically utilize screen reading technology, which converts on-screen text into spoken words. This technology enables the application to read aloud not only the main content of a page or document but also any headings, links, buttons, form fields, and other interactive elements. The text-to-speech engine can be adjusted to control the speed, volume, and voice characteristics to suit the user's preferences. By providing a self-voicing feature, applications enhance accessibility by minimizing barriers to accessing information and content. Users can interact with the application solely through speech, without relying on visual cues or inputs. This allows individuals with visual impairments to independently navigate through menus, perform actions, and interact with content that may otherwise be inaccessible. Self-voicing applications can be beneficial in various contexts, including communication, education, entertainment, and productivity. In communication apps, such as messaging or video conferencing platforms, self-voicing features enable users to read and respond to text-based conversations in real-time, transforming written messages into spoken words. In educational applications, self-voicing capabilities make it possible for students with visual impairments to listen to textbooks, articles, or assignments, facilitating learning and knowledge acquisition. Entertainment and productivity applications can also adopt self-voicing features to ensure that users with visual impairments can access content such as books, movies, presentations, or emails. Additionally, self-voicing applications are crucial for individuals with learning disabilities, such as dyslexia, who may experience difficulties with reading or comprehending text. The ability to hear the content read aloud can significantly enhance understanding and engagement, empowering these individuals to access and participate in digital environments effectively. In conclusion, self-voicing applications play a fundamental role in promoting accessibility for individuals with visual impairments and reading difficulties. By providing a built-in text-to-speech feature, these applications enable users to access digital content by listening to it read aloud. With self-voicing capabilities, individuals with visual impairments or learning disabilities can independently navigate, comprehend, and interact with various types of digital content, fostering inclusivity and empowerment in the digital world.

Semantic HTML

Semantic HTML refers to the practice of using HTML elements in a way that accurately represents the structure and meaning of the content on a web page. It is an important aspect of accessibility design as it helps users with disabilities to navigate and understand the content more effectively. Semantic HTML helps in providing meaningful information to users who rely on assistive technologies such as screen readers. By using appropriate HTML elements, the structure of the page can be conveyed in a way that makes sense to these technologies. For example, using the `` element for the main heading, `` for subheadings, and `` for paragraphs helps in creating a clear and logical content hierarchy. In addition to headings and paragraphs, semantic HTML includes elements such as ``, ``, ``, ``, ``, and ``. These elements provide semantic meaning to different sections of a web page. For instance, the `` element is used to mark up the navigation menu, the `` element represents the introductory content at the top of a page, and the `` element indicates the bottom section. Using semantic HTML also improves the overall usability of a website. Search engines rely on semantic markup to better understand and index web pages. By providing clear and descriptive HTML elements, search engines can easily determine the relevance and context of the content, leading to improved search engine optimization (SEO). Semantic HTML promotes separation of content and presentation. By using appropriate elements, it allows developers to focus on the structure of the content without worrying about its visual appearance. This separation is crucial for ensuring a consistent experience across different devices and platforms. It also makes it easier to update and modify the presentation of the content without affecting its underlying structure. Overall, semantic HTML is a fundamental principle in accessibility design that aims to provide a clear and meaningful structure to web content. By using appropriate HTML elements, it enhances the accessibility, usability, and search engine visibility of a website, making it easier for all users, including those with disabilities, to access and understand the information.

Sensory Impairments

Sensory impairments refer to disabilities that affect one or more of the five senses: sight, hearing, touch, taste, and smell. In the context of accessibility design, sensory impairments primarily focus on ensuring that digital content and interfaces are accessible to individuals who have limited or no use of one or more senses. When designing for individuals with visual impairments, considerations must be made to ensure that content is accessible to those who are blind or have low vision. This can be achieved through various techniques such as providing alternative text descriptions for images, using proper headings and semantic markup for screen readers, and ensuring sufficient color contrast for individuals with color blindness. For individuals with hearing impairments, accessibility design aims to provide alternatives to audio-based content. This can involve providing closed captions or transcripts for videos, providing text-based alternatives for audio-only content, and ensuring that important auditory cues are also available in a visual or tactile format. Tactile impairments relate to the sense of touch, and accessibility design targets individuals who may have limited or no sensation in their fingers or hands. Design considerations include ensuring that touch targets are large enough, allowing for alternative forms of input like keyboard navigation, and providing tactile feedback through haptic vibrations or audio cues. Taste and smell impairments are less commonly addressed in digital accessibility design but may still be relevant in certain contexts. For example, individuals with taste impairments may require additional labeling or descriptions for food-related content, while individuals with smell impairments may require alternatives for olfactory cues in certain scenarios. In conclusion, sensory impairments encompass a wide range of disabilities that affect one or more of the five senses. Accessibility design aims to address these impairments by ensuring that digital content and interfaces are accessible to individuals who have limited or no use of certain senses, through techniques such as alternative text, closed captions, tactile feedback, and other forms of sensory alternatives.

Sign Language Interpretation Agencies

Sign Language Interpretation Agencies are organizations that provide professional interpreter services for individuals who are deaf or hard of hearing. These agencies play a crucial role in facilitating communication between deaf individuals and hearing individuals in various settings, ensuring accessibility and inclusion for the deaf community. Sign Language Interpretation Agencies typically employ interpreters who are fluent in sign language and have a deep understanding of deaf culture. These interpreters use American Sign Language (ASL) or other sign languages to convey spoken language to deaf individuals and interpret sign language into spoken language for hearing individuals. Sign Language Interpretation Agencies work in a wide range of settings to meet the diverse needs of their clients. They may provide interpretation services in educational institutions, such as schools or universities, where deaf students may require interpreters to access their education. These agencies also work in healthcare settings, ensuring that deaf patients can communicate effectively with healthcare providers and understand important medical information. In addition to educational and healthcare settings, Sign Language Interpretation Agencies may also provide services in legal settings, business meetings, conferences, and public events. They may offer on-site interpretation services, where interpreters are physically present, or remote interpretation services, where interpreters provide services through video or teleconferencing platforms. Accessibility design involves considering the communication needs of individuals with disabilities and finding ways to make information and services accessible to them. Sign Language Interpretation Agencies are a vital component of accessibility design as they bridge the communication gap between deaf individuals and the hearing world. By providing professional interpreters, these agencies ensure that deaf individuals have equal access to education, healthcare, legal services, employment opportunities, and social integration.

Sign Language Interpretation Services

Sign Language Interpretation Services refer to the provision of trained professionals who assist in facilitating communication between individuals who are deaf or hard of hearing and those who do not understand or utilize sign language. This service is crucial in ensuring access to information, services, and opportunities for individuals with hearing impairments and is a key component of accessibility design. Sign language is a visual-gestural language that uses hand shapes, facial expressions, and body movements to convey meaning. It is a distinct language with its own grammar and syntax, and differs from spoken languages. Many individuals who are deaf or hard of hearing rely on sign language as their primary means of communication. Sign language interpretation services are needed in a variety of settings, including educational institutions, workplaces, healthcare facilities, government offices, and public events. A sign language interpreter acts as a mediator, conveying spoken language into sign language and vice versa, allowing effective communication between all parties involved. Effective sign language interpretation services require highly skilled and qualified interpreters who possess a deep understanding of both sign language and the spoken language(s) being used. They must have a strong command of language, be able to accurately convey subtle nuances and idiomatic expressions, and have a broad knowledge base to handle diverse subject matter. In addition, interpreters must adhere to a code of ethics that includes principles of confidentiality, impartiality, and cultural sensitivity. Accessibility design aims to create an inclusive environment that eliminates barriers and ensures equal access for all individuals, including those with disabilities. Sign language interpretation services are a crucial component of accessibility design, allowing individuals who are deaf or hard of hearing to fully participate in a wide range of activities and engagements. By providing sign language interpretation, organizations and individuals demonstrate their commitment to inclusivity and accessibility, promoting equality and diversity within society.

Sign Language Interpretation

Sign Language Interpretation Sign Language Interpretation refers to the process of conveying spoken languages into sign languages and vice versa for the purpose of communication between individuals who are deaf or hard of hearing and those who can hear. It plays a vital role in ensuring accessibility for the deaf community by providing a means of understanding and participating in conversations, public events, educational settings, and various types of media. In the field of accessibility design, sign language interpretation is a fundamental component that aims to bridge the communication gap between deaf and hearing individuals. It involves the use of visual-gestural language, utilizing hand movements, facial expressions, and body language to communicate meaning. Skilled sign language interpreters facilitate effective communication by accurately translating spoken content into sign language and vice versa, allowing deaf individuals to fully engage in different social and professional contexts.

Sign Language Recognition

Sign Language Recognition is a technology that aims to facilitate and improve accessibility for individuals who are deaf or hard of hearing. It involves the use of computer algorithms and machine learning techniques to interpret and understand the gestures and movements used in sign language. The goal of Sign Language Recognition is to enable communication between people who use sign language as their primary means of communication and those who do not understand sign language. By recognizing and interpreting the gestures and movements made by individuals using sign language, the technology can convert these into spoken or written language that can be understood by others. In the context of accessibility design, Sign Language Recognition plays a crucial role in ensuring equal access to information and communication for individuals with hearing impairments. It allows individuals who are deaf or hard of hearing to interact with technology, devices, and digital content more effectively, breaking down the barriers that can often exist in communication. By incorporating Sign Language Recognition into accessibility design, websites, applications, and other digital platforms can provide features that accommodate sign language users. This can include the ability to translate sign language gestures into text or spoken language, enabling real-time communication between sign language users and individuals who do not understand sign language. Sign Language Recognition technology can be implemented through various methods, such as using cameras to capture and analyze the movements of hands and facial expressions, or through input devices that allow users to input sign language gestures directly. The technology then processes and interprets these gestures, matching them to a database of predefined signs or using machine learning algorithms to recognize and understand new signs. Overall, Sign Language Recognition is a crucial accessibility tool that promotes inclusivity and equal access to communication for individuals who are deaf or hard of hearing. By incorporating this technology into digital platforms and devices, designers can create more inclusive and accessible experiences for all users, supporting the integration and participation of individuals with hearing impairments in society.

Sign Language Translation Apps

Sign Language Translation Apps are mobile applications specifically designed to enhance accessibility for individuals who are deaf or hard of hearing. These apps utilize video recognition and artificial intelligence technology to translate spoken language into sign language, allowing deaf individuals to understand and communicate with hearing individuals more effectively. These apps typically function by analyzing spoken language through the device's microphone and then generating corresponding sign language animations or videos. The translations are often displayed in real-time, providing instant access to sign language interpretations. In addition to translation capabilities, many apps also offer features such as word dictionaries, instructional videos, and interactive quizzes to help users learn and improve their sign language skills.

Sign Language

Sign Language is a tactile visual language that allows communication with individuals who are deaf or hard of hearing. It is a complete language with its own grammar, syntax, and vocabulary, and is considered the natural language for individuals who are deaf. Sign Language is based on gestures, facial expressions, and body language, and involves the movement of hands, arms, and body to convey meaning. In the context of accessibility design, Sign Language plays a crucial role in ensuring effective communication for individuals with hearing disabilities. It provides them with a means to express themselves, understand others, and participate in society on an equal basis. By incorporating Sign Language into various elements of design, such as videos, presentations, and websites, accessibility can be ensured for individuals who rely on Sign Language for communication.

Single Switch Scanning

Single switch scanning is an accessibility design technique that allows individuals with limited mobility or dexterity to navigate and interact with digital interfaces using a single switch input device. This method is particularly beneficial for individuals who may not have the ability to use traditional input devices such as a keyboard or mouse. In single switch scanning, the user is presented with a series of choices or options on the screen one at a time, and they use the single switch to select the option they desire. The scanning process can be customized to suit the user's needs and preferences, with options for adjusting the scanning speed, direction, and pattern. To begin the scanning process, the user activates the single switch, which triggers the scanning to start. The system highlights or moves through each option on the screen, presenting them in a sequential order. The timing and movement pattern of the scan can be adjusted to accommodate the user's capabilities and preferences. When the desired option is highlighted, the user activates the single switch again to select it. This scanning technique often employs auditory, visual, or both types of feedback to assist users in keeping track of the scanning progress and identifying the current highlighted option. For example, auditory cues may be provided, such as a voice or sound indicating the current option being highlighted, while visual cues can include highlighting or color changes on the screen. Single switch scanning can be implemented in various digital environments, including software applications, websites, and mobile devices. It provides individuals with limited motor skills the means to independently access and interact with digital content, allowing them to navigate menus, select options, input text, and perform other tasks that would typically be achieved through traditional input devices. In conclusion, single switch scanning is an accessibility design technique that enables individuals with limited mobility or dexterity to navigate and interact with digital interfaces using a single switch input device. It offers customizable scanning options and utilizes feedback cues to assist users in making selections. By incorporating single switch scanning into digital environments, individuals with physical disabilities can experience greater independence and accessibility when engaging with technology.

Speech Disorders

A speech disorder is a communication disorder in which an individual experiences difficulties with speech production, voice quality, and/or the articulation of sounds. It affects the way a person speaks and can impact their ability to communicate effectively with others. Speech disorders can manifest in different ways, including difficulties with pronouncing words correctly, speaking fluently, or controlling the volume and pitch of their voice. These challenges can significantly impact the individual's ability to express themselves, be understood by others, and engage in meaningful conversations.

Speech Recognition Apps

Speech recognition apps are software applications that use advanced technology to convert spoken words into written text. These apps are designed with the aim of providing accessibility to individuals who may have difficulty typing or using traditional input methods, such as people with physical disabilities or those with limited mobility. By leveraging speech recognition technology, these apps allow users to dictate their thoughts, ideas, or commands to their devices, which are then transcribed into written text in real-time. This eliminates the need for manual typing and provides an alternative means of communication, making digital content accessible to a wider range of users.

Speech Recognition Software Companies

Speech recognition software companies are organizations that specialize in developing and providing technology solutions that enable computers or devices to understand and interpret spoken language. These companies work towards creating software applications and algorithms that can accurately convert spoken words into written text, enabling individuals with disabilities or challenges in conventional communication methods to interact with computers and technology more effectively. The primary objective of speech recognition software companies in the context of accessibility design is to make digital content and technology more inclusive and accessible to people with diverse needs and abilities. By leveraging advanced algorithms and machine learning techniques, these companies strive to develop applications that can understand and transcribe spoken words accurately, allowing individuals with vision impairments, motor disabilities, or learning difficulties to use computers, mobile devices, and other technology with ease. Through their research and development efforts, speech recognition software companies aim to enhance the user experience for individuals with disabilities, enabling them to navigate and interact with digital interfaces seamlessly. These companies collaborate with accessibility experts and disability advocacy groups to identify the unique challenges faced by different user groups and incorporate their feedback into the design and improvement of their software solutions. Speech recognition software companies also play a crucial role in the development of assistive technology for individuals with hearing impairments. By using speech-to-text conversion technology, they enable real-time transcription of spoken content, allowing deaf or hard-of-hearing individuals to participate in conversations, meetings, or presentations where spoken communication is the primary mode of interaction. In summary, speech recognition software companies are instrumental in driving advancements in accessibility design by developing innovative solutions that empower individuals with disabilities to communicate, navigate, and interact with digital content and technology effectively. Their expertise and focus on inclusion contribute to creating a more accessible and inclusive digital landscape.

Speech Recognition Software

Speech recognition software, in the context of accessibility design, refers to technology that enables individuals with disabilities to control their computer or device using voice commands instead of traditional input methods such as keyboard and mouse. This technology can recognize and interpret spoken language, allowing users to perform various tasks on their device hands-free. By using speech recognition software, individuals with mobility impairments, visual impairments, or other disabilities that affect their ability to use traditional input devices can access and interact with digital content and applications more easily. They can navigate through menus, open applications, compose emails, browse the internet, and perform various other tasks by speaking simple commands or dictating text instead of manually typing or clicking. The software converts spoken words into text or executes predefined actions based on recognized voice commands.

Speech Recognition

Speech recognition in the context of accessibility design refers to the technology that enables individuals with disabilities to interact with digital devices and applications using their voice. It allows users to dictate text, control devices, and navigate through interfaces without relying on traditional input methods such as keyboard and mouse. Speech recognition utilizes natural language processing algorithms to convert spoken words into text or commands. These algorithms analyze the acoustic signal of the user's voice and match it to a database of recognized words and phrases. The process involves capturing audio input, digital signal processing, feature extraction, and pattern recognition. Once the speech is recognized, it can be used for various purposes, such as transcribing speech into text, executing commands, or triggering actions. The integration of speech recognition in accessibility design aims to provide an inclusive user experience for individuals with motor or dexterity impairments, visual impairments, or learning disabilities. By enabling users to control digital devices and applications using their voice, it eliminates barriers and enhances accessibility. Speech recognition is particularly beneficial for individuals who have difficulty using traditional input methods, such as those with limited mobility, repetitive strain injuries, or dyslexia. In accessible design, speech recognition can be implemented in various ways. It can be embedded within operating systems, web browsers, or specific applications. Integration with screen readers, text editors, and other assistive technologies allows users to navigate and interact with content using their voice. Speech recognition can also be utilized in communication tools and accessibility extensions, allowing individuals to dictate emails, compose documents, or navigate websites hands-free. However, it is important to note that speech recognition technology may have limitations and challenges. Various factors, such as ambient noise, accents, or speech disorders, can affect the accuracy and reliability of the recognition process. Additionally, speech recognition may require training or calibration to better understand an individual user's speech patterns and preferences. Overall, speech recognition plays a crucial role in accessibility design by enabling individuals with disabilities to interact with digital devices and applications using their voice. By eliminating reliance on traditional input methods, it enhances inclusivity and empowers users to access and engage with digital content.

Speech Synthesis

Speech synthesis, in the context of accessibility design, refers to the technology that converts written text into spoken words. It allows individuals with visual impairments or those who have difficulty reading, to access and understand digital content. By utilizing speech synthesis, web developers and designers can ensure that their websites and applications are inclusive and accessible to all users. This technology is particularly beneficial for individuals who rely on screen readers or other assistive technologies to navigate and interact with digital content.

Speech-To-Text Software

Speech-to-text software, also known as voice recognition software, is a technology designed to convert spoken words into written text. It enables individuals with communication impairments, such as those with hearing or speech disabilities, to interact and communicate more effectively in various contexts. This software serves as an assistive tool for individuals who may struggle with traditional methods of communication, such as typing or writing. By using speech-to-text software, individuals can dictate their thoughts, ideas, or messages, which are then converted into written form, either in real-time or as a transcript. This allows them to express themselves more easily and efficiently.

Sticky Keys

Sticky Keys is an accessibility feature in computer systems that aims to assist individuals with physical disabilities or limitations, allowing them to use keyboard shortcuts more easily. This feature is specifically designed for users who have difficulty pressing multiple keys simultaneously. When Sticky Keys is enabled, users can press and release modifier keys such as Shift, Ctrl, Alt, or the Windows key one at a time while still having the same effect as holding them down. It eliminates the need for simultaneously pressing multiple keys, which can be challenging for individuals with motor impairments, limited dexterity, or conditions like arthritis.

Structured Data

Structured data, in the context of accessibility design, refers to the organization and presentation of information in a way that allows people with disabilities to easily understand and navigate web content. It involves the use of semantic HTML markup and proper labeling of elements to ensure that assistive technologies, such as screen readers, can accurately interpret and convey the meaning and structure of the content to users with disabilities. Structured data is essential for creating an inclusive and accessible web experience for all users. By using semantic HTML tags, such as headings, paragraphs, lists, and tables, accessibility can be greatly enhanced. These tags provide important cues to assistive technologies about the structure and relationships of content on a web page, enabling individuals with disabilities to navigate and comprehend the information effectively.

Subtitles

Subtitles are an integral part of accessibility design that provide a textual representation of the spoken words in a video or audio content. They aim to assist individuals who are deaf or hard of hearing, as well as non-native speakers, in understanding the content being presented. In the context of accessibility design, subtitles are typically displayed at the bottom portion of the screen and synchronize with the audio or video to provide a meaningful and inclusive viewing experience for all users. They are commonly used in movies, TV shows, online videos, and other forms of multimedia content. The primary objective of subtitles is to convey spoken dialogue, sound effects, and other relevant audio information to individuals who may have difficulty hearing or comprehending auditory content. By offering a written representation of the dialogue, subtitles allow users to follow along with the content and fully grasp the intended message. Subtitles also play a significant role in ensuring accessibility for individuals with hearing impairments. They provide an alternative means of understanding and enjoying audiovisual content, allowing these users to access information that would otherwise be limited or inaccessible. Moreover, subtitles can be designed to enhance the accessibility of content for individuals with cognitive or language disabilities. By providing a visual aid alongside the auditory content, subtitles can assist with comprehension, making the content more easily digestible for users who struggle with language processing or understanding complex dialogue. In terms of technical implementation, subtitles are typically created using specific file formats such as SubRip (.srt), WebVTT (.vtt), or Timed Text Markup Language (.ttml). These file formats contain timecodes that synchronize the display of the subtitles with the audio or video content. By embedding these files within the HTML structure, developers ensure that the subtitles are properly rendered and displayed to the user. In summary, subtitles are a crucial component of accessibility design, enabling individuals with hearing impairments or language barriers to fully participate in and understand audiovisual content. By providing a written representation of dialogue and other audio information, subtitles enhance inclusivity and make digital media accessible to a wider audience.

Subtitling Services Providers

Subtitling Services Providers encompass a range of solutions aimed at ensuring accessibility to audiovisual content for individuals with hearing impairments. These providers specialize in creating and embedding captions or subtitles into multimedia presentations, including films, videos, television shows, and online content. The purpose of subtitling is to facilitate comprehension and enhance the viewing experience for people who are deaf or hard of hearing. By offering subtitling services, providers play a crucial role in promoting inclusive design and equal access to information and entertainment. They employ various techniques, such as transcription and time coding, to accurately capture the spoken dialogue, sound effects, and relevant audio cues in a video. Subsequently, these captions or subtitles are presented on screen in a synchronized manner to correlate with the corresponding audio elements, ensuring coherent and seamless viewing.

Subtitling Services

Subtitling Services in the context of accessibility design refer to the process of providing captions or subtitles for audiovisual content to ensure that it is accessible to individuals with hearing impairments or those who cannot fully understand the spoken language in the video. Subtitles are typically displayed at the bottom of the screen in the same language as the audio, allowing viewers to read along with the dialogue and understand the content. They provide a textual representation of the spoken words and other important audio elements, such as sound effects or background music.

Subtitling Software

Subtitling software is a type of software designed to provide accessibility to individuals with hearing impairments or language barriers. It is primarily used to display text captions or subtitles alongside audio-visual content such as movies, television shows, or online videos. The software translates and synchronizes the spoken dialogue or audio cues into written text that is displayed on the screen in real-time. Accessibility design refers to the practice of creating products, services, or environments that are inclusive and usable by individuals with disabilities. In the context of subtitling software, accessibility design focuses on ensuring that the software meets the specific needs of individuals with hearing impairments or language barriers.

Switch Access

Switch Access is an accessibility feature in design that allows individuals with limited mobility to interact and operate digital devices or software using a switch instead of traditional input methods such as a keyboard or mouse. It is primarily designed to cater to individuals with physical disabilities or conditions that restrict their movement, making it difficult for them to navigate through digital interfaces or perform certain tasks. The switch used in Switch Access can be any external device that is compatible with the device or software being used. The most common form of switches used includes specialized buttons, foot pedals, or even eye-tracking devices. These switches are connected to the device or software via wired or wireless connections, depending on the specific accessibility requirements or capabilities of the device or software.

Symbol Communication

The concept of symbol communication in the context of accessibility design refers to the use of visual symbols or pictograms to convey information, instructions, or messages to individuals who may have difficulty with traditional written or spoken language. It is an inclusive approach that aims to provide equal access to information for people with different abilities, including those with cognitive impairments, learning disabilities, or limited language skills. Symbol communication is an important aspect of accessibility design as it helps bridge the communication gap between individuals with diverse abilities and the information or services they need. By using symbols that are universally understood or easily recognizable, designers can ensure that their content is accessible and comprehensible to a wider audience.

Tabindex Attribute

The tabindex attribute is an HTML attribute that allows developers to control the tab order of interactive elements on a webpage. It helps improve the accessibility of a website for users who navigate through the site using keyboard-only. The tabindex attribute assigns a numerical value to an element, determining the order in which it receives focus when the user presses the Tab key. When a user interacts with a webpage using a keyboard, they rely on the proper tab order to navigate through the interactive elements. By default, the tab order follows the document structure, which means elements are focused in the order they appear in the HTML source code. However, this order may not always be logical or intuitive for all users. To address this issue, developers can use the tabindex attribute to override the default tab order and provide a more meaningful navigation experience. The tabindex attribute can be applied to various HTML elements, such as links, buttons, form controls, and interactive content. The tabindex attribute's value can be either positive, zero, or negative. Elements with a positive tabindex value are focused first, in ascending order. Elements with a higher positive value receive focus before those with a lower value. When multiple elements have the same positive value, the order follows the document structure. Elements with a tabindex of zero are focused after those with a positive tabindex value. They follow the natural tab order but can be focused out of order if necessary. This allows important elements, such as navigation links or search fields, to receive focus earlier. Negative tabindex values (tabindex="-1") remove an element from the tab order altogether. These elements can still be focused programmatically using JavaScript but are skipped during regular keyboard navigation. This feature is useful for elements that should not be reachable via keyboard navigation, such as hidden or off-screen content. It's important to note that modifying the tab order using tabindex should be done thoughtfully, considering the logical flow of the webpage's content. Overriding the default order can potentially confuse users if it deviates too much from their expected navigation patterns. The tabindex attribute should be used sparingly and purposefully to enhance accessibility without sacrificing usability. However, it is worth mentioning that relying too heavily on tabindex may indicate underlying accessibility issues that could be better addressed through proper semantic structure and ARIA attributes. The tabindex attribute should be used as a last resort when other accessibility techniques are not sufficient. In conclusion, the tabindex attribute is an HTML attribute that allows developers to control the tab order of interactive elements on a webpage. By using tabindex, developers can enhance the accessibility of a website for keyboard-only users by providing a more meaningful and logical navigation experience.

Table Headers

Table Headers in the context of accessibility design refer to the information that is placed at the top of each column or row in a table to provide a clear and concise description of the content within that column or row. They serve as an aid to assistive technologies, such as screen readers, in presenting the information in a structured and meaningful way to users with visual impairments. In HTML, table headers can be defined using the element. The element is similar to the element used for regular data cells in a table, but it carries special significance as a header cell. It represents a header for a group of table cells. There are two types of table headers: column headers and row headers. Column headers, also known as "table header cells," describe the content of a column. They are typically placed in the first row of the table. Column headers help users understand the relationship between the data in each column and provide context for the information contained within the table cells in that column. Row headers, on the other hand, describe the content of a row. They are usually placed in the first column of the table. Row headers assist users in understanding the relationship between the different rows of data, allowing them to navigate and interpret the information more easily. To create column headers in HTML, each element is placed within a element, which represents a row in the table. The table headers are then placed within the appropriate tags. For example: Column 1 Column 2 Column 3 Data 1 Data 2 Data 3 In this example, "Column 1," "Column 2," and "Column 3" are the column headers. Similarly, to create row headers, the elements are placed within the elements, just like regular table data cells. For example: Row 1 Data 1 Data 2 Data 3 Row 2 Data 4 Data 5 Data 6 In this example, "Row 1" and "Row 2" are the row headers. By properly marking up table headers using the element, assistive technologies can convey the table structure and relationships to users with disabilities. This allows them to navigate and understand the content more effectively and ensures equal access to the information presented in the table.

Tactile Communication

Tactile communication in the context of accessibility design refers to the use of touch-based interactions to convey information and engage users with diverse sensory abilities. It involves the integration of tactile elements and haptic feedback within digital interfaces, physical objects, or environments to ensure a more inclusive and interactive experience for individuals with visual impairments or other sensory limitations. Tactile communication plays a crucial role in making information more accessible to individuals who rely on touch as their primary means of perception. It enables users to navigate and interact with digital content, physical interfaces, or spatial environments through the sense of touch, opening up new ways to receive and interpret information. In digital accessibility, tactile communication is often achieved by incorporating tactile cues, such as raised or embossed elements, Braille labels, or tactile diagrams, on touch screens or physical surfaces. These cues provide tactile feedback to individuals who are blind or visually impaired, allowing them to locate and operate interactive elements or understand the layout and structure of a user interface. Similarly, in the design of physical products or environments, tactile communication can be facilitated through the use of tactile textures, shapes, or patterns. By employing materials with different textures or incorporating tactile symbols and indicators, designers can enhance the usability and comprehension of a product or space for individuals with limited vision. Tactile communication also extends to the provision of haptic feedback, which refers to the use of subtle vibrations or forces to provide touch-based feedback in response to user actions. Haptic feedback can be used to convey information, such as confirmation of a button press or the presence of an object, enhancing the overall user experience and enabling individuals with visual impairments to engage more effectively with digital interfaces or physical objects. By incorporating tactile communication into accessibility design, designers can create more inclusive experiences that go beyond visual and auditory stimuli, enabling individuals with visual impairments or other sensory limitations to access and interact with information and the environment more effectively.

Tactile Feedback

Tactile feedback, in the context of accessibility design, refers to the provision of physical or tactile sensations to individuals with visual impairments or other disabilities in order to enhance their understanding and interaction with digital or physical interfaces. When it comes to accessibility, it is crucial to consider the needs of individuals who may have limited or no vision. Providing tactile feedback allows them to access and engage with various technologies, devices, or user interfaces more effectively.

Tactile Graphics Printing Companies

Tactile Graphics Printing Companies are organizations that specialize in creating tactile graphics for individuals with vision impairments. Tactile graphics are 2D representations of visual information that can be felt rather than seen, allowing individuals with visual impairments to access and understand visual content. These companies use various techniques and materials to produce tactile graphics, including embossing, thermoforming, and printing with specialized inks. They work closely with designers, educators, and accessibility experts to ensure that the tactile graphics are accurate, clear, and effectively communicate the visual information.

Tactile Graphics Software

Tactile Graphics Software is a specialized tool designed to create tactile graphics, which are raised representations of visual information that can be felt by touch. This software is primarily used in the field of accessibility design to ensure that individuals with visual impairments have the same access to information as those with sight. Tactile graphics are an essential component of inclusive design, as they allow people with visual impairments to access and understand visual information, such as maps, diagrams, charts, and graphs. Tactile graphics software enables designers to convert visual content into tactile representations, making it accessible to individuals who are blind or visually impaired.

Tactile Graphics

Tactile graphics refer to the visual representations of information that are created using raised surfaces, textures, and other materials to be perceived through touch. These graphics are specifically designed to provide accessibility for individuals with visual impairments, allowing them to access and understand visual content in a tactile format. Unlike traditional visual graphics that rely on sight, tactile graphics provide a means for individuals with visual impairments to use their sense of touch to gather information. By using different textures, patterns, and raised surfaces, tactile graphics convey various aspects of visual content, such as shapes, lines, colors, and textures.

Tactile Keyboards

Tactile keyboards are a type of input device designed to enhance accessibility for individuals with visual impairments. These keyboards are equipped with tactile features that provide physical feedback to users, allowing them to navigate and interact with the digital environment more effectively. The primary purpose of tactile keyboards is to address the challenges faced by visually impaired individuals when using traditional keyboards, which rely mainly on visual cues. By incorporating tactile elements, these keyboards enable users to locate keys more easily and accurately, improving their typing speed and accuracy.

Tactile Paving

Tactile paving, also known as tactile ground surface indicators (TGSI), is a type of pavement surface that is designed to provide sensory cues to individuals with visual impairments or other disabilities. It is an important feature in accessibility design, aimed at ensuring a safe and inclusive environment for all pedestrians. Tactile paving consists of a series of raised, textured patterns that can be detected by touch or with a cane. These patterns are generally placed at key locations such as pedestrian crossings, stairs, ramps, and platforms to provide guidance and alert individuals to potential hazards or changes in the environment.

Tactile Warning Strips

Tactile warning strips are a type of accessibility design element that is used to provide tactile cues to individuals with visual impairments or low vision. These strips are typically made of a contrasting colored material or have raised patterns that can be felt with the fingertips. The purpose of tactile warning strips is to alert individuals to potential hazards or changes in their environment, allowing them to navigate safely. These strips are commonly found in various public spaces and transportation facilities, such as sidewalks, pedestrian crossings, train platforms, and stairs.

Telecommunications Relay Service (TRS)

The Telecommunications Relay Service (TRS) is an accessibility service that allows individuals with hearing or speech disabilities to communicate through the telephone system. TRS ensures that individuals who are deaf, hard of hearing, or have speech impairments can effectively make and receive phone calls, bridging the communication gap between them and the general public. TRS works by using relay operators who act as intermediaries in the conversation. These operators facilitate communication by relaying the messages between the parties involved, following strict guidelines to ensure accuracy and confidentiality. When a person with a hearing or speech disability wants to make a phone call, they dial a designated TRS number. The relay operator then answers the call and assists the person by converting their speech into text or using sign language interpreters to interpret their signs into speech. The operator then relays the conversation in real-time to the other party on the line, and also transcribes their responses back to the person with the disability. This process allows for smooth and effective communication between individuals using different modes of communication. TRS is an essential tool for accessibility in today's society, as it allows individuals with hearing or speech disabilities to participate in everyday communication. It enables them to make important phone calls, such as contacting emergency services, making appointments, or engaging in business conversations. In addition to traditional telephone calls, TRS also supports other communication methods, such as text messaging and video calls. This versatility ensures that individuals with different communication needs can access the service and communicate in a way that is most comfortable for them. To guarantee the availability and reliability of TRS, it is regulated by the Federal Communications Commission (FCC). The FCC sets and enforces standards for TRS providers, ensuring that the service is accessible to all who require it. Overall, the Telecommunications Relay Service plays a vital role in promoting accessibility and inclusivity for individuals with hearing or speech disabilities. By bridging the communication gap, TRS empowers individuals to fully participate in society and engage in meaningful interactions with the world around them.

Text Readability

Text readability, in the context of accessibility design, refers to the level of ease with which written content can be comprehended and understood by a wide range of users. It encompasses several factors, such as the complexity of vocabulary, sentence structure, and overall writing style. Accessible text should be tailored to cater to individuals with diverse reading abilities, including those with cognitive or learning disabilities, non-native speakers, and individuals with visual impairments using screen readers or other assistive technologies. By ensuring that text is easily readable, designers can enhance the usability and inclusivity of their digital products or platforms.

Text-To-Speech Apps

Text-to-Speech (TTS) Apps are software applications that convert written text into spoken words, allowing individuals with visual impairments, learning disabilities, or other reading difficulties to access and comprehend digital content. These apps are designed with the aim of promoting inclusivity and accessibility in online resources, applications, and services. By utilizing TTS apps, users can listen to textual content instead of reading it visually, thus bypassing barriers posed by limited sight or difficulties in processing written information. The apps employ advanced algorithms and synthesized speech technology to accurately convert text into spoken words, maintaining natural inflections and intonations for enhanced comprehension.

Text-To-Speech Software Developers

Text-to-Speech software developers are individuals or teams responsible for creating and improving software programs that convert written text into spoken words. This technology is designed to enhance accessibility for individuals with visual impairments or other disabilities that make reading difficult or impossible. The main objective of text-to-speech software developers is to create tools that enable people to listen to the written content instead of reading it visually. By utilizing natural language processing techniques, these developers aim to generate high-quality and human-like speech output, allowing users to comprehend and consume information more easily. Text-to-speech software development involves advanced algorithms and techniques that convert text into phonetic representations. These representations then undergo a process of voice synthesis, where they are transformed into audible speech. Developers work on various aspects of the software, including the accuracy, speed, and naturalness of the generated speech to ensure a seamless and pleasant user experience. In the field of accessibility design, text-to-speech software developers play a crucial role in making digital content more inclusive and accessible to a wider audience. By providing a means for individuals with visual impairments or reading difficulties to access written information through auditory means, these developers help bridge the accessibility gap and promote equal opportunities for all. Furthermore, text-to-speech software developers collaborate with accessibility experts and organizations to ensure that their tools meet the specific needs and requirements of users with disabilities. They engage in user testing, feedback collection, and continuous improvement cycles to enhance the usability and effectiveness of their software. In conclusion, text-to-speech software developers are instrumental in creating and improving software programs that convert written text into spoken words. Through their efforts, they contribute to the accessibility design field by enabling individuals with visual impairments or reading difficulties to access and comprehend information in a more accessible and inclusive manner.

Text-To-Speech Software

Text-to-Speech (TTS) software refers to a tool or program that converts written text or electronic documents into spoken words. It aims to assist individuals with visual impairments or reading difficulties by providing an auditory representation of the text content. TTS software is a key component of accessibility design, as it promotes equal access to information and enhances the user experience for individuals who rely on auditory communication. Typically, TTS software operates by analyzing the text using Natural Language Processing techniques, interpreting the structure and meaning of sentences and paragraphs, and generating an audio output that reflects the intended message. The software can be integrated into various devices and platforms, including computers, mobile phones, tablets, and even assistive technologies like screen readers. One crucial aspect of TTS software design is ensuring a clear and natural voice output. Developers strive to create high-quality synthesized voices that convey the intended emotions and nuances of the text effectively. These voices should be easy to understand and pleasant to listen to, enabling users to engage with the content effortlessly. TTS software offers various customization options to cater to individual preferences and needs. Users can adjust the speed, pitch, and volume of the synthesized voice according to their comfort. Some software even allows users to choose from different voice options, languages, and accents, further enhancing the user experience and personalization. The applications of TTS software are extensive. In addition to providing accessibility for visually impaired individuals, it can be utilized in educational settings to support students with reading difficulties or language challenges. It also finds utility in industries such as call centers and customer service, where automated voice systems can provide efficient and consistent responses to customers. In conclusion, Text-to-Speech (TTS) software is an essential tool in accessibility design, benefiting individuals with visual impairments or reading difficulties by converting electronic text into spoken words. Its development focuses on creating clear and natural synthesized voices that can be customized to suit individual preferences. TTS software plays a crucial role in promoting equal access to information and enhancing the user experience for a diverse range of users.

Text-To-Speech (TTS) Software

Text-to-Speech (TTS) software is a vital tool in the context of accessibility design. It is a technology that converts written text into spoken words, allowing individuals with visual impairments or other reading difficulties to access and comprehend written information with ease. TTS software works by using advanced algorithms to analyze and interpret written text, converting it into natural-sounding human speech. This technology enables individuals with disabilities to effectively consume content that would otherwise be inaccessible to them.

Text-To-Speech

Text-to-Speech, also known as TTS, is an accessibility design feature that converts written text into spoken words. This technology allows individuals with visual impairments or reading difficulties to perceive and comprehend textual content through audio output. TTS synthesizes natural-sounding speech by processing and interpreting written text, enabling users to listen to the content read aloud instead of having to visually read it. TTS plays a pivotal role in making digital content more accessible and inclusive. By providing an alternative way of consuming information, it ensures that individuals with visual impairments or reading challenges can access and engage with various forms of textual content, such as websites, articles, documents, or digital books. Through the implementation of TTS, accessibility designers strive to eliminate barriers faced by individuals who struggle with traditional reading methods.

Touch Gestures

Touch gestures are a set of interactive movements and actions made with one or more fingers on a touch-sensitive device, such as a smartphone or tablet. These gestures are designed to allow users to navigate, interact with, and control digital content and applications, making them an essential element of accessibility design. By utilizing touch gestures, designers can create a user-friendly and intuitive interface that accommodates individuals with diverse abilities and disabilities. These gestures rely on a combination of finger movements, taps, swipes, pinches, and presses to provide users with a seamless and efficient browsing experience.

Trackball

A trackball is a type of input device used in accessibility design that provides an alternative way to control the movement of the cursor on a computer screen. Unlike a traditional computer mouse, which requires the user to move the device across a surface, a trackball is stationary and uses a ball on top that can be rotated with the user's fingers or palm. This rotation of the ball translates into movement of the cursor on the screen.

Universal Accessibility Symbols

Universal Accessibility Symbols are graphical representations that are used in the field of accessibility design to communicate information about the accessibility features and facilities available in a particular space, environment, or service. These symbols provide a visual language that improves communication and understanding, ensuring that individuals with diverse abilities can access and navigate public spaces and facilities with ease. The symbols are designed to be easily recognizable and universally understood, transcending language and cultural barriers. They are typically displayed on signs, maps, websites, and other communication materials to indicate the presence of accessible features such as wheelchair ramps, accessible parking, elevators, bathrooms, and assistive listening systems. The most commonly used universal accessibility symbol is the International Symbol of Access (ISA), also known as the wheelchair symbol. This symbol consists of a stylized figure of a person seated in a wheelchair, indicating that the facility or service is accessible to individuals with mobility impairments. The ISA is often accompanied by additional symbols that represent specific accessibility features, such as a tactile symbol for accessible pathways or a symbol for hearing loop systems for individuals with hearing impairments. In addition to the wheelchair symbol, other symbols may be used to indicate different types of accessibility, such as a symbol representing a person with a white cane for individuals with visual impairments, or a symbol representing a person with a communication board for individuals with speech impairments. These symbols help individuals with disabilities identify the resources and support available to them in a particular environment. It is important for designers, architects, and organizations to incorporate universal accessibility symbols into their designs and communication materials to ensure that individuals of all abilities can navigate and access public spaces and services independently and with dignity. By using these symbols, we create a more inclusive and welcoming environment for everyone, regardless of their abilities. The use of universal accessibility symbols promotes equal access, independence, and social inclusion for individuals with disabilities. It enhances their ability to participate fully in society, access employment opportunities, and enjoy cultural and recreational activities. By implementing these symbols, we demonstrate our commitment to diversity and inclusion, and the creation of accessible environments for all.

Universal Design Assessment Services

Universal Design Assessment Services is a comprehensive evaluation and consulting process that focuses on ensuring accessibility and inclusivity for people with disabilities in various environments and settings. This assessment service aims to assess the level of accessibility in built environments, technology, products, and services, and provide recommendations for improvement to meet the needs of individuals with diverse abilities. Universal Design Assessment Services involves a systematic and methodical approach to identify and address barriers that may prevent people with disabilities from fully participating and accessing resources, services, and facilities. It aims to create an inclusive and equal opportunity environment for all individuals, regardless of their age, ability, or disability.

Universal Design Assessment

Universal Design is an approach to design that aims to create products, environments, and systems that are accessible and usable by all people, regardless of their age, ability, or background. It is a concept that originated in the field of architecture but has since been applied to various other disciplines, including web design, product design, and graphic design. The key principle of Universal Design is to ensure that individuals with disabilities are able to independently and safely use a product or environment, without the need for adaptation or specialized design. This is achieved by incorporating inclusive design features that accommodate a wide range of abilities and characteristics, including physical, sensory, cognitive, and neurological. In the context of accessibility design for the web, Universal Design means creating websites and web content that are accessible to all users, including those with disabilities. This includes people with visual impairments who may use screen readers or magnification tools, individuals with hearing impairments who may rely on captions or transcripts, and those with mobility impairments who may use assistive devices such as switches or keyboard alternatives. To ensure the accessibility of a website, several aspects of Universal Design need to be considered. This includes providing alternative text descriptions for images, using clear and concise language, ensuring proper color contrast for text and background, providing keyboard navigation options, and designing flexible layouts that can adapt to different screen sizes and resolutions. Universal Design also extends beyond accessibility to consider the diverse needs and preferences of all users. This means designing for a wide range of devices and technologies, considering cultural and linguistic differences, and providing customization options that allow users to personalize their experience. By embracing Universal Design principles, designers can create inclusive and user-friendly experiences that benefit all individuals, regardless of their abilities or disabilities. Universal Design not only increases accessibility for people with disabilities but also improves usability for all users, resulting in a more inclusive and equitable digital environment. Universal Design Assessment therefore plays a crucial role in ensuring that websites and digital content are accessible to all individuals, providing equal opportunities and equal access to information and services.

Universal Design Principles

Universal Design Principles refer to a set of guidelines and considerations that ensure the accessibility and usability of products, environments, and services for individuals with diverse abilities and disabilities. These principles are specifically designed to eliminate barriers and create inclusive designs that can be used by everyone, regardless of their age, size, or ability. The first principle of Universal Design is equitable use, which means that the design should be useful and accessible to individuals with different abilities. This involves providing the same means of use for all users, avoiding segregating or stigmatizing any particular group. For example, providing ramps and elevators alongside stairs in a building ensures equitable use for individuals with mobility impairments. The second principle is flexibility in use, which focuses on designing products and environments that cater to a wide range of user preferences and abilities. This principle allows users to choose the most comfortable and convenient way of interacting with a product. For instance, designing a website with multiple navigation options, such as keyboard shortcuts and voice commands, ensures flexibility in use for individuals with varying motor abilities. Simple and intuitive use is the third principle of Universal Design, emphasizing the importance of making products and services easy to understand and operate for all users. This principle aims to eliminate complexity and provide clear instructions and feedback. For example, using clear and concise language in user interfaces helps individuals with cognitive disabilities better comprehend and navigate through a system. Perceptible information is the fourth principle, which focuses on presenting information and feedback in a way that is perceivable by all users, including those with sensory impairments. This involves using multiple modes of communication, such as text, images, and audio, to convey information effectively. For instance, providing closed captions or transcripts for videos ensures that individuals with hearing impairments can access the content. Tolerance for error, the fifth principle, aims to minimize the consequences of mistakes and provide a forgiving design that allows users to easily recover from errors. This principle is important for individuals with cognitive impairments, as it reduces frustration and allows them to navigate through a system without facing significant barriers. Using clear error messages and providing options to undo or correct actions are examples of implementing this principle. The final principle is low physical effort, which focuses on minimizing the physical effort required to use a product or service. This principle benefits individuals with physical disabilities by reducing fatigue and strain associated with interactions. Implementing this principle may involve using ergonomic designs, reducing repetitive motions, and providing alternatives to manual manipulations.

Universal Design For Learning (UDL)

Universal Design for Learning (UDL) is an approach to designing and delivering instruction that ensures accessibility and inclusivity for all learners. It is a framework that provides educators with strategies and guidelines to create flexible learning environments that can be accessed and used by individuals with diverse needs and abilities. UDL is rooted in the principles of accessibility, equity, and inclusivity. It recognizes that learners differ in their abilities, preferences, and learning styles, and aims to provide multiple means of representation, expression, and engagement to meet these diverse needs. By doing so, UDL promotes equal opportunities for all learners to access and participate in the learning process.

Universal Design

Universal design in the context of accessibility design refers to the concept of creating products, environments, and systems that are inherently accessible and usable by people with diverse abilities, without the need for specialized adaptations or modifications. This approach to design aims to ensure equal access and inclusion for all individuals, regardless of their age, size, mobility, sensory abilities, or cognitive capabilities. By integrating accessibility features into the initial design process, universal design eliminates the need for retrofits or accommodations, ultimately promoting inclusivity and independence.

Usability Testing With Disabilities Consultancies

Usability testing with disabilities consultancies refers to the process of evaluating the accessibility and usability of a product, service, or website by involving individuals with disabilities, who are often represented by specialized consultancies or organizations.These consultancies specialize in providing feedback and recommendations based on the unique needs and perspectives of individuals with disabilities. They conduct usability tests using various assistive technologies, adaptive devices, and alternative input methods to simulate the experiences of people with diverse disabilities.

Usability Testing With Disabilities Tools

Usability Testing with Disabilities Tools refers to a set of tools and techniques used in the field of accessibility design to evaluate the usability of digital products and services for individuals with disabilities. These tools aim to identify potential barriers and challenges that users with disabilities might encounter when interacting with a website, application, or other digital interfaces. By conducting usability testing with disabilities tools, designers and developers can gain valuable insights into the user experience of individuals with various impairments, including but not limited to visual, auditory, motor, and cognitive disabilities.

Usability Testing With Disabilities

Usability Testing with Disabilities is a research method used in the context of accessibility design to evaluate the effectiveness and efficiency of a website or application for individuals with disabilities. It involves observing and recording the experiences of users with disabilities as they interact with the digital product, with the aim of identifying barriers and areas for improvement in the design. The purpose of Usability Testing with Disabilities is to ensure that digital products are accessible to individuals with disabilities, including but not limited to visual, auditory, motor, and cognitive impairments. By involving users with disabilities in the testing process, designers and developers can gain insights into how the design may impact these users' ability to navigate, understand, and interact with the digital product.

Usability Testing With People With Disabilities

Usability testing with people with disabilities refers to the process of evaluating the accessibility and user experience of a website or application by involving individuals with different disabilities. This testing is conducted to ensure that the design, functionality, and content of a digital product can be easily accessed and used by people with various impairments. Inclusive design aims to create products that are accessible to all users, regardless of their disabilities. Usability testing with people with disabilities plays a crucial role in achieving this goal. By actively involving individuals with disabilities in the testing process, designers and developers can identify and address accessibility barriers that may hinder their ability to use the product effectively. During the usability testing, participants with disabilities are given tasks to perform on the website or application while researchers observe and record their interactions. This testing is conducted in a controlled environment, allowing researchers to collect qualitative and quantitative data on the user experience, ease of navigation, and overall accessibility of the product. People with disabilities who are involved in usability testing may have a range of impairments, such as visual, hearing, cognitive, or motor limitations. The testing process takes into account their specific needs and uses assistive technologies or adaptive strategies that they commonly rely on to navigate digital interfaces. This ensures that the product is optimized for compatibility with screen readers, alternative input devices, voice control applications, or other assistive technologies. The insights gained from usability testing with people with disabilities provide valuable feedback for improving the accessibility and usability of a digital product. Designers and developers can identify and rectify any issues or barriers that prevent people with disabilities from effectively using the product. This can include making content more perceivable and understandable, improving keyboard navigation, providing alternative text for non-text elements, and optimizing color contrast. In conclusion, usability testing with people with disabilities is an essential component of the accessibility design process. By involving individuals with disabilities in the testing phase, designers and developers gain valuable insights into the usability and accessibility of their digital products. This ensures that the final product meets the needs of all users, regardless of their abilities or impairments.

Usability Testing

Usability testing, in the context of accessibility design, refers to the systematic evaluation of a website or application to determine how effectively and efficiently users with disabilities are able to interact with and navigate through the digital product. During usability testing, individuals with various disabilities are given specific tasks to perform within the website or application. These tasks are designed to assess the ease of use, comprehensibility, and overall accessibility of the digital product. Testers may include individuals with visual impairments, hearing impairments, motor disabilities, cognitive impairments, and other types of disabilities.

Usability For People With Disabilities

Accessibility design focuses on creating products, services, or environments that can be easily used by individuals with disabilities. Usability for people with disabilities refers to the extent to which individuals with disabilities can effectively and efficiently use these accessible designs. Accessibility design aims to remove barriers and create inclusive environments where everyone, regardless of their abilities, can independently access and use products or services. Usability plays a crucial role in achieving this goal. It ensures that individuals with disabilities can seamlessly interact with and derive benefits from accessible designs, without facing unnecessary challenges or disadvantages. People with disabilities may have various impairments, such as vision or hearing loss, motor disabilities, cognitive impairments, or reduced dexterity. Usability for people with disabilities ensures that these individuals can navigate, perceive, understand, and interact with accessible designs in a way that meets their unique needs, preferences, and abilities. For individuals with visual impairments, usability includes features such as alternative text for images, consistent and logical page structure, resizable text, and compatibility with screen readers. These features allow users to access and understand the content of a website or application, even if they cannot rely on visual cues. People with hearing impairments require usability features like captions and transcripts for audio content, visual notifications for sounds, and clear visual cues to indicate important information. These features enable individuals to comprehend and engage with multimedia content effectively, regardless of their hearing ability. Motor disabilities may necessitate usability aspects like keyboard navigation, large clickable areas, and customizable input options, which allow users to interact with accessible designs using alternative input devices or modifications. Such features ensure that individuals with motor impairments can efficiently operate and control devices or interfaces. Cognitive impairments may require usability considerations like clear and concise language, consistent and intuitive navigation, logical information structure, and error prevention techniques. These features make it easier for individuals to understand, remember, and follow the flow of information within a design. Usability for people with disabilities goes beyond accommodating individual impairments. It encompasses a user-centered approach that considers the diverse needs and abilities of people with disabilities, ensuring that they can independently and effectively use accessible designs. In conclusion, usability for people with disabilities refers to the extent to which individuals with disabilities can effectively interact with and benefit from accessible designs. By considering the needs and abilities of individuals with disabilities, usability in accessibility design aims to create inclusive experiences that empower and enable all users, regardless of their disabilities, to access and use products or services.

User Agent

A user agent, in the context of accessibility design, refers to the software or device used by individuals to access and interact with digital content. It can include web browsers, assistive technologies, and other applications that facilitate the presentation and interaction of content on various devices. The primary purpose of user agents is to render content in a way that is perceivable and operable for users. In the context of accessibility, user agents play a crucial role in ensuring that individuals with disabilities can access and navigate digital content effectively.

User Experience Accessibility

User experience accessibility refers to the practice of designing digital products and services in a way that ensures they can be accessed and used by individuals with diverse abilities and disabilities. It involves creating inclusive user experiences that remove barriers and provide equal access to information, functionality, and interactions. When designing for accessibility, it is crucial to consider the needs and limitations of various user groups, including those with visual, motor, hearing, cognitive, and neurological impairments. This entails employing design principles, techniques, and assistive technologies that enhance usability and address specific accessibility challenges.

User Experience For Accessibility

User-Centered Design

User-Centered Design, in the context of accessibility design, refers to the approach of creating digital products or services that prioritize the needs and abilities of all users, including those with disabilities. It is an inclusive design process that puts the user at the center, ensuring that their diverse needs and preferences are considered and addressed. In user-centered design, every stage of the design process is guided by a deep understanding of the target users. This involves conducting user research to gain insights into their behaviors, needs, and challenges. By understanding the experiences and goals of people with disabilities, designers can create more inclusive and accessible digital experiences. Accessibility is a key aspect of user-centered design, aiming to remove barriers that may prevent people with disabilities from accessing and interacting with digital products. This includes considerations for various disabilities, such as visual impairments, hearing impairments, cognitive impairments, and motor limitations. By applying accessibility principles, designers can ensure that information is perceivable, operable, understandable, and robust for all users. The user-centered design process typically involves iterative design and testing cycles, where prototypes and designs are evaluated by users with disabilities. User feedback is gathered and incorporated into the design to improve the overall usability and accessibility. This ensures that the final product or service meets the needs of a diverse range of users. By prioritizing accessibility in user-centered design, organizations can not only create inclusive products but also comply with legal requirements, such as the Web Content Accessibility Guidelines (WCAG). These guidelines provide a set of recommendations and best practices for making web content more accessible to people with disabilities. In summary, user-centered design in the context of accessibility is an inclusive approach that considers the diverse needs and abilities of users, particularly those with disabilities. It involves understanding their experiences, conducting user research, and incorporating accessibility principles throughout the design process. This ensures that digital products and services are accessible and usable by everyone, regardless of their abilities.

Video Accessibility Consultants

Video Accessibility Consultants are professionals who provide expertise and guidance on the design and implementation of accessible video content. Their role is to ensure that videos are inclusive and can be effectively accessed by individuals with disabilities. These consultants work closely with organizations and content creators to ensure that their videos meet the accessibility standards and guidelines specified by various regulatory bodies, such as the Web Content Accessibility Guidelines (WCAG). They possess in-depth knowledge of accessibility requirements for different types of disabilities, including visual, hearing, cognitive, and motor impairments. In their role, video accessibility consultants conduct thorough assessments of the video content and identify any barriers or limitations that may hinder individuals with disabilities from fully accessing and comprehending the content. They analyze factors such as video quality, closed captioning, audio descriptions, and interactive features to determine if they meet the necessary accessibility standards. Based on their findings, these consultants provide recommendations and strategies to improve the accessibility of the video content. They may suggest, for example, adding closed captions for individuals with hearing impairments, providing audio descriptions for those with visual impairments, or ensuring that interactive elements are accessible via keyboard for individuals with motor impairments. Video accessibility consultants also play a crucial role in educating content creators and organizations on best practices for video accessibility. They keep themselves updated with the latest advancements and guidelines in the field of accessibility design and proactively share their knowledge and expertise with clients. In summary, video accessibility consultants help ensure that video content is inclusive and accessible to all individuals, regardless of their disabilities. Through their expertise and recommendations, they play a pivotal role in creating an inclusive digital environment that allows everyone to access and engage with video content equally.

Video Accessibility Tools

Video accessibility tools refer to a range of technologies and strategies designed to make videos more accessible to individuals with disabilities. These tools aim to remove barriers and provide equal access to video content for people with visual, hearing, or cognitive impairments. One key component of video accessibility tools is closed captioning. Closed captions display a text version of the audio content, allowing individuals with hearing impairments to read along while watching the video. Captions also benefit individuals who prefer to watch videos without sound or in loud environments where audio may not be audible. Another important accessibility tool is audio description. Audio description provides a verbal narration of visual elements, such as actions, settings, and facial expressions, to assist individuals who are blind or have low vision in understanding the visual content of a video. By providing this additional auditory information, individuals can fully comprehend the video's context and visual details. Sign language interpretation is another significant accessibility tool for videos. This involves the presence of a sign language interpreter or the inclusion of sign language overlays to facilitate understanding for individuals who are deaf or hard of hearing. Sign language interpretation ensures that important auditory information is conveyed through sign language visuals, enabling individuals to comprehend and engage with the video content. Some video accessibility tools also focus on cognitive accessibility. For instance, videos can include visual cues, such as color contrast, large text, and clear typography, to support individuals with cognitive disabilities. Additionally, features like transcript availability and searchable captions contribute to cognitive accessibility by allowing users to easily navigate and find specific information within a video. In conclusion, video accessibility tools are crucial in ensuring that videos are inclusive and accessible to individuals with disabilities. By incorporating these tools into the design and production of videos, content creators can provide equal access to information, entertainment, and educational resources for all individuals, regardless of their abilities.

Video Relay Service (VRS)

Video Relay Service (VRS) is an accessibility design that enables individuals who are deaf, hard of hearing, or speech-impaired to communicate in real-time using sign language. VRS allows these individuals to make telephone calls to hearing individuals through a sign language interpreter, effectively bridging the communication gap. VRS is typically provided through a videophone, which consists of a camera and screen for video communication. The user signs to the interpreter through the camera, and the interpreter relays the message by speaking to the hearing individual on the other end of the call. The interpreter also signs the response back to the user, allowing for a seamless conversation. VRS offers several benefits for individuals with hearing impairments or speech disabilities. It provides them with the ability to independently make phone calls without relying on text-based communication or third-party assistance. This allows for more natural and efficient communication, as sign language is the user's preferred mode of communication. In addition to facilitating one-on-one conversations, VRS can also be used in group settings. Multiple individuals can participate in a call, with each person using their own videophone and connected through the interpreter. This allows for inclusive communication among people who use sign language, regardless of their physical location. Furthermore, VRS enhances accessibility in emergency situations. When an individual with hearing impairments or speech disabilities needs to contact emergency services, they can use VRS to quickly communicate their needs and receive assistance. The interpreter acts as a vital link between the individual and emergency personnel, ensuring that crucial information is accurately conveyed.

Visual Accessibility

Visual accessibility is a design aspect that aims to make digital content accessible to individuals with visual impairments or disabilities. It involves creating webpages, applications, and documents in a way that accommodates the diverse needs of visually impaired users, enabling them to perceive, understand, and interact with the content effectively. In the context of accessibility design, visual accessibility primarily focuses on ensuring that visually impaired individuals can access and comprehend digital content through various assistive technologies, such as screen readers, magnifiers, and braille displays. It involves considering aspects such as color contrast, text size, font type, and layout to optimize the readability and usability of the content for a wide range of users. Color contrast is a crucial component of visual accessibility as it ensures that individuals with low vision or color blindness can distinguish between different elements on a webpage or application. Sufficient contrast between text and background helps in enhancing readability and ease of navigation, allowing users to perceive and comprehend the information presented. Text size and font type play a significant role in visual accessibility. Providing options to adjust the text size ensures that visually impaired users can personalize the content to their needs, enhancing legibility. Additionally, using clear, sans-serif fonts makes it easier for users with visual impairments to read the text, as these fonts are generally more accessible and well-suited for screen reading technologies. Layout and structure are essential in visual accessibility as they help users navigate and comprehend digital content efficiently. Clear headings, logical structure, and consistent formatting facilitate the overall understanding of the content. Properly organized content ensures that visually impaired users can quickly locate and access the information they are seeking. Visual accessibility also includes alternative text descriptions for images, charts, and graphs, allowing visually impaired users to understand the visual context through assistive technologies. These descriptions provide a textual representation of the visual elements, enabling users to perceive the content's intent accurately. In summary, visual accessibility is an integral aspect of accessibility design that focuses on making digital content accessible to individuals with visual impairments. By considering elements such as color contrast, text size, font type, layout, and alternative text descriptions, visual accessibility ensures that visually impaired users can perceive, understand, and interact with digital content effectively, promoting inclusivity and equal access to information.

Visual Impairment Aids

Visual impairment aids refer to assistive devices or technology that have been specifically designed to enable individuals with visual impairments to access and interact with their environment more effectively. These aids aim to compensate for, or overcome, the limitations imposed by their visual impairment, thereby promoting their independence and improving their overall quality of life. One category of visual impairment aids are magnification devices. These devices use various technologies such as lenses, digital displays, or cameras to enlarge printed material, images, or objects. They allow individuals with low vision or partial sight to read texts, view photographs, or see distant objects more clearly. Examples of magnification aids include handheld magnifiers, stand magnifiers, and video magnifiers. Another category of aids are braille and tactile devices. These devices convert visual information into tactile or auditory output, enabling individuals with visual impairments to access textual information and navigate their surroundings. Braille displays, for instance, are devices that convert digital text into braille characters, which can be read with the fingers. Tactile maps, on the other hand, provide spatial information through raised surfaces and textures, allowing users to understand the layout of unfamiliar places. Audio devices are an essential component of visual impairment aids. These devices convert visual information into audio output, making it accessible to individuals with visual impairments. Screen readers, for example, use speech synthesis technology to read aloud the content displayed on a computer or mobile device screen. Voice assistants, such as Amazon's Alexa or Apple's Siri, also aid in accessing information and performing tasks through voice commands. Navigation aids play a crucial role in enabling individuals with visual impairments to move around independently and safely. These aids include white canes, which act as extensions of the user's sense of touch, helping them detect obstacles and changes in the environment. Global Positioning System (GPS) technology has also been incorporated into wearable devices to provide turn-by-turn directions and alerts for users navigating unfamiliar or complex spaces. In conclusion, visual impairment aids encompass a wide range of devices and technologies that enhance the accessibility and functionality for individuals with visual impairments. These aids aim to compensate for vision loss, allowing users to carry out daily tasks, access information, and navigate their surroundings with greater ease and independence.

Voice Commands For Accessibility

Voice commands for accessibility refers to the use of spoken language as a means of interacting with digital devices and applications in order to enhance accessibility for individuals with disabilities. This form of human-computer interaction allows users to control and navigate technology using their voice, reducing the reliance on traditional input methods such as keyboards or touchscreens. Through the use of voice commands, individuals with limited dexterity or physical impairments are able to access and interact with digital content and applications more easily. This technology is particularly beneficial for individuals with mobility impairments, such as those with spinal cord injuries or conditions like arthritis, who may find it challenging to use traditional input devices.

Voice Commands

Speech recognition or voice commands refer to the technology that enables users to interact with a device, application, or website by using their voice instead of traditional input methods like typing or clicking. It involves converting spoken words into text and then using that text to perform various tasks or commands. In the context of accessibility design, voice commands play a crucial role in making digital content and interfaces more inclusive and accessible to individuals with disabilities. People with mobility impairments, visual impairments, or conditions that limit their ability to use their hands or fingers can benefit greatly from voice commands as an alternative input method. By incorporating voice command capabilities into design, developers can provide individuals with disabilities an accessible means of navigating and interacting with digital content. Voice commands can be used to perform a wide range of functions, including but not limited to: 1. Navigation: Users can use voice commands to navigate through menus, websites, or applications. For example, they can say "Go back," "Open settings," or "Scroll down" to perform these actions. 2. Content control: Voice commands can be used to control various aspects of digital content, such as playing or pausing media, adjusting volume, or switching between different sections. 3. Form filling: Instead of manually typing in form fields, users can use voice commands to input text or select options, making it easier for individuals with dexterity impairments or limited hand function. 4. Search: Voice commands can be used to initiate searches within apps or websites, providing users with the ability to find information or perform actions quickly without the need for manual input. 5. Virtual assistant integration: Voice commands can be utilized to interact with virtual assistants like Siri, Google Assistant, or Cortana, enabling users to perform tasks, ask questions, or receive information through voice interaction. By incorporating voice commands, designers can ensure that individuals with disabilities have equal access to digital content and services. This technology enhances usability and removes barriers for those who may struggle with traditional input methods. Through accessibility-focused design practices, websites and applications can create a more inclusive experience for all users.

VoiceOver (Accessibility Feature)

VoiceOver is an accessibility feature designed to assist individuals with visual impairments in navigating and interacting with digital content on Apple devices. It is a screen reader that provides spoken feedback, allowing users to hear descriptions of on-screen elements and perform various gestures and actions using only their voice or a compatible external input device. With VoiceOver enabled, users can navigate through the user interface by swiping their finger on the screen or by using specific gestures on external input devices like a Braille display or a keyboard. As the user moves their focus, VoiceOver announces the name and type of each element, such as buttons, links, headings, and form fields. This audible feedback enables individuals with visual disabilities to understand the layout and structure of a page, facilitating independent navigation. Additionally, VoiceOver offers various customization options to enhance usability for each user's specific needs. Users can adjust the speech rate, volume, and pitch of the spoken feedback, as well as enable sound effects to provide auditory cues. The rotor feature allows users to navigate through different types of content on a page, such as headings or links, by rotating their finger on the screen or using rotor-specific input commands on external devices. Furthermore, VoiceOver provides contextual information and guidance to help users interact with elements on the screen. For instance, it can describe the purpose or action associated with a button or notify users when they need to perform additional gestures to access certain functionalities. VoiceOver also supports text recognition, providing spoken feedback for text within images or other visual objects, enabling users to access information that may otherwise be inaccessible. Overall, VoiceOver plays a crucial role in creating an inclusive digital environment by allowing individuals with visual impairments to independently access and interact with the content on Apple devices. By providing spoken feedback, customizable settings, and contextual information, VoiceOver empowers users to navigate interfaces, complete tasks, and engage with digital experiences, facilitating equal access and participation for all.

VoiceOver (IOS)

VoiceOver is an accessibility feature on iOS devices that assists individuals with visual impairments in navigating and using the device. It is a screen reader that provides spoken descriptions of on-screen elements, allowing users to interact with apps, websites, and other content. When VoiceOver is enabled, it reads out the names of buttons, text fields, icons, and other interface elements, as well as any content displayed on the screen. It also provides auditory cues to indicate gestures and actions, such as swiping, tapping, and scrolling. Users can navigate through the elements on the screen by swiping their fingers or by using gestures specific to VoiceOver. VoiceOver is highly customizable, allowing users to adjust the speed and volume of the spoken feedback, as well as the verbosity of the descriptions. This allows individuals to tailor the experience to their specific needs and preferences. In addition to the basic functionality, VoiceOver offers advanced features to enhance usability. For example, it supports braille displays, so individuals who read braille can connect their device to a braille display and read the on-screen content through the display. It also provides rotor navigation, a gesture-based mechanism that allows users to quickly navigate through different types of content, such as headings, links, and tables. VoiceOver is an important tool for making iOS devices accessible to people with visual impairments, enabling them to independently use and enjoy their devices. It enables individuals to access a wide range of apps, communicate through various means, browse the web, and perform tasks that were previously challenging or impossible. VoiceOver encourages inclusivity and ensures that individuals with visual impairments can fully participate in the digital world.

WCAG 2.1 Testing Tools

WCAG 2.1 Testing Tools are tools used in the context of accessibility design to assess and evaluate the compliance of web content with the Web Content Accessibility Guidelines (WCAG) version 2.1. These tools provide a means to test and measure the accessibility of websites, applications, and digital content, allowing designers and developers to identify areas where improvements are needed to ensure accessibility for all users. WCAG 2.1 Testing Tools typically include automated tools, such as web accessibility checkers and validators, which scan web pages and detect common accessibility issues, such as missing alternative text for images or improper use of headings. These tools provide feedback and reports on the identified issues, assisting designers and developers in understanding the areas where their content may not be fully accessible and allowing them to make necessary adjustments. In addition to automated tools, WCAG 2.1 Testing Tools may also include manual testing techniques. This involves conducting manual evaluations and assessments to identify accessibility barriers that automated tools may not detect. Manual testing may involve keyboard navigation, screen reader usage, and other assistive technologies to simulate the experience of users with disabilities. By directly experiencing the digital content and its interaction, designers and developers can gain insights into potential barriers and make appropriate modifications to improve accessibility. WCAG 2.1 Testing Tools are essential in the field of accessibility design as they provide a systematic and structured approach to assessing the accessibility of web content. By using these tools, designers and developers can ensure that their digital products and services are usable by individuals with disabilities and align with recognized accessibility standards. By addressing accessibility issues early in the design and development process, WCAG 2.1 Testing Tools contribute to creating an inclusive digital environment where all users can access and interact with the content in a meaningful and equitable manner.

WCAG 2.1

WCAG 2.1, or Web Content Accessibility Guidelines 2.1, is a set of guidelines developed by the World Wide Web Consortium (W3C) to ensure that web content is accessible to individuals with disabilities. These guidelines provide standards and criteria that designers and developers can follow to create websites and web applications that are usable for all users, regardless of their abilities or impairments. The main focus of WCAG 2.1 is to address the accessibility needs of individuals with various disabilities, including visual, auditory, physical, speech, cognitive, and neurological disabilities. By following these guidelines, designers can ensure that their websites are perceivable, operable, understandable, and robust for all users.

WCAG Compliance

WCAG Compliance refers to adherence to the guidelines provided by the Web Content Accessibility Guidelines (WCAG) for designing and developing accessible digital content. WCAG is a set of principles and technical specifications created by the World Wide Web Consortium (W3C) to ensure that people with disabilities can perceive, understand, navigate, and interact with websites and web-based applications. WCAG Compliance is essential in ensuring that digital content is accessible to all users, including those with disabilities. By following the WCAG guidelines, designers and developers ensure that their websites provide equal access and usability for individuals with visual, auditory, physical, cognitive, and neurological disabilities. WCAG Compliance addresses various aspects of web accessibility, including the use of clear and concise language, proper presentation of text alternatives for non-text content such as images, videos, and audio, consistent navigation and site structure, providing resizable text and content, and enabling keyboard accessibility for individuals who cannot use a mouse. Additionally, WCAG Compliance emphasizes the importance of designing websites that are compatible with assistive technologies such as screen readers, magnifiers, alternative keyboards, and voice recognition software. This includes providing sufficient color contrast, clear and consistent heading structures, and meaningful link text. WCAG Compliance involves conforming to three levels of accessibility standards: Level A, Level AA, and Level AAA. Level A addresses the most basic requirements for web accessibility, while Level AA covers a wider range of issues and is the recommended level of compliance. Level AAA represents the highest level of accessibility and includes additional guidelines that enhance usability for individuals with disabilities. By achieving WCAG Compliance, designers and developers promote inclusivity and ensure that their digital content is accessible to all individuals, regardless of their abilities or disabilities. This not only improves user experience but also helps businesses comply with legal requirements, such as the Americans with Disabilities Act (ADA) in the United States. In conclusion, WCAG Compliance is crucial for designing and developing accessible digital content that enables equal access and usability for individuals with disabilities. Adhering to WCAG guidelines ensures that websites are compatible with assistive technologies and provide a barrier-free experience for all users.

WCAG (Web Content Accessibility Guidelines)

WCAG (Web Content Accessibility Guidelines) are a set of internationally recognized standards that provide guidelines for making web content accessible to people with disabilities. These guidelines are created and maintained by the World Wide Web Consortium (W3C), an international community that develops open standards for the web. WCAG is designed to ensure that people with disabilities, such as auditory or visual impairments, physical disabilities, or cognitive limitations, can access and interact with web content effectively. It provides a framework for web developers and designers to follow in order to create websites and web applications that are inclusive and usable by everyone. WCAG guidelines cover a wide range of accessibility requirements, including but not limited to: 1. Perceivable: The content should be presented in a way that can be perceived by all users, regardless of their sensory abilities. This includes providing alternative text for images, captions for videos, and clear and concise content structure. 2. Operable: The content and functionality of the website should be operable through a variety of input methods, such as keyboard navigation or voice commands. It should also be easy to navigate and understand, with clear headings, labels, and consistent navigation elements. 3. Understandable: The website should be designed in a way that is easy to understand for all users. This includes using clear and simple language, providing instructions and feedback in a way that is easy to comprehend, and avoiding any elements that may cause confusion or distraction. 4. Robust: The website should be developed using technologies that are compatible with assistive technologies, such as screen readers or speech recognition software. It should also be able to adapt to different platforms and devices, ensuring a consistent and accessible experience for all users. By following WCAG guidelines, web designers and developers can create websites that are accessible to a wide range of users. This not only provides equal access to information and services for people with disabilities but also benefits other users, such as those using mobile devices or in situations where accessibility is limited. WCAG is an essential resource for ensuring that the web is inclusive and accessible to everyone, regardless of their abilities. It sets a standard for accessibility and encourages the development of accessible technologies that can be enjoyed by all users.

Web Accessibility Auditing Firms

A web accessibility auditing firm is a company that specializes in evaluating the accessibility of websites and digital content for individuals with disabilities. Their primary goal is to ensure that websites are designed and developed in a way that allows equal access and usability for all users, regardless of their disabilities or impairments. These firms conduct comprehensive audits and evaluations of websites, mobile applications, and other digital platforms to identify any barriers or limitations that may prevent individuals with disabilities from accessing or navigating the content effectively. They assess the compliance of websites with accessibility standards and guidelines, such as the Web Content Accessibility Guidelines (WCAG).

Web Accessibility Auditing Tools

Web Accessibility Auditing Tools refer to software programs or online services that are designed to evaluate the accessibility of a website or web application. These tools analyze the digital content and code of a web page to identify any potential barriers for individuals with disabilities, such as visual impairments, hearing impairments, motor disabilities, cognitive limitations, or other accessibility needs. The main purpose of web accessibility auditing tools is to help web developers and designers ensure that their websites are accessible and usable for all users, regardless of their abilities or disabilities. These tools provide feedback and recommendations on how to improve the accessibility of a website, following established guidelines and standards, such as the Web Content Accessibility Guidelines (WCAG) developed by the World Wide Web Consortium (W3C). Web accessibility auditing tools typically use automated tests and algorithms to scan web pages, evaluate the markup and structure of the content, and check for compatibility with assistive technologies, such as screen readers or voice recognition software. They can detect issues like missing alternative text for images, improper semantic structure, lack of keyboard accessibility, insufficient color contrast, or non-semantic use of HTML elements. Some web accessibility auditing tools can also simulate the experience of users with disabilities by emulating different assistive technologies or impairments. For example, they might allow the tester to navigate the website using only a keyboard, simulate screen reader output, or display the content with different color contrasts. These features help identify and address accessibility barriers that may not be apparent to designers and developers without disabilities. Web accessibility auditing tools can generate reports or provide detailed information about the accessibility issues found, including recommendations for remediation. However, it is important to note that these automated tools can only identify certain types of accessibility issues and might not catch all potential barriers. Manual testing and user feedback from individuals with disabilities are also essential for comprehensive web accessibility assessment and continuous improvement.

Web Accessibility Evaluation Tools

A web accessibility evaluation tool is a software tool or online service that helps evaluate and assess the accessibility of a website or web application. It analyzes the website's HTML, CSS, and JavaScript code, as well as its content and structure, to identify potential accessibility barriers and issues. These tools are used by web developers, designers, and content creators to ensure that their websites are accessible to people with disabilities. They help identify and fix common accessibility issues such as inadequate color contrast, missing alternative text for images, improper use of heading structure, and inaccessible forms or navigation.

Web Accessibility

Web Accessibility refers to the design and development of websites, web applications, and digital content that can be accessed and used by all individuals, regardless of their abilities or disabilities. It aims to ensure that people with visual, auditory, physical, cognitive, and neurological impairments can perceive, navigate, and interact with web content effectively and without barriers. Accessibility design focuses on creating inclusive and equal opportunities for all users to access and use information and services available on the web.

Web Content Accessibility Standards (WCAG)

Web Content Accessibility Standards (WCAG) are guidelines and principles that are developed and recommended by the World Wide Web Consortium (W3C) to ensure that digital content is accessible to people with disabilities. These standards are designed to provide a clear framework for developers, designers, and content creators to follow when designing and developing websites, applications, and other digital content. WCAG is based on four key principles: perceivable, operable, understandable, and robust. Perceivable means that all information and user interface components must be presented to users in a way that they can perceive. This includes providing alternatives for non-text content, ensuring content is adaptable to different sensory abilities, and making it easier for users to see and hear content. Operable means that users must be able to interact with all controls and interactive elements on the website. This includes making sure that keyboard accessibility is supported, providing enough time for users to read and interact with content, avoiding content that may cause seizures, and providing multiple ways to navigate and find information. Understandable means that content should be presented in a way that users can understand. This includes using clear and concise language, organizing content in a logical manner, providing instructions and feedback that are easy to understand, and helping users to avoid and correct mistakes. Robust means that web content must be compatible with a wide range of assistive technologies and future technologies. This includes using markup that can be parsed reliably by assistive technologies, ensuring that content is compatible with different browsers and operating systems, and using technologies that are accessible to users with disabilities. WCAG provides specific success criteria within each principle, ranging from basic to advanced levels of accessibility. These success criteria provide concrete measures and guidelines for designers and developers to ensure that their digital content meets the needs of people with disabilities. By adhering to WCAG, website owners and developers can create a more inclusive and accessible digital environment for all users.

WebAIM Contrast Checker

The WebAIM Contrast Checker is a web-based tool that helps ensure that the color contrast between text and its background meets accessibility guidelines. Accessibility design refers to designing websites and applications that can be easily accessed and used by people with disabilities. The purpose of the WebAIM Contrast Checker is to assess and determine if the contrast between text and background colors is sufficient for individuals with low vision or color blindness to perceive and read the content comfortably. These individuals may rely on high contrast for improved legibility and comprehension. The tool analyzes the color values of the text and background and provides a pass/fail result based on the WCAG (Web Content Accessibility Guidelines) standards. To use the WebAIM Contrast Checker, you provide the hexadecimal color codes, or select colors from their respective color pickers, for the text and background of the web element in question. The tool will then calculate the contrast ratio between the two colors. A contrast ratio of at least 4.5:1 is recommended for normal text and 3:1 for large text, according to WCAG 2.1. The tool instantly displays the contrast ratio result and whether it meets the accessibility standards. The WebAIM Contrast Checker allows web designers and developers to quickly test various color combinations and make informed decisions regarding the accessibility of their content. By using this tool, they can ensure that their websites comply with the established accessibility guidelines and provide an inclusive and user-friendly experience for all visitors. By validating color contrast, the WebAIM Contrast Checker contributes to enhancing the readability and usability of web content for individuals with visual impairments. It assists in preventing issues such as text blending into the background or being unreadable due to insufficient contrast. With increased accessibility, more people can access and engage with digital content, regardless of their disabilities or visual limitations. In summary, the WebAIM Contrast Checker is a valuable tool for web designers and developers to evaluate and improve the color contrast of their websites. By adhering to the recommended contrast ratios, they can facilitate equal access to information and create a more inclusive online environment for everyone.

WebAIM

WebAIM is an organization dedicated to promoting web accessibility for individuals with disabilities. They provide guidance and resources to help designers and developers create websites and web applications that are inclusive and usable for all visitors. Web accessibility refers to the practice of designing and developing websites that can be accessed and used by people with disabilities. This includes individuals with visual impairments, hearing impairments, mobility impairments, and cognitive impairments. In order to ensure web accessibility, designers and developers need to consider various factors. They should make sure that website content is perceivable, meaning that it can be perceived by all users regardless of their sensory abilities. This includes providing text alternatives for non-text content such as images, videos, and audio files, so that individuals who are blind or have visual impairments can still understand the information. Additionally, designers should make sure that website interfaces are operable, meaning that users can navigate and interact with them using different input methods. This includes providing keyboard accessibility, so that users who cannot use a mouse can still navigate through the website using only the keyboard. Web accessibility also involves ensuring that website content is understandable, so that users with cognitive impairments or language barriers can comprehend the information. This can be achieved by using clear and simple language, avoiding jargon and complex sentence structures. Lastly, designers and developers should make sure that websites are robust, meaning that they are compatible with a wide range of assistive technologies such as screen readers and voice recognition software. This involves using standard HTML markup, avoiding deprecated or proprietary technologies, and testing the website with different assistive technologies. By following WebAIM's guidelines and recommendations, designers and developers can create accessible websites that provide equal access and equal opportunity to individuals with disabilities. Web accessibility is not only a legal requirement in many countries, but it is also an ethical consideration, as all individuals should be able to fully participate and engage with the digital world. To summarize, WebAIM is an organization that promotes web accessibility and provides valuable resources and guidelines for designing and developing inclusive websites. By ensuring that websites are perceivable, operable, understandable, and robust, designers and developers can create accessible web experiences for all users.

WebSockets Accessibility Tools

WebSockets Accessibility Tools are web development tools specifically designed to ensure that WebSocket-based applications are accessible to all users, including those with disabilities. These tools assist developers in creating WebSocket applications that adhere to accessibility standards and guidelines, making them perceivable, operable, understandable, and robust for individuals with various impairments. Accessibility tools for WebSockets typically provide a range of features and utilities to aid developers in creating inclusive applications. Some of these tools include: 1. WebSocket Accessibility Testing: These tools allow developers to test the accessibility of their WebSocket applications. This includes checking for compatibility with assistive technologies, evaluating keyboard navigation, and ensuring proper implementation of focus and ARIA roles. 2. Code Analysis and Recommendations: These tools analyze WebSocket application code and provide recommendations to improve accessibility. They can highlight potential accessibility issues, suggest appropriate ARIA attributes, and help developers make their applications more accessible to assistive technologies. 3. Assistive Technology Simulation: To enhance testing and debugging, these tools simulate the behavior of various assistive technologies. They allow developers to experience their WebSocket applications as users with disabilities would, providing insights into potential accessibility barriers and helping in the identification and resolution of issues. 4. Documentation and Guidelines: WebSockets accessibility tools often come with resources, guidelines, and best practices for developers to refer to during the development process. These documents provide instructions on implementing accessibility features, techniques for optimizing WebSocket application accessibility, and strategies for addressing common accessibility challenges. By utilizing WebSockets Accessibility Tools, developers can ensure that WebSocket applications are usable and accessible to everyone, regardless of their abilities. These tools play a crucial role in promoting digital inclusion, enabling individuals with disabilities to access and interact with WebSocket-based applications on par with their peers.

WebSockets Accessibility

WebSockets accessibility refers to the design and implementation of the WebSocket protocol with the goal of ensuring equal access and usability for all individuals, regardless of their abilities or disabilities. WebSockets is a communication protocol that provides full-duplex communication channels over a single TCP connection. It allows for real-time, bi-directional communication between a client (typically a web browser) and a server, facilitating interactive and dynamic web applications. In the context of accessibility design, it is important to ensure that WebSockets can be used by individuals with various disabilities, including those who rely on assistive technologies for web browsing.

WebSockets

WebSockets are a communication protocol that enables interactive, real-time communication between a client (typically a web browser) and a server. Unlike traditional HTTP connections, which are stateless and require a new request to be made for each server response, WebSockets provide a persistent and bidirectional connection that allows for constant communication between the client and server. WebSockets play a crucial role in accessibility design by facilitating the development of inclusive and interactive web applications. They offer several benefits that enhance the accessibility experience for users with disabilities. Firstly, WebSockets support real-time updates, enabling developers to create dynamic content that can be immediately communicated to the user. This is particularly beneficial for individuals with visual impairments who rely on screen readers or assistive technologies. With WebSockets, changes in content can be instantly conveyed to users, creating a more seamless and responsive user experience. Moreover, WebSockets enable the implementation of accessible chat features, which are essential for individuals with hearing impairments or who rely on alternative means of communication. By establishing a persistent connection between the client and server, users can receive real-time updates in chat conversations, ensuring that they are not left out of important discussions or updates. WebSockets also play a crucial role in accessibility by enhancing the performance of web applications. With traditional HTTP connections, requests for server updates must be made continuously, resulting in increased latency and slower application performance. By using WebSockets, developers can establish a constant connection that significantly reduces the overhead associated with repetitive requests, resulting in faster and smoother performance for all users, including those with disabilities. In conclusion, WebSockets are a communication protocol that provides a persistent and bidirectional connection between a client and server. In the context of accessibility design, WebSockets enhance the user experience for individuals with disabilities by enabling real-time updates, facilitating inclusive chat features, and improving web application performance. By incorporating WebSockets into their designs, developers can create more accessible and user-friendly applications for all users.

Wheelchair Accessibility

Wheelchair Accessibility refers to the ability of individuals using wheelchairs or other mobility devices to access and navigate a physical environment with ease and safety. It encompasses the design, layout, and features of buildings, public spaces, transportation systems, and other facilities, ensuring equal opportunities for people with disabilities to participate in society. In the context of accessibility design, wheelchair accessibility aims to remove barriers and provide inclusive environments for people with mobility impairments. It involves creating spaces and infrastructure that accommodate individuals using wheelchairs, both manually propelled and motorized versions. This includes ramps, elevators, wider doorways, accessible parking spaces, tactile indicators, and other features that enable smooth and independent movement for wheelchair users.

Windows Narrator

Windows Narrator is an accessibility feature in the Microsoft Windows operating system designed to provide screen reading capabilities for individuals with visual impairments. It is a built-in tool that uses synthetic speech to read aloud the content displayed on the screen, enabling users to navigate and interact with their computer without relying solely on visual cues.Windows Narrator enhances accessibility by providing a way for visually impaired individuals to access and interact with the digital world. It allows users to listen to documents, emails, web pages, and other content, enabling them to independently perform tasks and access information. By converting text into speech, Windows Narrator provides an auditory interface, allowing visually impaired users to perceive and comprehend the visual elements on the screen.

Wired Mouse

A wired mouse is an input device used in computer systems, designed to provide accessibility to users with mobility impairments or who prefer an alternative to the touchpad or trackpad. It is connected to the computer via a wire, providing a constant and reliable connection. The primary purpose of a wired mouse is to allow users to control the cursor on the screen and interact with various graphical user interfaces (GUI). It consists of a body that fits comfortably in the hand, with buttons and a scroll wheel that can be easily pressed or rotated to perform different functions. The movement of the mouse is translated into cursor movement on the screen, enabling users to navigate through different applications, click on icons or buttons, select text, and perform other tasks. The accessibility design of a wired mouse takes into consideration the needs of individuals with limited dexterity, coordination, or hand strength. It often features a shape that conforms to the natural curvature of the hand, reducing discomfort and fatigue during extended use. The size and positioning of the buttons and scroll wheel are also optimized to accommodate different hand sizes and minimize strain. For individuals with motor impairments, the sensitivity of the mouse can be adjusted to meet their specific needs. This allows users to control the cursor with precision, compensating for reduced hand movement or tremors. Some wired mice also incorporate programmable buttons, enabling users to assign custom functions or shortcuts to specific actions, increasing efficiency and reducing the need for extensive hand movement. The wired connection of the mouse ensures a reliable and consistent communication with the computer, minimizing input lag and ensuring accurate cursor control. It eliminates the need for batteries or charging, providing uninterrupted accessibility to users. In conclusion, a wired mouse is a vital tool in accessibility design, offering users with mobility impairments or personal preferences an alternative and ergonomic means of interacting with computer systems. Its design considerations, such as comfort, adjustability, and reliable connectivity, contribute to a user-friendly experience for individuals who require accessible input options.

Wireless Mouse

A wireless mouse is an electronic input device that is designed to provide easy and convenient control over the cursor on a computer screen without the need for a physical connection. In the context of accessibility design, a wireless mouse plays a crucial role in enhancing the usability and accessibility of computers for individuals with physical disabilities or limitations. By eliminating the need for restrictive cables, a wireless mouse offers greater flexibility and freedom of movement, enabling users to position themselves comfortably and operate the computer from a distance.

Word Prediction Apps For Accessibility

A word prediction app is an assistive technology tool designed to enhance accessibility for individuals with disabilities, particularly those who have difficulty typing or generating text. This application predicts the word or phrase a user intends to type based on input patterns and offers suggestions in real-time, which minimizes the effort required for typing and improves overall typing speed and accuracy. Word prediction apps are primarily used by individuals with motor disabilities, physical impairments, or cognitive disabilities that affect their ability to communicate effectively through traditional means of typing. These apps provide an effective way for individuals to express their thoughts, ideas, and messages by reducing the physical and cognitive effort associated with typing.

Word Prediction Apps

Word Prediction Apps in context of accessibility design refer to software or applications that assist individuals with disabilities in writing or typing by predicting words or phrases based on the input provided. These apps are specifically designed to be inclusive and accessible, aiming to improve the user experience for individuals with different types of disabilities, such as motor impairments, cognitive difficulties, or visual impairments. The primary objective of word prediction apps is to enhance the efficiency and accuracy of typing for individuals who may have challenges with traditional keyboard or touch input methods. By suggesting words or phrases as the user types, these apps aid in reducing the amount of time and effort required for text entry, while also minimizing errors. The predictions are typically based on algorithms that analyze the input text and generate a list of likely options. The user can then select the desired word or phrase from the list, which is inserted into the text field. For individuals with motor impairments, who may have limited dexterity or control over their movements, word prediction apps can be particularly useful. By reducing the amount of typing required, these apps help individuals complete their writing tasks more efficiently. Additionally, word prediction apps can offer features such as customizable interfaces, adjustable prediction settings, or the ability to integrate with alternative input devices, further enhancing accessibility for users with motor impairments. Furthermore, individuals with cognitive difficulties or learning disabilities can benefit from word prediction apps as well. These apps can provide additional support by reducing the cognitive load associated with typing, as users can rely on the app's predictions instead of having to recall and type out entire words or phrases. The predictive nature of these apps can improve the user's overall writing fluency, allowing them to focus on their thoughts and ideas rather than struggling with the mechanics of typing. In the case of individuals with visual impairments, word prediction apps can assist by offering auditory feedback options. By providing spoken suggestions for word predictions, these apps enable users with visual impairments to interact with the app and select the desired words or phrases through audio cues. Additionally, word prediction apps that are designed with accessibility in mind often adhere to guidelines and standards, such as providing sufficient color contrast or supporting screen readers, ensuring that they can be fully utilized by individuals with visual impairments.

Word Prediction Software

Word prediction software in the context of accessibility design refers to a technology that helps individuals with physical and cognitive disabilities to improve their typing speed, accuracy, and overall communication. This software analyzes the user's input and suggests words or phrases that are most likely to be intended based on context, frequency, and previous usage. The primary objective of word prediction software is to reduce the effort and time required for individuals with disabilities to create written content. By suggesting words or phrases, the software assists users in completing their sentences more quickly, effectively increasing their productivity. This can be particularly useful for individuals with conditions such as motor impairment, learning disabilities, or limited vocabulary.

ZoomText Screen Magnifier

ZoomText Screen Magnifier is an assistive technology tool designed to enhance accessibility for individuals with visual impairments. It is specifically developed to address the needs of people with low vision by providing a range of screen magnification features. ZoomText Screen Magnifier works by enlarging and enhancing the content displayed on a computer screen, making it easier for individuals with visual impairments to read and interact with digital content. Its primary function is to magnify on-screen text, graphics, and other visual elements, allowing users to see and comprehend information more clearly.